MU00624033

"Ayman Ibrahim has produce(of Islam and neighbors of M clarifies important terminology and historical data, providing the reader with information about the Islamic faith while shedding light on Muslims who practice it. He writes a fair treatment of the issues and ideas while not refraining from describing some of the lesser-known internal conflicts and inconsistencies within Islamic thought and practice. Ibrahim brings to the table the mind of a scholar and the heart of an evangelist. This book will be a welcome companion to all who desire to better understand the faith of their Muslim friends. I cannot recommend it strongly enough."

—**J. Keith McKinley**, associate professor of Christian missions, director of the Bevin Center for Missions Mobilization, The Southern Baptist Theological Seminary

"To 'love your neighbor as yourself' requires both caring and understanding. In this thoughtful work, Ayman Ibrahim opens windows into our Muslim neighbors' worldview by clearly explaining Islam's key concepts and vocabulary. He shows not only how these terms are used in Islamic texts and movements throughout history but also what they mean for the matters of faith and practice by which these neighbors live. An excellent resource for healthy dialogue."

—**George Bristow**, senior research fellow, Institute for the Study of Religion in the Middle East (ISRME)

"Ayman Ibrahim provides an invaluable resource in *A Concise Guide to Islam*. For those working or serving among Muslims, this book will be the go-to reference to better understand Islamic concepts or words. For the novice or veteran Christian missionary, *A Concise Guide to Islam* meets an important felt need, while also serving as a resource for anyone wanting to understand more about the Islamic faith."

—**Carol B. Ghattas**, author and speaker with over thirty years in cross-cultural ministry among Muslims

"Without knowledge of the meaning of basic terms and concepts, one is merely 'flailing in the wind' in the attempt to understand any particular religion. Ibrahim has provided a work that will be kept close, not only by those who are initially seeking to understand Islam and its adherents but also by any who find themselves needing a clear definition or explanation of a term or concept related to Islam. An exceptional resource for all who wish to understand Islam!"

"This is a valuable book, incorporating up-to-date scholarship in an easy-to-read style. Ibrahim has provided a versatile volume that promises to be frequently consulted and will be at home both in a university library or on a pastor's bookshelf."

"In his latest, aptly named book, Ayman Ibrahim brings welcome clarity to this influential world religion. Writing for beginners, he focuses on key Muslim beliefs and practices, delivering a compendium of a hundred-plus terms and concepts. The entire itinerary, from Islamic texts and history through jurisprudence to Islamic movements, will considerably enrich general readers who go the distance. Serious travelers (and day-trippers) will also benefit from this ready reference tool as they return to it time and again."

A
CONCISE GUIDE TO
ISLAM

A
CONCISE GUIDE TO
ISLAM

DEFINING KEY CONCEPTS
AND TERMS

Ayman S. Ibrahim

Baker Academic

a division of Baker Publishing Group
Grand Rapids, Michigan

Published by Baker Academic
a division of Baker Publishing Group
Grand Rapids, Michigan
www.bakeracademic.com

Printed in the United States of America

Library of Congress Cataloging-in-Publication Data
Names: Ibrahim, Ayman S., 1973– author.
Title: A concise guide to Islam : defining key concepts and terms / Ayman S. Ibrahim.
Description: Grand Rapids : Baker Academic, a division of Baker Publishing Group,
    2023. | Series: Introducing Islam | Includes bibliographical references.
Identifiers: LCCN 2023008950 | ISBN 9781540966667 (paperback) | ISBN
    9781540966803 (casebound) | ISBN 9781493442768 (ebook) | ISBN 9781493442775
    (pdf)
Subjects: LCSH: Islam.
Classification: LCC BP161.3 .I257 2023 | DDC 297—dc23/eng/20230306
LC record available at https://lccn.loc.gov/2023008950

Quotations from the Quran (indicated by the letter Q) are the author's translation.

Baker Publishing Group publications use paper produced from sustainable forestry practices and post-consumer waste whenever possible.

23 24 25 26 27 28 29   7 6 5 4 3 2 1

Contents

Islamic History   23

Islamic Faith and Belief   41

Islamic Practices and Religious Duties   77

Islamic Jurisprudence   127

Islamic Movements   149

Acknowledgments

I am grateful to my supervisors and colleagues at Southern Seminary, who constantly encourage me in my writing. My students inspire me. Through their diligence in research and questions in the classroom, they open new dimensions for me and give me direction for avenues to pursue in my books. I am grateful for the support and resources I always receive from my team at the Jenkins Center for the Christian Understanding of Islam at The Southern Baptist Theological Seminary. In a true fulfillment of its vision and mission, the Center encourages my writing projects, particularly providing financial resources when needed. Thanks in particular to staff member Tracy Martin, who edits our writing projects.

At Baker Academic, I thank Jim Kinney, Anna Gissing, Melinda Timmer, and Julie Zahm. They are supportive, professional, and dedicated to exceptionalism.

My wife is the hero behind all this. Her love, encouragement, and constant support for me and my work allow me time and space to write. To all, with gratitude, I say *shukran*!

Pronunciation Guide

This word list is intended to serve as an easy-to-use, practical pronunciation guide for native English speakers. The capitalized portion of the word indicates the syllable that should be stressed. An apostrophe at the end represents a glottal stop.

aaya: EYE-ya
Abbasids: ab-bah-SEEDS
abd: abd
abu: ah-boo
adhan: a-THAN or a-ZAN
ahl al-kitab: ah-l al-kee-TAB
ahl al-Quran: ah-l al-kor-AHN
Ahmadiyya: ah-ma-DAY-uh
akhbari: ukh-BERR-ee
alhamdulillah: al-HAM-doo-le-leh
Allah: al-LUH
Allahu Akbar: al-LUH-hu ukk-bar
ansab: an-SEHB
aqida: ah-KEE-duh
asbab: as-BEHB
Ashuraa': ah-SHOO-ruh
asmaa' Allah: as-MEH al-LUH
as-salaamu 'alaykum: as-sa-LEH-muh ah-LAY-koom
'awra: our-uh

baraka: BAH-rah-kuh
basmala: bahs-meh-luh
bid'a: bid-AH
bint: bint

daar al-harb: DAR ul-HARB
daar al-islaam: DAR ul-ess-LAM
da'wa: DAH-uh-wah
dhimmi: THIM-mee
du'aa': doo-WAH

eid: eyed

fatwa: FAT-wuh
fiqh: fik-h ("h" sound at end)
fitna: fit-nuh
futuh: foo-tooh ("h" sound at end)

hadith: ha-DEETH
hajj: hahj
halal: ha-laal
haram: ha-rom
hijab: hih-JAHB
hijra: hij-ruh
hoor: hoh-oor
hudud: hoh-dood

ibn: ibn
ihsan: ih-sehn
i'jaz: ee-jazz
ijmaa: ihj-mayah
imam: ih-MAM (mam sounds like "ma'am")
iman: ih-MAN
Injil: in-jeel
inshallah: in-shah-al-LUH
Islam: is-LAM (lam rhymes with "ram")
'isma: eye-smuh
isnad: is-NAHD

jahannam: ja-HAHN-num
jahiliyya: ja-hee-LEE-yuh

janna: JAN-nuh
jihad: jee-had (had rhymes with "bad")
jinn: jihn
jumu'a: joo-moo-AH

Ka'ba: KAH-ha-bah
kafir: KAF-fur
kalam: ka-LAM (lam rhymes with "ram")
khutba: KHUT-buh (khut rhymes with "put")

laylat al-qadr: lay-lat al-kod-der

madhhab: MADH-heb
madrasa: MAHD-rah-suh
maghazi: ma-GHEH-zee
mashallah: ma-sheh-al-LUH
masjid: mass-jihd
maslaha: moss-la-hah
mihna: MEH-nuh
mu'min: mo-min (glottal stop sound between syllables)
murtad: moor-ted (roll the *r*)
mushaf: moos-hahf
mushrik: moosh-rick
mut'a: moot-ah
Mu'tazilism: maw-teh-zeh-lism

nabi: nab-BEE (nab rhymes with "cab")
naskh: nas-kh
nikaah: nee-kay-ah

qadar: kahd-dar (roll the *r*)
qadi: kah-dee
qibla: kib-LEH
qira'at: kee-rah-AWT
Quran: kor-AHN
Quraysh: koo-roysh

Ramadan: rah-mah-DON (don rhymes with "on")
Rashidun: raw-shee-doon
rasul: ra-SOOL
ribaa: re-bah

Salafism: SAH-la-fism
salat: sah-LAHT
salla allahu alayhi wa sallam: sul-LUH al-LUH-hu al-lay-hee weh
   sal-LUM
Shahada: shah-HAHD-duh
sharia: sha-REE-uh
Shiism: SHEE-ism
sira: SEE-ruh
Sufism: SOOF-ism
sunna: SOON-nah
Sunnism: SOO-nee-ism
sura: SOO-ruh
Suryaani: soo-ree-YAN-nee

tafsir: tef-seer
talaaq: tah-lock
taqiyya: tah-KAY-uh
tarikh: tah-reekh
tawakkul: tah-wah-KOOL
tawba: taw-buh
tawhid: taw-HEED
Tawrah: taw-ruh
tilaawa: tee-LAH-wuh

ulamaa': oh-leh-MEH
Umayyads: ooh-my-yadz
umm: ohm
umma: OHM-mah
umm al-kitab: ohm al-kee-TAB

Wahhabism: wah-HAHB-ism
wahy: WAH-yuh
wudu': woo-DOO

yawm al-qiyaama: yowm al-KEE-yah-muh

Zabur: zah-BOOR
zakat: zah-CAT
zinaa: zee-nah

Introduction

How Can One Define Islam?

I grew up in Cairo, Egypt. During my childhood, most of my neighbors and classmates were committed Muslims who used Islamic terms in daily conversation. To be sure, we all spoke the same language—Arabic, with a wonderful Egyptian dialect—but the terms Muslims repeatedly used were not just Arabic; they were Islamic. In conversations—with other Muslims or with Christians present—my Muslim friends did not shy away from terms that conveyed their identity and beliefs.

Muslims cherish terms such as *jihad, halal, haram, fatwa, masjid, madrasa,* and *Allahu Akbar* and repeat them daily. Some Muslims assume, wrongly, that these terms are well understood by non-Muslims, but they in fact convey uniquely Islamic concepts. For example, Muslims believe there is a difference between the ritual prayer and a mere petition or supplication. They use a unique word to describe their concept of religiously legitimate banking—which differs from banking in the Western world. Even an official marriage differs from a temporary pleasure marriage, with different rules and regulations for each. Most non-Muslims cannot understand these terms and concepts without adequate explanation, especially since some of these words involve sophisticated theological notions and challenging pronunciations. These terms and concepts are part of a unique vocabulary distinct to Islam. Any solid understanding of Islam must begin with understanding these words.

My aim in this book is to provide readers with a concise guide to Muslim terms and concepts. This introduction briefly highlights two foundational matters—What is Islam? and What is a Muslim?—before explaining the structure and special features of this book.

What Is Islam?

Today, Islam is a world religion with over 1.6 billion followers. A follower of Islam is called a Muslim. The deity of Islam is known as Allah. The founder of Islam is Muhammad, who is viewed by Muslims as a divinely guided prophet sent by Allah to humankind in general and to the Arabs in particular. The story of Islam's founding is told in Islamic traditions in significant detail. We are told that Muhammad was born around 570 in a city called Mecca, in today's Saudi Arabia. He died in 632 in a nearby city (actually more like an oasis in the desert) called Yathrib, which was later renamed Medina. The word *Medina* means "the city," which, for Muslims, basically identifies it as the city of their prophet. Muhammad's birthplace, Mecca, was known as a pagan city where idol worship was flourishing, especially in a shrine in its midst named the Ka'ba. The shrine contained 360 idols that were worshiped by local Arabs and traveling pilgrims. The Ka'ba was an essential contributor to the local income and the wealth of Muhammad's tribe, the Quraysh. Life in Mecca was colored by tribal hierarchy and aristocracy. Even though Muhammad's tribe was powerful, his family was not part of its wealthy or influential branch. Muhammad's father, Abdullah, died four to six months before Muhammad was born. Muhammad's mother, Amina, raised him with the help of his uncle and grandfather, but she died when Muhammad was around seven years old. Because they were Meccan, Muhammad's parents and relatives were likely idol worshipers, but the Muslim traditions convey competing messages about their religious leaning, most likely in an attempt to depict Muhammad's family as believers even before Muhammad became Allah's prophet.

In his youth, Muhammad worked as a shepherd and trader. Traditions claim that Muhammad never worshiped idols like his family members. He was known as faithful and honest in his trading, to the extent that a wealthy woman, Khadija, was impressed with his integrity. Although she was fifteen years older than Muhammad, she proposed marriage. He accepted the proposal, and they married when he was twenty-five and she was forty. She was Muhammad's first wife, but she had at least two husbands before him. Muhammad did not marry other women during Khadija's lifetime, but after her death he amassed at least nine wives and many concubines. Khadija supported him financially and spiritually, as he used to go to a secluded mountain to worship the one true deity.

When Muhammad was forty, the story claims, the angel Gabriel appeared to him during one of his visits to the mountain. Muhammad was terrified. However, Gabriel assured him that he brought a divine message that would enable Muhammad to lead his people out of polytheism and into monotheism. Muhammad rushed to tell Khadija, and she was the first to believe in his divine calling—known later as the religion of Islam. After her, a handful of men believed in Muhammad's message. After preaching in secret for three years without gaining significant followers, he then went public with his message. Immediately, the Meccan pagans began to harass and persecute him and his followers, as he reportedly threatened their business related to the idol worship in the Ka'ba. For ten more years, he continued to bear oppression from the idol worshipers.

Although Muslims insist that Muhammad was a monotheist during his time in Mecca, Muslim traditions reveal a uniquely disturbing incident. Nine years after he allegedly received the divine revelation, Muhammad was reportedly deceived by Satan into advocating for three pagan goddesses as intercessors. He uttered satanic words, which made their way into the Quran for some time, until Allah removed them. The incident, as found in Islamic traditions, portrays Muhammad as a polytheist, at least temporarily.

Due to persecution from the Meccans and their rejection of his message, Muhammad was forced to emigrate from Mecca to Medina when he was fifty-three. He then lived in Medina for the last ten years of his life, during which time he was able to preach Islam more freely—especially because he gained power through a series of raids and expeditions against other Arab groups. These raids made him tribally powerful and wealthy. In Medina, the Muslim community consolidated their control and advanced their influence over many parts of Arabia, especially the western region known as the Hijaz. Before Muhammad's death in 632, he was known as the king of Arabia by many of his opponents. His followers, on the other hand, viewed him as both a messenger of Allah and a commander in chief. Their raids differed from other tribal incursions in that those carrying them out felt they were following the will of Allah. A couple years before Muhammad's death, many of the Arab tribes submitted to Muhammad's rule by declaring their conversion to Islam. Their conversions in this setting probably represented declarations of loyalty and tribal submission rather than religious conviction. Still, their conversions from paganism to Islam represented, for Muslims, the growth of Muhammad's influence as a proclaimer of monotheism in Arabia. Islam's two components, religious guidance and military power, were essential in the advancement of the Muslim community. Both are still important aspects of the religion, which is viewed by many Muslims as both faith and state, worship and leadership.

Nonetheless, after Muhammad's death, many of the Arab tribes abandoned Islam partially or entirely. Muhammad's successor, Caliph Abu Bakr, launched the Apostasy Wars, fighting to restore the Arabs to Islam. He succeeded in bringing many back to following Islam and to continuing the practice of paying the religious tax. After the success of the Apostasy Wars, Muslim armies continued to advance. What began as raids of small armies throughout Arabia turned into major military conquests that challenged the superpowers of the time: the Byzantine and Persian Empires. Within a century after Muhammad's death, Muslims had established an empire ruling over a vast territory, stretching from China to West Africa and Spain. Muslim rule brought more and more people to embrace the religion of the rulers. Three or four centuries after Muhammad, Muslims made up the majority of this region's population.

From a theological standpoint, Islam is built on two major foundations: Muhammad and the Quran. For Muslims, Muhammad is Allah's final prophet and the Quran is Islam's scripture, which, for Muslims, is Allah's inerrant, perfect, and final message to humankind. They believe that Muhammad is the example that should be imitated, as he fulfilled Islam's scripture and followed it to the letter. Thus, Islam, at its core, is a religion adhering to a book as exemplified in the life of one man, Muhammad. Muslims believe, however, that as a religious message, Islam is not new—it is Allah's religion that was followed by many pre-Islamic prophets. Abraham, Isaac, Ishmael, and Jacob were essentially Muslims (Q 2:127–33). Theologically, Islam is an exclusive religion; it specifies that only those who adhere to its teaching, believe in its prophet, and follow its tenets are accepted by the deity. Allah had sent previous prophets—including Moses and Jesus—but their messages, according to most Muslims, have been corrupted. The only remaining authentic message is Islam and its scripture. The exclusive nature of Islam is also evident in its eschatology, where humankind is divided into two camps: believers and unbelievers. The afterlife includes paradise for believers and hellfire for everyone else. This judgment will take place according to one's deeds, which include choosing Islam as the right path.

From a sectarian standpoint, Islam contains various sects, although its two major branches are Sunnism and Shiism. While many claim that the difference between Sunnis and Shiites is mainly political, this is incorrect. There are major disagreements on faith and practice between the two sects. In fact, each sect accuses the other of being misguided and straying from the true religious path. In addition to the two sects, marginal groups exist—like the newly founded Ahmadiyya sect—although they are dismissed by the mainstream sects and viewed as heretical.

In practice, Islam is a works-based religion with a significant emphasis on religious duties. In essence, good works—including divinely prescribed duties—are a means to gain Allah's favor and ultimately inherit a blissful afterlife. While a list of ways to guarantee a blissful afterlife does not exist, believers who perform good works are on the right path toward securing a dwelling place in paradise. The emphasis on works appears to be a continuation of the pre-Islamic worship system. In many aspects, Muhammad seems to have accepted and adopted the practices of pre-Islamic pagan Arabs, with some minor adjustments. The pilgrimage to the Ka'ba in Mecca is a glaring example. Many of the rituals of the pre-Islamic pilgrimage to Mecca continued well into Islam, without any change or with only minor tweaks. The pre-Islamic pagan rite of kissing the black stone—as one of the rituals of the Ka'ba pilgrimage—is required in Islam as a major religious duty. To make the kissing of a stone religiously plausible in Islam, many traditions were later forged to establish its celestial origin and supernatural sacredness. Similarly, the walking or running between two hills, Safa and Marwa, as part of the pre-Islamic pilgrimage, continued into Islam and is practiced by Muslim pilgrims today. The same goes for other religious duties, including the circumambulation around the Ka'ba, ablution before the ritual prayer, and even the number of daily prayers. Even some of the various kinds of marriages in pre-Islamic Arabia were later endorsed by and adopted into Islam. Many of these duties and rituals were crucial in pre-Islamic Arabian life, and the emergence of Islam—as a religion of, from, and for the Arabs—necessitated some sort of religious continuity. The nascent religion needed a ritual system that shared similarities with pre-Islamic Arabian worship in order to appeal to Arabs.

In the same vein, it appears that Islam borrowed aspects from earlier revelations, including Judaism and Christianity. While this notion is often rejected by Muslims, many scholars have argued that Judaism and Christianity largely influenced Islam and its prophet. After all, Islam did not appear in a vacuum. The Quran is full of biblical stories, characters, and concepts. While Muslims insist that the preaching of the Quran began in a pagan city full of idols, the Quran itself seems to refute this claim, as it includes stories of Adam, Noah, Abraham, Isaac, Ishmael, Jacob, Moses, Jesus, and many other biblical figures. If the Quran was initially proclaimed to pagans, why did it include these biblical figures who were unknown to idol worshipers? Scholars believe that the Quran was formed over time and in conversation with Jews and Christians—a conversation that necessitated a narrative embedded in biblical material. Some passages in the Quran rely heavily on biblical accounts, whether canonical or apocryphal. We read stories of Jesus forming birds from clay in the Quran (chaps. 3 and 5). These stories have significant similarities to the apocryphal gospels. Both the Quran and Muhammad's traditions indicate not only that Jews and Christians lived where Muhammad allegedly proclaimed his message but also that he met some of them both before and after his supposed encounter with Gabriel. The first man to confirm Muhammad's revelation, we are told, was Khadija's cousin, Waraqa, who was a Christian linguist and scholar. While he reportedly affirmed Muhammad's prophethood, Waraqa did not convert to the new religion. Similarly, many years earlier, Muhammad was on a journey to Syria with his uncle. They both met a Syrian monk who foretold of Muhammad's prophethood. Contrary to Muslim claims, biblical material seems to have significantly influenced Islam, as evidenced in the various biblical aspects that permeate Islam's religious system.

Against this background, one may question the major Muslim premise that Islam as a religious system came down from heaven—as if it appeared in a vacuum—and never borrowed elements from pre-Islamic Arabia or any other religion. An examination of Muslim sources and religious practices suggests that the religion of Islam emerged and developed in conversation with pre-Islamic religious systems, both pagan and biblical. In a sense, Islam has been influenced not only by that which came before it but also by the environment and religious communities within which it emerged and took shape. The notion that Islam is a religious system that dropped from heaven is just that. This point is further explained in entries on sunna and tarikh, among others.

While Islam is indeed a religion in that it is a set of beliefs and practices, in practical terms it extends beyond that. This is evident in the way Muslims live out this religion in their daily lives. When one interacts with Muslims, one realizes that Islam is more of a cultural identity and even a nationalistic movement. It influences Muslims far beyond mere religious tenets. This begs the question: What is a Muslim?

What Is a Muslim?

A Muslim is a follower of the religion of Islam. While Muslims largely share beliefs, tenets, and practices, they differ significantly in their understanding of these beliefs, their interpretation of these tenets, and their commitment to adhering to these divinely prescribed practices. The reality is that Islam is lived out in many different ways by Muslims based on their views and dispositions. In terms of practices and interpretations, we can roughly identify three major groups among Muslims: cultural, practicing, and radical. These categories demonstrate the diversity among Muslims in their approaches to Islam. Yet because these categories may overlap in some cases, it is better to think of Muslims as existing on a spectrum rather than as distinct groups.

A cultural Muslim is a nominal Muslim, meaning they are Muslim in name only and follow Islam simply as the religion of their birth. Many cultural Muslims do not seek sophisticated understanding of their faith, its tenets, or its interpretations but instead follow customs and practices dictated by their social and cultural contexts. This category is by far the largest among Muslims. It is reflected in the so-called folk Islam, where the faith is highly colored by the culture of the person. For cultural or nominal Muslims, Islam serves as their social identity and nationalistic sentiment. They are Muslims because they were born into Muslim families and because Islam is part of their social and cultural identity. In such cases, Islam is not sophisticated beliefs they follow or advance; it is simply a part of their family, relationships, habits, customs, and social activities. For these Muslims, abandoning Islam is impossible, as it is a part of everything they do and know. They cannot see themselves as anything but Muslim. Not surprisingly, some of the deeds and customs of cultural Muslims are considered heretical by mainstream Islam. For instance, cultural Muslims may seek to visit the graves of pious dead people to acquire blessings, and they may use amulets to bring about healing or cast away evil spirits. These practices are considered unorthodox by mainstream Islam, which largely relies on a set of sacred texts.

A practicing Muslim is devout in the sense of following a particular form of Islam in matters of faith and practice. A practicing Muslim can be conservative, fundamentalist, modernist, liberal, or progressive. Most rely on sacred Islamic texts, but they view and interpret them in various and often competing ways. A fundamentalist or conservative Muslim may insist that an apostate must be killed based on Muhammad's command in the authentic tradition, while a modernist or progressive may accept the same tradition but argue that it was only for past generations and has no bearing on modern times. The same is true regarding views on women's rights, homosexuality, slavery, and so forth. While practicing Muslims insist they are following the sacred texts, they view and interpret them differently.

A radical Muslim is extreme in their views and interpretations of Islam's precepts and commands. Radicals are extreme in the eyes of those who disagree with them, not in their own eyes. They often follow texts as written and emphasize the political nature of Islam. For them, Islam is both faith and state, worship and leadership, divine text and military power. Examples of radicals can often be found in militant groups, such as al-Qaeda, the Taliban, Boko Haram, and ISIS. Members view themselves as devout Muslims who follow the letter of the sacred texts, while other Muslims and non-Muslims may view them as radical in their interpretations.

By and large, the vast majority of Muslims—particularly Sunnis—agree on two important sets of obligations, one related to practices and another detailing basic beliefs. The two sets define what Muslims do and what they believe. The practices are called the Five Pillars of Islam, and the beliefs are the Six Articles of Faith. The pillars are the prescribed divine duties that every Muslim should practice. They are the profession of faith, performing the five daily ritual prayers, almsgiving, fasting during Ramadan, and the completion of the pilgrimage once in a lifetime when able. The articles of faith are belief in Allah's oneness, his angels, his books, his prophets, his Day of Resurrection, and his predestination of all things. These two sets of obligations are shared by the vast majority of Muslims. However, their acceptance is not unanimous, as Shiites, for example, have some differences in their two sets.

Whether cultural, practicing, or radical, Muslims often experience a unique sense of unity and solidarity among themselves. This sense of cohesion is built on the religious concept of the umma (one unified community). Muslims, for the most part, view themselves as one united body of believers whose religious bond surpasses social measures and cultural backgrounds. This religious claim is believed and voiced by many Muslims, although it appears, at times, to be a theoretical assertion more than an ideal practice, especially in Muslim societies where social classes and economic measures govern human affairs. The umma—among many other concepts—is important when defining Islam, and this concept stands at the core of this book.

Structure and Special Features of This Book

My goal in compiling this material is to give those with limited exposure to Islam a clearer understanding. This book serves as a concise guide to over one hundred terms and concepts that define Islam, particularly its beliefs and practices. Each of these terms and concepts is explained in an entry. The entries are grouped under six headings: (1) Islamic Texts, (2) Islamic History, (3) Islamic Faith and Belief, (4) Islamic Practices and Religious Duties, (5) Islamic Jurisprudence, and (6) Islamic Movements. These six headings represent the major spheres that constitute the heart of Islam as a belief system. Each section begins with a brief introduction, followed by a logical flow of entries. When an entry could arguably fit under multiple headings, I chose the option that seemed most appropriate.

Each entry begins with a concise definition of the Islamic term or concept under consideration. The definition is then explained in more detail. This explanation includes linguistic, theoretical, practical, and lexical aspects. I also assist native English speakers with proper pronunciation by including a phonetic spelling that indicates which syllables should be stressed. A pronunciation guide located at the beginning of the book includes a compilation of these pronunciations for all the entries arranged alphabetically. Of course, for better pronunciations, readers will need to practice with Arabic-speaking friends.

In explaining the theoretical aspects of each entry, I relied primarily on the most trusted sources of Islam—particularly the Quran and Muhammad's traditions, which include his sayings, biographies, and histories. I relied on these sources because they are believed and cherished by the vast majority of Muslims. Many of these sources are found only in Arabic, and my goal is to make their contents available to all readers. However, I also realize that Muslims are not a monolith. They approach and interpret the contents of these primary sources differently, sometimes even in opposite ways. This is why when I explain the practical aspects of each concept—that is, how Muslims actually practice it—I do my best to explain the diversity of popular opinions. In particular, I highlight the major views of the two largest sects in Islam, Sunnism and Shiism. Sometimes Sunnis and Shiites agree on a particular practice, but in many cases they disagree. I attempt to explain these disagreements so that readers may gain a proper understanding of the different views among the majority of Muslims.

In addition to primary sources, I consulted reputable secondary sources and recent scholarly research. A list of these sources is provided at the end of the book. These secondary studies—Muslim and non-Muslim—add to the depth and breadth of each entry. To supplement many of the entries, I expand on the material found in my two previous resources, *A Concise Guide to the Quran* (2020) and *A Concise Guide to the Life of Muhammad* (2022). These two books include discussions related to Islam's beliefs and practices as well as ample scholarly resources. I highly recommend them, as they are foundational to understanding Islam and its tenets and practices. Although I consulted these two resources, in many cases my explanations here extend beyond them. Moreover, some of the terms and concepts explained in this book are not mentioned or discussed in the two earlier resources. In such cases, I was aided in my research by two important scholarly encyclopedias,

Encyclopaedia of Islam (2nd ed.) and *Encyclopedia of the Qur'ān*. They include excellent entries related to Islam and its particularities. In addition to these encyclopedias, I consulted reputable academic resources whose bibliographical information is listed at the end of this book in the "Sources Consulted" section.

I conclude this introduction with a few notes on style and content. First, this book is intended for beginners, which is why I avoid cumbersome footnotes and direct quotations. Even when referring to verses in the Quran, I simply provide the meaning of the verse followed by its reference (Q) and then the chapter and verse numbers. My hope is to present a helpful guide and readable text to nonspecialist interested readers. While I aim for a non-Muslim audience, I write with Muslims in mind. I appreciate their diversity and differences, and I do my best to convey their varying opinions and views. Nonetheless, I write as a critical scholar, and I understand that my conclusions may not coincide with those of other scholars, Muslim or non-Muslim.

Second, in terms of content, some entries are lengthier than others, as they required more depth and detail. Many entries are directly linked to others. When this is the case, bold type is used to indicate that supplemental information on the current topic can be found in another entry.

Third, a stylistic decision had to be made regarding Arabic words and their transliterations. Since this book aims to serve nonspecialists and I wanted to avoid complicating the readability of the text, I do not use transliteration for Arabic terms to indicate phonetics. While scholars may prefer renditions like Muḥammad and ʿUthmān, I simply use Muhammad and Uthman. Similarly, some Arabic words contain special Arabic letters that can be confusing. This is particularly the case with two Arabic marks, the hamza and the ʿayn. I render both of these symbols as an apostrophe. So while scholars may prefer Kaʿba or Kaʿba, I simply use Ka'ba.

Fourth, I often present various Muslim viewpoints. I then present a few critical observations that may assist readers in considering nontraditional views concerning Muslim claims. I understand that some may disagree with my presentation of these views. In the end, it is my sincere hope that non-Muslim readers will better understand Islamic beliefs and practices by gaining familiarity with significant terms and concepts that are cherished by our Muslim neighbors.

ISLAMIC TEXTS

This section identifies the major Islamic texts upon which Muslims build their understanding of the various spheres of their faith. These are the primary sources for knowledge of Islamic belief and practice. No sources are more important for Muslims than these ancient texts, which are revered, honored, and treasured, albeit in varying degrees. No other book is venerated and respected by Muslims like their scripture, the Quran, acclaimed as Allah's speech to humankind. While they view the Quran as the revelation given to Muhammad, the text itself does not reveal much about him. When Muslims want to learn about Muhammad's life, they refer to other texts, which are also respected and revered, though to a lesser extent than the Quran. These texts include Muhammad's sayings, biography, expeditions, and history. They form the Muslim understanding of the life and career of their prophet and collectively serve as Islam's tradition. In addition to these texts, Muslims study the history of Islam and its chronicles. They also refer to non-Muslim texts identified by Islam as valid and valuable resources. These include books revealed to Jews and Christians. Ultimately, this section serves as a guide for the most important primary texts for Muslims—those from which they learn their doctrines, convictions, and tenets.

1

Quran: Islam's scripture

The Quran, pronounced "kor-AHN," is the holiest book for over 1.6 billion Muslims. In English, the title is rendered in various ways, including "Kuran," "Koran," and "Qoran." Scholars of Islam render it as "Quran" (or "Qur'an" to indicate the glottal stop in the middle of the word). In its current form, the book is divided into 114 chapters—each called a **sura** in Arabic. Each sura is divided into verses. A verse is called an **aaya** in Arabic, and the word itself can mean "a verse in scripture" or "a sign or miracle." The Arabic Quran contains 6,236 to 6,616 verses, depending on the version. In the Arabic text, the number of a verse follows it. However, in translations of the Quran, the number precedes the verse, as is the custom in biblical texts. The Muslim community views a translation of the Quran not as a true Quran but rather as a rendition of its meaning. This is because Muslims believe the Quran is written in a perfect Arabic, which cannot be conveyed properly in any other language.

Muslims believe that in 610, when Muhammad was forty years old, he began to receive revelations of what was in the celestial tablet. The revelations were given by Allah through the angel Gabriel. For Muslims, Muhammad proclaimed the Quran as he heard it. Once it was proclaimed, Muslims wrote the verses down on different materials, including stones, palm tree leaves, and camel bones, to ensure the preservation of the proclamation. To the vast majority of Muslims, the text of the Quran is inerrant and infallible—it is the only perfectly preserved scripture. Muslim traditions state that other pre-Islamic scriptures, like the Bible, have been corrupted or altered. Today's Quran, Muslims argue, is the exact copy of the original heavenly tablet eternally existing next to the throne of the deity.

Regarding the literary features of the Quran, each sura has a title that was not in original manuscripts but was added later by medieval scholars. The title is often derived from a major theme or person mentioned in the sura. The titles of the suras include "Cow," "Prophets," "Ants," "Catastrophe," "Elephant," and "Infidels," among others. After the title of each sura, either Mecca or Medina is listed as the location where Muhammad allegedly received the chapter. Like the title of each sura, this location was not in the original. It was added by medieval Muslims. Each chapter—after the title and the presumed location of the revelation—also includes a statement: "In the name of Allah, Most Gracious, Most Merciful." The statement is known among Muslims as the **basmala**.

In today's Quran, the suras do not follow the chronological order of the alleged revelations. Later Muslims arranged the suras in decreasing length, with a few exceptions. For example, sura 114 is not the shortest sura, nor is sura 1 the longest. The longest chapter is actually sura 2, while the shortest is sura 108. In terms of chronology, Muslims claim that the first chapter revealed to Muhammad was sura 96.

The meaning of the word *Quran* is mysterious. While Muslims claim that the word *Quran* is a purely Arabic term that means "to read" or "recitation," some scholars trace the word to a pre-Islamic Christian Syriac term, *qeryana*, which means "a liturgical text." The argument for a Syriac root stems from the fact that this Semitic language was used by Middle Eastern Christians in the seventh century for liturgical purposes, and, scholars argue, it is plausible that the term *Quran* had roots in the liturgical language used by the believing community around Muhammad at that time.

hadith: a statement or tradition, primarily attributed to Muhammad

Linguistically, the basic meaning of the Arabic word *hadith* is "new," as opposed to old. It reflects erupting news or openly proclaimed words. In Islamic teaching, a hadith, pronounced "ha-DEETH," generally refers to a saying, statement, or report of any sort; however, for the most part, it is mainly a tradition attributed to Muhammad's words or actions. Hadith in Arabic is singular, and its plural form is *ahadith*; however, it is now common in English to use *hadiths*.

During Muhammad's lifetime, he reportedly forbade the writing of his statements and insisted that people recite and memorize only the Quran. This is probably why, in the first two centuries of Islam, Muslims had no record of Muhammad's sayings. However, in the third century of Islam, Muslims began to collect and circulate thousands of statements. Because they were attributed to Muhammad, these statements received authority and legitimacy. One particular group of Muslims, the traditionists (scholars of tradition), grew in number and power. These traditionists were known as the lovers, supporters, or people of the hadith. Despite Muhammad's reported command prohibiting the writing of his words, the people of the hadith compiled voluminous works allegedly containing the reliable statements of Muhammad, presumably to preserve his traditions.

The hadith scholars claimed that since Muhammad is the best example of humankind, the hadith collections are second in authority only after the Quran. Some went even further, affirming that since Muhammad received divine revelations, his statements are also divinely inspired words. Since the Quran appears at times general and ambiguous and the hadith statements are specific and straightforward, the authority of the hadith traditions grew rapidly. Muslims from opposing sects or competing political sympathies began to create their own hadiths and attribute them to Muhammad in order to settle religious or political debates. Any controversy, so to speak, could be settled if one party claimed that Muhammad had said such and such. The authority and power of the hadith grew even more once Muslims began writing commentaries on the Quran and historical works, including Muhammad's biography (**sira**), because all these texts relied heavily on hadith statements. Ultimately, these hadith traditions became extremely powerful and served as essential parts of Muhammad's **sunna** (accounts and reports about his conduct and teaching).

Not surprisingly, the two major sects of Islam, Sunnism and Shiism, accept different hadith collections. Sunnis have nine respected collections. Among them, two collections—one by **Imam** Bukhari (810–870) and another by Imam Muslim (821–875)—are considered the most reliable, trusted, and authentic. Shiites, on the other hand, have four major collections that include the sayings attributed to Muhammad and statements by his household, particularly his daughter Fatima and her husband, Ali, and their sons. Problematically, none of these Sunni or Shiite collections come from eyewitnesses of the time of Muhammad.

In Islamic texts, a hadith has two major parts: an **isnad** (a chain of transmitters) and a matn (text). A basic form of a hadith is "It is reported on the authority of person A who heard it from person B that Allah's Apostle said such and such." The isnad includes who heard and transmitted the statement, while the matn is the statement attributed to Muhammad. For Muslims, the isnad is what makes a hadith reliable.

sira: a life account or biography, particularly that of Muhammad

In Arabic, the term *sira*, pronounced "SEE-ruh," appears often in describing the life of an individual—the way a person lives, speaks, acts, and so forth. One may say that the sira of a man is full of testimonies of great accomplishments and honorable deeds. In Islam, the sira primarily refers to the life of Muhammad, the most important human figure for Muslims. While various Islamic texts detail the lives of other Muslims, such as Muhammad's closest companions, the term *sira* is often used to refer to and describe the entirety of the life of Muhammad—that is, his biography. Sira is a genre of Islamic literature that claims to detail the way Muhammad lived, the manners he used with his friends and enemies, and his military campaigns.

There is no extant biography of Muhammad written by contemporary eyewitnesses. The earliest sira we have for Muhammad was allegedly written by Ibn Ishaq (ca. 704–768), who died almost 120 years after Muhammad's death. Ibn Ishaq (pronounced "Ibn Is-hahk") was a hadith scholar who lived during the time of the powerful **Abbasid** caliph Mansur, who instructed him to write an account of Muhammad's life. The account, scholars observe, most likely aimed to embellish the image of the Abbasid Dynasty and legitimize their rule over the Muslims in the vast, growing empire. While some may question the reliability of the material about Muhammad's life—given the time gap between Muhammad and Ibn Ishaq—Muslims consider Ibn Ishaq's sira to be the most trusted biography of Islam's prophet. However, we do not actually have access to Ibn Ishaq's sira. Although it is now lost, Muslim tradition states that one of Ibn Ishaq's disciples, Ibn Hisham, found a copy of Ibn Ishaq's original. Ibn Hisham reportedly rearranged and amended Ibn Ishaq's account and removed sensitive and shameful material. Scholars identify this as censoring the sira. While we do not know what Ibn Hisham actually removed from or added to Ibn Ishaq's account, Muslims now consider Ibn Hisham's edited copy the official, authoritative, and standard sira of Muhammad. Its Arabic text was translated into English by British scholar Alfred Guillaume (1888–1965) and published by Oxford University Press in 1955.

As a genre of Islamic literature, sira is built on **hadith** traditions and actually developed from the earlier **maghazi** genre. The genre that started as maghazi—accounts of Muhammad's raids and expeditions—grew to include reports on other aspects of Muhammad's life in general. Still, the maghazi and sira genres are both built on hadith traditions, most often in the form of consecutive hadiths, allegedly supported by an **isnad** (a chain of transmitters). This is a general fact of early Islamic literature. The growth of the practice of writing hadith traditions—a century or so after Muhammad's death—resulted in the emergence of various genres of Islamic literature, all built on hadiths. Most of the early Muslim scholars, jurists, and historians—including Ibn Ishaq and Ibn Hisham—were compilers or, as skeptics say, authors of hadith traditions.

sunna: Muhammad's tradition, collectively

Linguistically, the word *sunna* means "a standard method, a unique custom, an exemplary manner, or a specific way of life." It is pronounced "SOON-nah." Muslims cherish the word and use it primarily in relation to Muhammad. Sunna collectively refers to his conduct, customs, practices, or deeds. When referring to a specific practice as admirable or commendable, Muslims often declare that it is "a sunna of Muhammad." They use this phrase to suggest that a reported deed or action was practiced or followed by Muhammad, which in turn makes the deed or action valued and praiseworthy to Muslims and, in many instances, legitimizes it. The word *sunna* is singular, and its plural form is *sunan*. Muslims often use the singular word *sunna* to refer to the collective tradition about Muhammad's life. This tradition includes thousands of reports that allegedly describe, in precise detail, everything related to Muhammad. For most Muslims, these reports are second in authority only to the Quran.

In truth, the reports were not documented during the time of Muhammad. Centuries after his death, Muslim scholars gathered traditions about his life—what he approved and forbade, said, did, or taught—and placed them in voluminous collections, declaring them truthful, sound, and authentic. While the late date of compilation casts doubt on the reliability, accuracy, and authenticity of such reports, Muslims often cherish them, viewing them as accurate and trustworthy narratives directly from or about Muhammad. One collection details his military activities (**maghazi**); another tells his biography (**sira**); a third reveals his sayings (**hadith**). Another collection provides interpretations of some verses in the Quran (**tafsir**). These collections make up a collective sunna of Muhammad, covering various genres of Islamic sacred texts.

But there is no one Islamic book—or set of books—titled *The Sunna*. We have collections of sunan (accounts deemed sacred by Muslims) about Muhammad's life. These collections consist of numerous narratives about Muhammad's life and deeds. These narratives come in a sequence of reports, each reflecting an aspect of Muhammad's sunna. The remarkable reality is that from the ample accounts of Muhammad's sunna, we know astonishing details and specifics about what he presumably did and said. We can learn his preferences regarding food, drink, hygiene, and even private manners with his wives. We can read about his customs before bed or after waking up. We can even create a picture of how he ate and what fingers he used to pick up his food.

In practical terms, the sunna of Muhammad is vitally important for every Muslim who seeks to imitate and follow Muhammad's example, but this sunna is also difficult to unravel for most Muslims, who are often cultural adherents of Islam and unversed in religious matters. These Muslims often rely on **imams**, educated clerics, and religious jurists to obtain Islamic knowledge and to learn the details of Muhammad's sunna. Today, many clerics utilize social media platforms to offer **fatwas** (religious rulings) for Muslims based on the Quran and Muhammad's sunna. If Muslims want to imitate Muhammad in a certain situation, they usually ask a religious preacher what the sunna of Muhammad says regarding the matter in question. The Muslim preacher usually begins with a verse from the Quran as the ultimate authority, then states a sunna of Muhammad, which comes next in authority after the Quran for most Muslims. The two major sects of Islam, Sunnism and Shiism, both cherish Muhammad's sunna, but they adopt different, often competing, traditions. The Arabic word *sunni* is an adjective describing relation or belonging to the sunna, so the name Sunni identifies a Muslim as a follower or a lover of Muhammad's sunna.

maghazi: Muhammad's military campaigns

The Arabic term *maghazi* is plural and means "military campaigns." It is pronounced "ma-GHEH-zee." Muslims use the term particularly in relation to Muhammad's raids and incursions. Some he led in person, and others he commissioned and entrusted to his skillful commanders. Muslims also use the term *maghazi* to refer to the genre of literature describing these campaigns. Muslims cherish the reports of Muhammad's military campaigns to the extent that early believers viewed Muhammad's life entirely as maghazi—a series of successful campaigns against non-Muslims. Before Muslims coined the term *sira* to describe Muhammad's biography, they used *maghazi* for his deeds and career. The maghazi were a matter of pride to the early Muslims, who viewed the success of the military campaigns as evidence of **Allah**'s confirmation of Muhammad's deeds and prophetic career.

In his lifetime, Muhammad led or commissioned over seventy military raids varying in strength, target, and number of Muslim soldiers. These maghazi took place in the final ten years of his life, particularly after he emigrated from Mecca to Medina in 622 in the major event known as the **hijra**. Some of the maghazi targeted Meccan pagans, while others were against believers of other religions, including Jewish or Christian tribes or settlements.

In practical terms, Muslims rely on the maghazi to learn about Muhammad's life and career, especially his military activity. However, the maghazi accounts did not come from eyewitnesses of Muhammad's life but rather from Muslims who lived centuries after the events. These accounts were basically composed of a series of **hadith** traditions. The emergence and growth of the hadith traditions led to other Islamic genres, including the one that describes Muhammad's military career. Medieval Muslims portrayed Muhammad as a shrewd military commander who initiated raids with talent and skill. These early Muslims described the raids as tactical and strategic campaigns, supported and advanced by Allah's divine favor. For these early Muslims, the term *maghazi* was not offensive when used to describe Muhammad because they did not feel it was odd or unfavorable to portray a prophet as a warlord. For some contemporary Muslims, the matter is different. These Muslims avoid claims that Muhammad initiated wars, and they argue that Muhammad's

maghazi were always for self-defense and for the proclamation of Islam—
although the Muslim accounts themselves demonstrate otherwise.

futuh: military conquests with religious significance

The Arabic term *futuh*, pronounced "foo-tooh," describes the military
conquests of non-Muslim lands by Muslim commanders after Muhammad's death as well as the literary genre that describes these conquests.
While the term *futuh* is often rendered as "conquests," its literal meaning
is "openings." Muslim historians did not view these military conquests
as invasions but instead as "opening" campaigns to bring the light of
Islam to the lands living in religious darkness. The term describes the
Islamic concept of wars with religious significance.

As a literary genre, the futuh is in many ways similar to the **maghazi**
of Muhammad. While the maghazi primarily describe Muhammad's
military expeditions, and the futuh details the Islamic expansion after his
death, some Muslim historians used the term *futuh* to describe Muhammad's major raids. Both maghazi and futuh genres describe historical
accounts (**tarikh**), although they are basically a series of hadith traditions. Many scholars voice skepticism regarding the reliability of many
accounts of the futuh, not only because of their late documentation and
contradictory details but also because of the apparent exaggeration in
the reports. For instance, some futuh accounts portray Muslims as significantly successful in conquests—even able to defeat hundreds of thousands of Christian Byzantines—although they were very few in number.

As for futuh reflecting the reality of Muslim military operations, it
appears that after Muhammad's death, Muslims expanded their rule
greatly. While Muhammad was able to control only the western parts
of what is today the Arabian Peninsula, after his death, Muslim caliphs
expanded their territory through conquests, controlling the entire land
of Arabia and defeating the superpowers of the day, the Byzantine and
Persian Empires. Within a century, Muslims ruled what we know today
as the Middle East and North Africa and controlled massive territories
from China to Spain and West Africa. Thus, the military conquests were
greatly successful, and they placed a minority of Muslims as rulers over
a vast territory of conquered people of other religions, including Judaism, Christianity, and Zoroastrianism.

tarikh: a history or historiography

The Arabic term *tarikh*, pronounced "tah-reekh," refers to both history—meaning the past or events of the past—and any writing about the past or the study of historical writings, technically described as historiography. While there is evidence that Muslims attempted to write their history from the earliest period of Islam, this tarikh did not reach us. Because the early historical accounts were lost between consecutive caliphates, it took over two centuries for the tarikh of Muslims to be formed and finalized. The fact is that three caliphates came to power in the first 120 years after Muhammad. The first (the **Rashidun** Caliphate, 632–661) did not seem to care much about documenting historical accounts, as it was embroiled in political turmoil and expansion. The second (the **Umayyad** Caliphate, 660–750) supported some attempts to document historical reports, but they were all lost or mostly censored by those who ruled after this caliphate. The third (the **Abbasid** Caliphate) came to power in 750. The Abbasid caliphs supervised the rewriting of Islam's tarikh and Muhammad's biography (**sira**) to support their claims to power among Muslims. Therefore, the Muslim tarikh, as we know it today, is a revised product, politically and religiously influenced to portray the version of Islam advanced by the Abbasid caliphs. This is why most of the accounts in the available Muslim tarikh disparage Umayyad leaders, depicting them as worldly and untrue Muslims, and portray Abbasid figures and ancestors as better Muslims who supported Muhammad and his prophethood from the start.

isnad: a chain of transmitters of Muhammad's tradition

Linguistically, the term *isnad*, pronounced "is-NAHD," is based on the noun *sanad*, which means "a pillar or foundation." The Arabic term *isnad* literally means "the act of leaning something against a strong support." It is a noun that describes the notion of supporting something by establishing a basis for it. This linguistic meaning helps to explain the technical Islamic meaning of the term *isnad*, which is used to highlight the support given to any saying (**hadith**) attributed to Muhammad. If a hadith has a strong isnad (support), then it is authentic and sound and, more importantly, is believed to trace back to Muhammad's words themselves. If the isnad is weak, then Muslims tend to be somewhat skeptical of the soundness and authority of the hadith. Technically, the word *isnad* refers to the chain of transmitters or informants who reported a hadith about Muhammad. If the informants are well known to Muslims and well connected to each other through generations, then the isnad is rigorous and solid; thus, the hadith becomes sound (sahih) and reliable.

In practical terms, the isnad of any hadith is basically a list of the people who repeated the hadith and conveyed it to the next person, often tracing back to Muhammad himself or to one of his earliest followers. A hadith can be as simple as a short statement: "Muhammad said that Friday is the best day of the week." This is the text (matn) of the hadith. To know how reliable this hadith is, Muslims check its isnad—that is, the chain of informants or transmitters who repeated it throughout the generations. The isnad precedes the text of any hadith: "It was reported on the authority of person A who heard it from person B who gathered it from person C who received it from person D who overheard it from Aisha the wife of the messenger of Allah who heard it from the Prophet himself concerning the days of any given week." Centuries after Muhammad, Muslim scholars created various religious tools to check the isnad of each hadith. Based on the soundness of the isnad, they distinguished hadiths, claiming some to be sound and others weak—meaning not as reliable as the sound ones—although they can still be valued to varying degrees.

Sunnis believe there are nine trusted collections of Muhammad's hadiths. Two collections are exceptionally trusted as reliable: the collection of **Imam** Bukhari (810–870) and the collection of Imam Muslim (821–875). The other seven collections are also reliable but are not of the same status as the first two. Shiite Muslims do not trust the Sunni collections, particularly those of Bukhari and Muslim. They have other collections of hadiths attributed to Muhammad and his household, known as the trusted Shiite imams.

tafsir: an interpretation of or commentary on the Quran

In Arabic, a tafsir is an explanation, interpretation, or commentary. The term *tafsir*, pronounced "tef-seer," is directly related to the **Quran** and refers to works on Quranic interpretation or exegesis. A commentary on the Quran, which seeks to explain or interpret the sacred Muslim text, is thus called a tafsir. The word *tafsir* is singular; its plural form is *tafasir* but is usually rendered in English as "tafsirs." Because the Quran, for Muslims, is divinely inspired, its words are beyond human comprehension. Still, Muslims believe that Muhammad explained the Quran during his lifetime to his earliest companions and that he was the best human who ever lived, exemplifying and fulfilling the Quran by his deeds and conduct. However, no tafsir of the Quran exists from Muhammad's time. The earliest extant commentary (tafsir) on the Quran is attributed to a non-Arab Muslim named Muqatil ibn Sulayman (ca. 702–767), who died about 140 years after Muhammad. This tafsir basically paraphrases every verse in the Quran and provides tales and stories to explain the text. Muqatil's tafsir is indeed the earliest commentary—and one of the shortest and least sophisticated, as compared to later commentaries.

With the expansion of the Muslim empire, non-Muslims—particularly Jews and Christians—continued to challenge Muslims about statements in the Quran. Consequently, Muslim scholars of the **hadith**—relying on the growing number of hadith traditions—began producing more works of tafsir. In technical terms, a tafsir on the Quran is basically a consecutive list of hadiths projected back in time, attributed to Muhammad, and alleged to provide an explanation of the Quran. When Muslim commentators faced contradicting verses in the Quran, they were forced to establish interpretive tools to explain the text. For example, Muslim scholars determined that when two verses contradict each other, the one revealed later abrogates—that is, cancels—the earlier one. This became known as the doctrine of **naskh** (abrogation). The growing number of tafsirs over time revealed many contradictions, although they all claimed to rely on statements given directly by Muhammad. As a result, many non-Muslim scholars in our day argue that the Muslim commentators were not necessarily attempting to interpret the Quran itself but were rather responding to questions posed by Muslims and non-Muslims at the time of writing.

Among Muslims, *ta'wil* is a term related to tafsir. It is pronounced "ta-wheel." While many refer to ta'wil as the equivalent of tafsir—that is, explaining and providing a commentary—some distinguish between the two terms, claiming that a ta'wil involves a deeper process than a tafsir. They argue that a tafsir is often focused on grammar and syntax, while a ta'wil aims to delve deeper into the meaning of the text, to where the human soul interacts with the text and digests it. Linguistically, the word *ta'wil* connotes returning something to its deeper origins. Some understand it to be close in meaning to allegorical exegesis and believe that it is used more in mystical Islam, like **Sufism**, as it seeks to meditate on the text and glean its treasures apart from its outer letter.

asbab: occasions, specifically of revealing verses of the Quran

The term *asbab*, which means "reasons, causes, or occasions," is very important to the Muslim interpretation of the **Quran**. It is pronounced "as-BEHB." It is the plural noun of the Arabic word *sabab*. For Muslims, to interpret the Quran properly, one needs to know the sabab or asbab of the revelation of a verse. Muslims often speak of asbab al-nuzul, meaning "the occasions of revelation of a specific verse," where the term *al-nuzul* means "the sending down or descending" of a specific verse. Thus, asbab al-nuzul is often rendered as "the occasions of revelation."

Asbab al-nuzul has become an Islamic science that is vital to the interpretation of the Quran. It has been argued that the Quran includes passages that appear to lack context; they do not reveal the time, place, or reason for the texts and thus cannot be understood on their own. Muslims must know asbab al-nuzul to unlock these vague texts. Whether a passage in the Quran is clear or ambiguous, Muslims seek to know its asbab al-nuzul in order to interpret it properly. While the earliest generation of Muslims did not have a way to identify the context of or the reasons behind the revelation of each verse in the Quran, later Muslims compiled volumes of asbab for this purpose. The earliest extant book of this genre comes from the fifth century after Muhammad's death. It relies on **hadith** traditions attributed to Muhammad and his immediate companions. While the earliest work on asbab al-nuzul is arguably late in its compilation, Muslims claim that the work relies on earlier traditions that circulated among Muslims for centuries. The rationale is this: Muhammad lived out the Quran in his lifetime, and before his death, he interpreted it all for his companions. His hadith traditions—Muslims claim—include asbab al-nuzul.

Asbab al-nuzul is a part of the broader **tafsir** genre of the Quran. They are intertwined and interconnected. In practice, most Muslims avoid comprehending the Quran on its own terms without relying on the traditions of asbab al-nuzul. Even if a passage is presumably clear, Muslims avoid interpreting it apart from tafsir or asbab al-nuzul. The traditions of asbab al-nuzul provide the context for every verse, passage, or chapter of the Quran—its time, place, and reason for revelation. This essentially means that later traditions—produced centuries after the supposed revelation of the Quran—provide its context to clarify and explain it. Still, most asbab traditions rely on hadith traditions projected back in time and attributed to Muhammad or one of his followers. In practical terms, these traditions aim to establish and advance specific interpretations and to suppress others. Political sympathies and sectarian loyalties were at work, as evidenced in how Sunni and Shiite traditions differ greatly in asbab al-nuzul of similar passages in the Quran.

ansab: genealogies

The Arabic term *ansab* refers to genealogies, and it is pronounced "an-SEHB." The singular form of *ansab* is *nasab*, which refers to lineage or genealogical links. Among the Arabs, especially during Muhammad's time but also still today, ansab were a source of pride and esteem. Free men in particular enjoyed prestige and assumed honor among the tribes due to their acclaimed nasab, which reflected their free—not enslaved—status. In Muhammad's tribe, the **Quraysh**, many members were known as ashraf, meaning "aristocrats" or "notables," because of their illustrious family nasab (lineage). A person known as one of the ashraf was assumed to have a pure and noble nasab and therefore was granted honor and status. In tribal social systems, a nasab provided a member with recognition and validation.

Among Muslims, nasab remains important today, especially in places where tribal considerations flourish (e.g., Saudi Arabia). Arabs, unlike those in individualistic societies, value a tribal lineage more than any personal status. The importance of nasab is evident in the fact that even today socially underprivileged individuals—who are not born with notable genealogy—often seek to receive honor by associating with honorable families. Currently, certain Muslims even claim to be descendants of the family of Muhammad. They claim to be ashraf (notables). This title grants them a noble status, which—in some Muslim-majority countries—offers them specific privileges. Here, again, we see how pre-Islamic tribal measures continued into Islamic times and permeated Islam's moral and social systems. However, for most Muslims, the religious concept of **umma**—Muslims as one unified and united community—often takes a higher priority over social considerations, even if only in theory.

Because ansab are of great significance to Muslims, many Muslim scholars have compiled volumes on genealogies. These volumes form a genre of Islamic texts called the ansab literature. This genre contains works on the ansab of the Quraysh, the ansab of the nobles among Arabs, the ansab of the famous poets, and the ansab of the hadith experts, among others. The earliest available ansab work was compiled by a Muslim scholar who lived about two centuries after Muhammad's death.

sharia: Islamic law, as prescribed by Allah

Linguistically, the word *sharia*, pronounced "sha-REE-uh," refers to a straight path or a pure source of water for people. Practically, the sharia, for Muslims, is Allah's will and divine law for all people. Because of its linguistic connotation, the sharia—Allah's law—is, according to Muslims, the perfect path and the best source for life. It is not only divine and inerrant but also superior to any human law and distinguished from any man-made precepts. Allah's sharia, for Muslims, is universal—it came down from Allah and is prescribed upon every human being, Muslim or non-Muslim. For cultural and religious Muslims, the sharia is sacred, just, and holy. It covers all aspects of life and worship, describing the way a Muslim should worship the divine and treat a fellow human being. Muslims cherish the claim that Muhammad was the best example of humankind applying Allah's sharia; thus, Muslims want to imitate him. They believe it is their sacred duty to establish states following the sharia's regulations. If Muslims follow the sharia, the rationale goes, the Islamic community will flourish and succeed. Many Muslims today believe that Islamic nations are in a state of decay, religiously and economically, because Muslims forsook Allah's sharia and its precise precepts.

But there is no book in Islam titled *Sharia*. The details of the sharia are found within ample Muslim traditions and are believed to be retrievable or extractable only by Muslim scholars. In reality, early Muslims did not know of anything called the sharia. Centuries after Muhammad's death, Muslim scholars needed to articulate the various aspects of Islamic worship and practice to a growing Muslim population, so they established regulations and rules based on the Quran and Muhammad's traditions. This resulted in the compilation of voluminous texts claiming to describe Allah's commands and define his sharia. Interestingly, with the passing of time and the growing number of Muslims, scholars needed to respond to ever-changing contemporary issues, and so they created more and more works allegedly specifying Allah's laws and precepts.

In general, the sharia, which contains specifics about religious, personal, cultural, and even political matters, covers every aspect of a Muslim's life. Not surprisingly, disagreement often arises between Muslim clerics as to what precisely the sharia says in regard to specific worship situations or life circumstances. The disagreements are sometimes minor (like whether a food is religiously clean) and other times major (like whether to accept the repentance of apostates as opposed to killing them). Also not surprisingly, since the Sunni and Shiite sacred sources—with the exception of the Quran—are not identical, the specific details of the sharia vary between Sunnis and Shiites.

In practice, cultural Muslims often face difficulty when determining the sharia precepts for themselves. Even for devout Muslim believers, finding answers is often difficult. The fact is that the keys to understanding Allah's sharia lie largely in the hands of Muslim clerics. In practical terms, the most influential person in the life of any Muslim is usually the **imam** of the local mosque. We should also note that when religious scholars do not find answers to a specific legal question in the Quran or Muhammad's teachings, they often try to apply analogy (qiyaas) or use a sophisticated procedure of religious reasoning to provide answers. This demonstrates even more the difficulty of determining what the sharia really is. Interestingly, because of the favorable nature of the word *sharia*, many Muslims tend to think that the best way to live is to apply Allah's sharia, even though they do not really know what it entails.

Injil: a revealed scripture given to Jesus, the Gospel

The Quran uses the term *Injil*, pronounced "in-jeel," to identify the heavenly scripture revealed by Allah to Jesus. In this context, Jesus is merely

one of Allah's prophets and messengers. He is known by the Arabic name
Isa (pronounced "ee-SUH") and was sent to the Israelites (Q 3:49). In
Islamic understanding, the Injil is not what Christians identify as the
New Testament, nor is it a collection of the four Gospels. The original
Injil—according to Muslim traditions—has been lost because Christians
intentionally corrupted it and created their own versions to satisfy their
evil desires. Although the Quran never explicitly states that the Injil was
corrupt or altered, Muslim traditions insist on this erroneous claim,
which has circulated among Muslims for over twelve centuries. One
reason for the claim of corruption is that Muslims believe the true Injil
contains a mention of Muhammad's advent. Since the current Gospels
do not include any explicit references to Muhammad, Muslim scholars
from the earliest days of Christian-Muslim encounters claimed the corruption of the Gospels. The case is similar with Jews and the Torah and,
in fact, with any other biblical scripture.

Muslims believe that the original Injil contains revelations similar to
those that Allah later gave to Muhammad in the Quran. After all, each
messenger of Allah, Muslims believe, is given a scripture. Like the Quran,
all previous revelations aim to proclaim **tawhid**, strict monotheism. In
fact, Muslims believe that all messengers—including Abraham, Moses,
and Jesus—were believers of Islam (Muslims) (e.g., Q 2:67; 5:52, 111;
10:84; cf. 3:19, 85). In addition to the Injil, the Quran refers to some other
pre-Islamic heavenly inspired books, including Moses's **Tawrah** (Torah)
and David's **Zabur** (Psalms) (e.g., Q 4:163; 5:43–45; 17:55; 21:105; 57:27).
Furthermore, the Quran refers to lesser-known scriptures (suhuf) sent by
Allah to Abraham and Moses (Q 20:133; 53:36; 80:13; 81:10; 87:18–19).
While these books may appear similar to sacred texts adopted by Jews,
Muslims believe they are not accessible any longer due to corruption.
However, they believe that the Quran now includes all that was in these
revelations.

Zabur: a revealed scripture given to David, the Psalms

The term *Zabur*, pronounced "zah-BOOR," appears three times in the
Quran (Q 4:163; 17:55; 21:105), where the first two references explicitly
describe it as a book divinely revealed to David. Thus, just as Allah sent
down the **Injil** to Jesus and the Torah to Moses, he did the same to David,

giving him the Zabur to proclaim to the Israelites. Scholars suggest that the Arabic word *Zabur* may be derived from a word referring to a song played on a wooden instrument similar to today's flute.

The Quran seems to directly quote the Zabur. In Q 21:105, Allah relays that he wrote in the Zabur that his righteous servants would inherit the earth. This assertion, according to many scholars, is a direct quote from the Bible in Psalm 37:29. This reference in the Quran about the Zabur is unique, as there is no other explicit reference of this sort in Islam's scripture.

In a **hadith** attributed to Muhammad, he mentions the Zabur and asserts that all previous divinely inspired scriptures—including the Zabur—contain the same contents, although the Quran has a unique chapter (Q 1) that was not in any of the previous revelations. The Quranic understanding of the Zabur is significantly different from the biblical perspective. For Christians and Jews, the psalms are songs written by David and others under God's inspiration. For Muslims, the Zabur is a heavenly scripture dictated by Allah to David. Furthermore, Muslims believe that the Zabur is now lost—that the book of Psalms used today is a corrupt version of what was initially revealed as the Zabur. For Muslims, now there is no need for the Zabur, as its entire content is found in the Quran, only better and more complete and, of course, completely preserved until the end of times.

Tawrah: a revealed scripture given to Moses, the Torah

For Muslims, the Arabic term *Tawrah*, pronounced "taw-ruh," refers to a dictated scripture given to Moses by Allah. It refers to the Torah. Unlike with the **Zabur**, which is associated with David in the Quran, there is no explicit association in Islam's scripture between the Tawrah and Moses. However, the Islamic understanding is that all three scriptures—the Tawrah, the Zabur, and the **Injil**—were sent to the Israelites, who rejected the prophets and persecuted them. Thus, just as the Zabur and the Injil were given to David and Jesus, respectively, so the Tawrah came down to Moses. More importantly, for Muslims, Moses did not write the Torah. He merely received it.

Just as the original Zabur and Injil—in the Islamic understanding—are nonexistent due to corruption by evil Jews and Christians, the same goes for the Tawrah. The claims of corrupting the Tawrah cannot be substantiated by the Quran, which explicitly affirms its trustworthiness (Q 5:43–44, 46). Muslims believe that all pre-Islamic divine revelations, including the Zabur and the Injil, can be found in the message of the Quran, which surpassed and replaced them as the only perfectly preserved scripture. One reason for the insistence of Muslim scholars that the Tawrah was corrupted may lie in the fact that the Quran states that Muhammad is mentioned in the Tawrah (Q 7:157). Since Muhammad is not mentioned in today's Torah, Muslim scholars deduced that it must have been altered. Nonetheless, Muslim traditions contain a unique hadith attributed to Muhammad in which he meets with a group of Jews who ask him about his ruling against an adulterous man. Muhammad responds by holding the Torah in his hand and stating that he believes in it and in Allah, who revealed it. For Muslims who believe the hadith traditions, this one refutes claims of corruption of the Torah.

The Quran seems to quote the Torah. In Q 5:44–45, we read of the famous Jewish ruling of an eye for an eye. This appears to quote Exodus 21:24–25, although with some variation. The Quran also affirms that Jesus (Isa) not only received the Injil but also learned the Tawrah and the wisdom books thoroughly (Q 5:110).

akhbari: a Muslim historian or chronicler

In Arabic, akhbar is news or chronicles. The term *akhbar* is plural, and its singular is *khabar*, which refers to a short piece of news or a brief historical report. An akhbari, pronounced "ukh-BERR-ee," is someone who reports news or details chronicles. In early Islam, an akhbari was basically a hadith scholar (or traditionist) who reported historical accounts in the form of a series of traditions, supporting them with an **isnad** (a chain of transmitters). Muslims wrote voluminous works with the word *akhbar* in their titles, purporting to detail historical events and life accounts of major Muslim figures.

The tendency among Muslims is to view the akhbaris (chroniclers or historians) of early Islam as pious hadith scholars who were keen to report the news of Islam's origins to educate later generations. However, the original Muslim accounts reveal that these akhbaris were paid to create biased reports for the powerful caliphs. We read of the powerful

Umayyad caliph Mu'awiya, who hired Muslim narrators to fabricate reports against his enemy, Muhammad's cousin Ali. We also learn of a major Muslim historian, Waqidi, who made a living in the **Abbasid** caliphal court by generating historical akhbar in order to pay off his debts.

In Shiism, an akhbari is synonymous with a hadith scholar but with an additional emphasis: it refers to a devoted transmitter of the teachings of the infallible twelve **imams** (descendants of Ali, Muhammad's cousin and son-in-law). For Shiite Muslims, these akhbaris were pious Muslims who did not imitate the spirit of their age, nor did they use human reasoning in matters of religion. Rather, they served as devotees to the imams by delivering and transmitting only sound and reliable rulings in the form of Shiite traditions.

ISLAMIC HISTORY

This section highlights important places, people, and events related to Islam's past and origins. Muslims view their past not as mere history but instead—for the most part—as sacred history. For most Muslims, the earliest generations of Islam were the best and most faithful to Islam. Islam's history, for these Muslims, is exemplary and unmatched—if Muslims wish to live well, the rationale goes, they must strive to follow the example of Muhammad and his companions. The veneration of these old days among certain groups of Muslims is simply unmatched. Today, many Muslims lament the state of affairs in Muslim countries and voice the frustration that Muslims are far from implementing Islam as the historical forefathers did. Many believe that if Muslims would return to their origins and apply Islam's basic principles, then their culture and society would thrive and they would become the most successful and powerful among the nations of the world. This sentiment reflects how Muslims cherish and value their history as a model for life. Although the historical accounts of Islam do not paint such a utopian picture of the early generations of Islam, many Muslims still pine for the earliest days of Islam to be revived and relived. This section includes important terms related to Islamic history, as any basic understanding of the Muslim past must involve a reflection on these elementary terms. While the explanation of each term attempts, first of all, to underscore the term's significance in relation to Muslim history in general, it also aims to relay how the place, person, or event impacted the formation of Islam and was related to other historical episodes.

jahiliyya: the pre-Islamic age of ignorance

The term *jahiliyya*, pronounced "ja-hee-LEE-yuh," refers to the pre-Islamic age of ignorance. It is an Islamic term that connotes the spiritual darkness and religious ignorance of the age before Muhammad came with guidance and light for his people through the message of Islam. It is related to the Arabic noun *jaahil*, an ignorant person, and another noun, *jahl*, which means "ignorance." The term appears several times in the Quran and always compares the time of Muhammad to what came before, indicating Allah's disapproval of jahiliyya as a time of falsehood, immodesty, and fuming tribalism (Q 3:154; 5:50; 33:33; 48:26).

The term reflects an Islamic ideology that depicts the pre-Muhammad era as religiously inferior to the glorious state of life and practice that Islam initiated. While the term directly describes the pre-Muhammad Arabs as idol worshipers, it extends beyond them to include all humankind, portraying humans as being in a state of disarray, waiting for the light of Islam. The Islamic rationale goes like this: Before Muhammad, Persians worshiped fire, Southern Arabia adored skies and stars, Meccans bowed to idols, and even Jews and Christians corrupted their faiths—then Islam came with its religious guidance to remedy the ignorance of humankind. Nonetheless, these ideological claims do not consider the fact that Islam itself seems to have adopted various customs and aspects of pre-Islamic Arab life. These aspects may include several features of the **hajj** (pilgrimage) and the practice of tribal raids—both of which continued well into Islam with some adjustments. Also, while Muslims insist that Islam changed jahiliyya views of women by elevating their status, Muslim sources themselves highlight the respected status some women, such as Muhammad's wife Khadija, had before Islam.

Due to its lexical meaning and ideological connotation, the term *jahiliyya* is used by Muslims today to refer to any ungodly or immoral state of affairs. Thus, in conservative Islamic societies, a Muslim may identify an unveiled woman as living in jahiliyya. The same goes for a man who does not practice his religion properly—he may be accused of living in jahiliyya. In Western societies, devout Muslims may refer to sexually vulgar Hollywood movies as jahiliyya.

Ka'ba: the cubic shrine in Mecca, the most sacred Islamic place on earth

The Ka'ba, pronounced "KAH-ha-bah," is the most sacred Muslim shrine on earth. It is a cubic structure, totally covered in black, located at the center of the sacred mosque (al-**masjid** al-haram) in today's Mecca in Saudi Arabia. For Muslims, if Mecca is the most sacred city (as the birthplace of Muhammad and thus Islam), then the Ka'ba is the most sacred spot in the most sacred city. The Ka'ba is thus the holy of holies in Islam. Among Muslims, it is not viewed as merely a shrine—it is Allah's house (Bayt Allah). Every follower of Islam longs—and often works diligently by saving money for years—to visit the Ka'ba at least once in their lifetime in order to fulfill the religious duty (fard) of performing the **hajj** (pilgrimage). When millions of Muslims gather for the hajj in Mecca, a significant part of their worship involves walking several times around the Ka'ba. This is a major ritual without which the hajj becomes invalid.

The history of the Ka'ba is mysterious and disputed even by Muslims. However, its sacred status stems from the many traditions that claim it was built by the great patriarch Abraham and his son Ishmael (not Isaac). Some other traditions claim that Adam, the first human, was actually the true builder of the Ka'ba. After the angels assisted Adam in building the Ka'ba, traditions claim, he became the first human to perform the hajj. Contradictory traditions indicate that the Ka'ba was actually created forty years before the creation of the earth. Then, after Allah created Adam, he sent him down to earth to choose the location of the Ka'ba. These traditions establish the Ka'ba's status and reverence. Many Muslims even believe that Muhammad claimed that one prayer in the Ka'ba is equal to a hundred thousand prayers elsewhere.

In today's Ka'ba—its walls covered by highest-quality black silk worth $4 million—nothing is more valuable than the sacred black stone (al-hajar al-aswad) located in its corner. Muslims believe it descended from heaven and thus has miraculous powers. It was white, we are told, but the sins of humans turned it black. While some skeptics may question whether there are rocks in heaven or whether a stone can actually change color due to human sins, devotees do not question these traditions. Due to the sacred status of the Ka'ba and its stone, the performance of the hajj can be invalidated if a Muslim is unable to touch or kiss the black stone.

Muslims believe that fighting has been absolutely forbidden in Mecca since the day Muhammad was declared its sole leader, about three years before his death. While these claims are shared and cherished by most Muslims, their own historical accounts reveal a completely opposite picture: today's majestic Ka'ba has been frequently destroyed, even by Muslim fighters themselves. A few decades after Muhammad's death, a huge Muslim civil war (fitna) erupted in Mecca; the Ka'ba was destroyed by fire during this conflict. This was not the only time. Shiites attacked the city in the 900s, seizing the black stone and holding it for over twenty years. While Muslim accounts about the Ka'ba are hardly persuading, they reveal the revered status of the cubic shrine in the heart of Mecca.

Quraysh: Muhammad's tribe

Quraysh, pronounced "koo-roysh," is the name of Muhammad's tribe, which was reportedly one of several major tribes in Mecca. The origin of the name is ambiguous. Some Muslims believe that Quraysh was the surname or nickname of a major ancestor from the tribe who existed many generations before Muhammad—some claim he was the tenth or twelfth grandfather of Muhammad. Some traditions claim that the name Quraysh was a reference to a sea creature and was later assigned to the tribe. Others believe the term is based on an Arabic noun denoting the collection of resources in business, which highlights what the Quraysh practiced—that is, trading and exchanging merchandise. According to Muslim traditions, the Quraysh controlled life in Mecca through their caravan trade—which reached throughout Arabia—and the managing of the **hajj** (pilgrimage) to the **Ka'ba**. These claims come from Muslim accounts written centuries after Muhammad. Non-Muslim sources contemporary or near-contemporary with Muhammad do not mention the Quraysh, nor do they refer to their Meccan location or trade.

The Quran includes a **sura** (chapter) titled "The Quraysh" (Q 106), which has four verses. The sura refers to Allah's rewards and his blessings on the tribe and the way the tribe should work to preserve these benefits. Ample **hadith** traditions attributed to Muhammad also praise and commend the Quraysh. Muhammad reportedly praised Muslims who recited the Quraysh sura (Q 106), promising they would receive numerous divine rewards (in some hadiths, tenfold more than people who reside in the sacred mosque). Muhammad also claimed that the caliph of the Muslims—the authority or ruler—will always come from the Quraysh, even if there are only two humans remaining on earth. While scholars highly doubt the reliability of these traditions, they drive claims of the superiority of Muhammad's tribe over other Arab tribes. Some view these traditions as forged accounts created by religious narrators who sought to please later rulers from the Quraysh.

The Quraysh, according to Muslim traditions, was the first context for Muhammad's preaching. After he allegedly received the divine revelations, he began preaching to his relatives, but he was unable to gain followers. When he went public with his **da'wa** (calling people to Islam), the Quraysh became hostile toward him, as they feared his message would jeopardize their professions and accumulation of wealth. The majority of the Quraysh opposed Muhammad, rejected his preaching, and mistreated him and his new followers. This, in part, resulted in emigration attempts by these Muslims. They tried to emigrate from Mecca to the nearby town of Ta'if but failed, then to Abyssinia (roughly today's Ethiopia) and succeeded. Still, they later found a better home: Yathrib. This was later called Medina (the city), denoting it as the homeland or residence of Muhammad. Three years before Muhammad's death, he returned victoriously to Mecca and ruled over it, thus defeating the Quraysh. Many of the members of the tribe hastened to embrace Islam and to surrender to the new leader. Some of the elites and aristocrats of the Quraysh were still reluctant to embrace Islam, but Muhammad gave them financial incentives that induced them to convert to Islam.

hijra: emigration

In Arabic, *hijra* refers to departing one place for another or simply emigration. The noun *hijra* is pronounced "hij-ruh" and is based on a verb meaning "the disassociating of oneself from social ties to move to a different place." In Islam, the hijra is a major point in Muhammad's life and refers to the emigration of Muhammad and his few followers from Mecca to a nearby oasis called Yathrib, which was later named Medina, "the city"—that is, the prophet's city.

The hijra event, according to Muslim traditions, was much needed, because Muhammad and his handful of believers were severely persecuted in Mecca by the pagan idolaters, particularly from Muhammad's tribe, the **Quraysh**. In world history, the hijra event coincides with the year 622. Years after Muhammad's death, the second caliph of Islam, Umar, designated this event as the beginning of the Islamic calendar, which is called the hijri calendar. Unlike the Christian calendar, the hijri calendar is lunar. It has twelve months, varying between twenty-nine and thirty days. The beginning of the month is determined by the appearance of the crescent moon. If it is seen after sunset, then the following day begins the next month.

According to Muslim traditions, Muhammad's hijra from Mecca to Medina was not the first hijra. Initially, Muslims attempted to emigrate from Mecca to Ta'if, but its inhabitants were not hospitable to Muslims and rejected them. Then the Muslims traveled to the kindgom of Abyssinia, while Muhammad stayed behind in Mecca. This was the first hijra, and Muslims were protected by the Christian king for a few years. The hijra to Abyssinia occurred almost eight years before the hijra to Medina. According to tradition, the Muslims who had emigrated from Mecca to Abyssinia thought the Muslims and pagans had reconciled, so many of them moved back to Mecca—although some chose to remain in the Christian kingdom.

Muhammad's reported hijra divides his prophetic career into two important parts—about thirteen years in Mecca and ten in Medina. His career as a prophet began in Mecca in 610, and he remained there until 622. This Meccan period, traditions claim, was colored by hostility and persecution by the pagans of the Quraysh and resulted in very few people accepting his religious message. In 622, the hijra to Medina occurred. There Muhammad began to act as a statesman and military commander, commissioning or leading raids against the Meccan pagans, the Jews of Medina and its surroundings, and some Christian tribes on the frontier of the Byzantine Empire. His time in Medina ended in 632 after he had subdued all his enemies and become the sole leader of western Arabia.

Not only was the hijra important for Muslims strategically, but it was also crucial for them exegetically. They believe that since the Quran was revealed to Muhammad in both Mecca and Medina, its chapters correspond to these different contexts. For Muslims, the Quran has two major parts—Meccan chapters and Medinan ones. The early passages are colored with tolerance, while the latter ones are marked by fighting and military prowess. For most Muslim commentators on the Quran, if two of its chapters conflict with each other, the Medinan abrogates the Meccan.

fitna: sedition, trial, or a Muslim civil war

The Arabic term *fitna* means "a challenging trial, severe affliction, distressful conflict, or distracting enticement." The term is singular (pronounced "fit-nuh"), and its plural form is *fitan*. Linguistically, the term refers to purifying or refining metals, especially gold and silver, with fire. While the meaning appears positive, the term itself almost always has a negative connotation in Arabic literature. The fitna is thus a distinguishing test.

In the Quran, the term *fitna* appears over thirty times and conveys many notions. Most of the occurrences seem to reflect the meaning of affliction, trial, or unbearable test (Q 5:71; 21:35; 22:111; 64:15). It also refers to affliction due to fighting (Q 8:73) and is used to highlight human sin and transgression (Q 9:49), sometimes pointing to shirk (polytheism) and kufr (unbelief or infidelity) (Q 8:39). It connotes the evil act of creating doubts in the hearts of people with the aim of leading them away from true beliefs (Q 3:7). The term can also indicate the act of harming people purposefully (Q 29:10) or creating chaos and disorder in the lands (Q 2:191, 217; 9:47). The term also appears as a divine punishment (Q 24:63).

In Muslim history, the term *fitna* is often associated with several civil wars that occurred among Muslims. According to historical accounts, the first fitna erupted about twenty-three years after Muhammad's death, during the reign of the third caliph, Uthman (d. 656). This fitna refers to the conflict that divided the Muslims into many factions before and after Uthman's assassination. When the caliph reportedly filled the most important government positions with his **Umayyad** relatives, other Muslims were dissatisfied. They declared him unfit to rule, and some claimed he was a **kafir** (infidel). His Muslim enemies surrounded his home and killed him. Soon after, the schism between his supporters and his enemies widened and resulted in more wars, leading to the deaths of tens of thousands of Muslims—including Muhammad's cousin Ali (the first Shiite **imam** and fourth caliph) and his son Husayn. This fitna not only led to the creation of the second caliphate in Islam, the Umayyad Dynasty, but also advanced the earliest manifestation of the conflict between the Shiites (supporters of Ali) and the anti-Shiites (who, generations later, became Sunnis). While this is arguably the first major fitna, some Muslims claim that the first fitna occurred immediately after Muhammad's death, when Muslims abandoned Islam, causing Caliph Abu Bakr to launch the Apostasy Wars to restore them to Islam.

Rashidun: the rightly guided caliphs

The term *Rashidun* means "the rightly guided." It identifies the first four successors of Muhammad (called caliphs) as divinely guided in following and applying Muhammad's **sunna** (example and conduct). The term is pronounced "raw-shee-doon." It is used only by Sunnis, since Shiites believe that the first three caliphs were wicked and did not imitate Muhammad and that only the fourth was rightly guided. Shiites thus refer to the era of the first four caliphs as merely "early Islam."

The first four caliphs were Abu Bakr, Umar, Uthman, and Ali. They ruled over the Muslim community from 632 until 661. Their time is known as the Rashidun Caliphate. Sunni Muslims identify each of the four as Muhammad's caliph (Arabic: khalifa), which means "deputy" or "successor." For Sunnis, these four caliphs are the perfect example of Islamic rulers. Their rule was, Sunnis claim, the golden time in Islamic history because they applied the **sharia** (Islamic law), as exemplified in Muhammad's life, in the most orthodox way. However, this idealistic picture is starkly contradicted by Muslims' own historical accounts, which depict religious tension, political fighting, and social unrest taking place within the Muslim community under the Rashidun.

Abu Bakr was Muhammad's first caliph and ruled for about two years, from 632 to 634. He became the caliph on the day Muhammad died. Abu Bakr is known among Sunnis as al-Siddiq, which means "the faithful and trustworthy," while Shiites consider him an evil infidel who grabbed power illegitimately with the help of major Meccans. He was three years younger than Muhammad. Abu Bakr's daughter, Aisha, was reportedly Muhammad's favorite and youngest wife. According to history, Abu Bakr's major achievements lie in launching the Apostasy Wars against those who abandoned Islam and refused to pay the **zakat** (obligatory charitable payment) and initiating conquests against Christian Byzantine lands such as Syria and Persian territories in Iraq. Sunnis largely view Abu Bakr as a protector of the faith who followed Muhammad's example perfectly. By the end of his reign, all of Arabia was under Islam, and the territory was expanding to the frontiers of the superpowers of the day. According to historical accounts, Abu Bakr died of fever, although some skeptics argue that he was killed by his successor.

Umar was the second caliph. He was about ten years younger than Abu Bakr, who designated him as his successor with a direct caliphal decree before he died. According to traditions, Umar had been a close friend of Abu Bakr and was influential in getting him chosen as Muhammad's successor in the major event known as the saqifa (a Bedouin roofed structure where the caliph was elected). This may indicate why Abu Bakr chose him, although traditions claim that Umar's merits inevitably led to the choice. Umar reigned from 634 to 644 and successfully directed the great conquests of the Persians and the Byzantines that brought Iraq and Syria under Muslim control and opened the gate wide for the continued expansion of the Islamic state based in Medina. He also succeeded in controlling Jerusalem, the third-most-important city in Islam. Among Umar's accomplishments was the establishment of the **hijri** calendar and the diwan, a bureaucratic registry to organize the finances of the caliphate in general and the salaries and rewards of the Muslim soldiers in particular. One of Umar's major consequential decisions was appointing Mu'awiya as the governor of the newly conquered Syria. Mu'awiya was a shrewd political commander from the **Umayyad** family, which included the cousins—and, largely, opponents—of Muhammad's family, especially Ali. Mu'awiya later became the first caliph in the second Muslim caliphate, the Umayyad Dynasty. Umar was assassinated by Fayruz, a Persian convert to Islam, who stabbed him. Many Sunnis believe that Fayruz was a false Muslim or a closet Shiite; other sources identify him as a Zoroastrian, Jew, or Christian. Umar survived for three days after the stabbing. He did not designate a successor, but on his deathbed, Muslims claim, he created a council of six aristocratic Meccans from whom the caliph would be chosen.

Uthman was chosen as Umar's successor. Like Mu'awiya, Uthman was from the Umayyad family. He ruled from 644 to 656 and was married to two of Muhammad's daughters. While he continued the expansion of the Islamic state, reaching more inland in the Persian and Byzantine territories, his tenure was colored by unrest among the Muslims, especially because he favored his Umayyad relatives for government positions. While his major achievement was compiling the Quran, he made many Muslims furious. Like Umar, Uthman was assassinated; an angry group of Muslims traveled all the way to Medina from Egypt and killed him in his own home in 656.

Ali succeeded Uthman as the caliph in 656. Shiites believe he was the rightful leader who remained faithful despite the wicked people in power. Mu'awiya sought revenge for the death of his relative Uthman, but the new caliph believed that maintaining peace was necessary. Since Mu'awiya was now the powerful governor of Syria who had consolidated power for over seventeen years, he and other Muslims openly opposed Caliph Ali. This rebellion was identified as the first fitna, or civil war, among Muslims. Two major wars occurred, thousands of Muslims died, and chaos spread throughout the empire. Some Muslims attempted to murder Mu'awiya and Ali, but they succeeded in murdering only the caliph in 661. This opened the way for Mu'awiya to continue his plan of establishing a new caliphate and elevating his Umayyad family over Muhammad's household, Ali's descendants, generally known as Shiites.

The Rashidun Caliphate is respected by most Muslims. In particular, today's Sunnis honor and revere the four caliphs for their supposed piety. Sunnis strive to apply Islam following the example of the Rashidun, calling their generation the best salaf (forefathers). The term *salaf*, from which the adjective *salafi* comes, is important among Sunnis. It refers to a follower of the example of the salaf in applying Islam. Nonetheless, these positive conceptions and affirmative views are merely religiously driven portrayals, as Muslim traditions do not describe a golden era or

faultless caliphs. During the twenty-nine years of the Rashidun Caliphate, there were assassinations, thefts of the treasury, and many wars that
targeted fellow Muslims in addition to non-Muslims.

Umayyads: the clan of Umayya, caliphs of the second caliphate

The noun *Umayyads*, pronounced "ooh-my-yadz," refers to the sons
of Umayya—a large family that was part of Muhammad's tribe, the
Quraysh. The Umayyads were also relatives of Muhammad's family, known as the sons of Hashim or the Hashimites. Both the sons of
Umayya and the sons of Hashim share a grandfather named Abd Manaf.
The enmity between the two branches of the family began long before
Muhammad's life and has long been asserted in Muslim traditions. It
was clear during Muhammad's life and continued after his death. Most
members of the Umayyad family rejected Muhammad's prophethood.
They did not convert to Islam or submit to Muhammad's leadership
until about three years before his death, when he conquered Mecca and
subdued everyone under his leadership. The Umayyads surrendered to
Muhammad, but they openly opposed him. Many of them received financial incentives to convert to Islam. Upon Muhammad's death, the key
Umayyad leaders, who reportedly hated the sons of Hashim, were influential in dissuading the Muslims from choosing Muhammad's cousin Ali
as his successor. Once the third caliph, Uthman, was in power, he began
a strategic plan to assign his Umayyad relatives important positions in
the **Rashidun** Caliphate.

When Uthman was killed, Mu'awiya—who was from the Umayyads—
declared an open rebellion against the new caliph, Ali, who was from
the Hashimites. The first **fitna** (civil war) erupted, and Ali was killed
a few years later. Mu'awiya seized the opportunity and strategically
planned for himself and his son to establish a new caliphate. In the
Muslim sources, Mu'awiya is known as an astute politician who used
money and bribery to make allies and to buy the loyalty of enemies.
Some reports even claim that Mu'awiya bribed Ali's son Hasan and
then later had Hasan's wife poison Hasan to ensure that power would
be solely in the hands of the Umayyads. Mu'awiya moved the capital of
the Muslim empire to Damascus in Syria, where he had been in control
as a governor for about two decades. He became the first caliph in the

Umayyad Caliphate and was followed by his sons; thus, it became the Umayyad Dynasty.

Mu'awiya reigned from Damascus for about twenty years and died in 680. His reign saw relative rest and some continued expansions in Asia and West Africa. However, the caliphate was weakened after his death due to sectarian and political conflicts. Mu'awiya appointed his son Yazid as his successor. Historical reports depict Yazid as one of the most ungodly caliphs of all time. Some declare him an outright **kafir** (infidel) who openly insulted the Quran and Muhammad's prophethood. He planned the massacre of Ali's second son, Husayn, to ensure that no Shiite (supporter of Ali) would rise against him to demand political authority. This marked the beginning of more turmoil among Muslims, sparking the second fitna in 680. Yazid also fought fellow Muslims—particularly in Medina—who rejected his immoral lifestyle and rebelled against him. He was followed by several Umayyad caliphs, including most importantly Abd al-Malik, who reigned from 685 to 705. In 749, the Umayyads were overthrown by the **Abbasids**, who were supported by the Shiites.

The Umayyad Caliphate lasted from 661 to 749; however, the historical reports present a major problem in that they come to us from the time of the Abbasids. The Umayyads are often portrayed in these historical sources as lustful for power and worldly desires. The family of Muhammad included Abbasids and Hashimites, both of whom are often portrayed as pious Muslims, while the Umayyads are often depicted as weak Muslims who embraced Islam only for economic or political gain. Since the primary sources of Islam were documented under the Abbasids, hardly any accounts show the Umayyads in a good light.

Abbasids: descendants of Muhammad's uncle, the third caliphate

The term *Abbasids*, pronounced "ab-bah-SEEDS," refers to the descendants of Abbas, Muhammad's uncle. Their control over the Muslim empire began in 749 after they led a successful revolution to overthrow the **Umayyads** and established the third Islamic caliphate. The revolution succeeded in part because the Abbasids united with two marginalized groups: the Shiites and the descendants of Ali (known as the Alids). This alliance crippled the Umayyads, who had already been weakened due to wars, plagues, and famines. The Abbasids and the Alids come from the sons of Hashim (Hashimites), who rivaled the Umayyads, although they all share a grandfather, Abd Manaf. One reason the Alids and the Shiites supported the Abbasids was that they shared the same enemy: the Umayyads, who reportedly targeted the descendants of Ali (Alids) and Ali's supporters (Shiites). However, once the Abbasids came to power, they began to distance themselves from the Alids and systematically targeted the Shiites to ensure that the Abbasids had no rivals in the caliphate.

To legitimize their rule over the Muslims, the Abbasids declared themselves good Muslims, contrasting themselves with the worldly and wicked Umayyads. Particularly, the Abbasids advanced themselves as the descendants of Muhammad's family through his uncle Abbas (d. 653), who was also one of the elite aristocrats of the **Quraysh**, Muhammad's tribe. Because they could trace their lineage to Abbas, the Abbasids claimed they had inherited the leadership (imamate) of the Muslims through their connection to Muhammad, depicting their ancestor as the most supportive of Muhammad. Additionally, to win over the hearts of the descendants of Ali, the Abbasids claimed that Ali and his grandson had given a bequest to the Abbasids to lead the Muslims. Thus, either by inheritance from Abbas or by a bequest from Ali's descendants, the Abbasids claimed authority and enforced it. Furthermore, the Abbasid caliphs began a new Islamic practice—they dressed following customs claimed about Muhammad and adopted regnal titles that incorporated the divine name into their designations. Thus, we have caliphs Mansur (victorious by Allah), Rashid (guided by Allah), Amin (faithful and entrusted by Allah), and so forth.

The Abbasids also added one more feature to the Islamic caliphate. While the Umayyads reportedly insisted on the Arabness of Islam, advancing the religion as mostly an Arabian product and emphasizing Arab Muslims as superior to Muslims with non-Arab origins, the Abbasids claimed that the caliphate was universal, accessible to both Arabs and non-Arabs. The Abbasid caliphs readily elevated non-Arab Muslims, particularly Persians. In the major posts of the caliphal court, the Abbasids relied on Persian converts to Islam who essentially built the empire through their experience in their former Persian Empire. The Abbasids also relied on Christians and Jews, especially to translate literature from other languages into Arabic. This was in the earliest generations of the Abbasid Caliphate, often known as its golden age.

Perhaps the most important accomplishment of the Abbasids was their creation of what we now know of Islam's origins. The caliphs commissioned and supervised the writing of Islam's most important and arguably earliest sources. Under their patronage, Muslim writers wrote numerous works of many Islamic genres. The third Muslim century is known as the golden century for Islamic writing. Scholars argue that the sources we now possess were created primarily to legitimize the Abbasids and their rule and to create propaganda against the Umayyads. While the Umayyads most likely supervised some works, none of them have reached us, mostly due to censorship by their Abbasid rivals.

The Abbasids did not advance politically, as the earlier two caliphates did. For the most part, the Abbasid caliphs attempted to secure their vast territories, maintaining what the **Rashidun** and **Umayyads** had already accomplished. The Abbasid Caliphate lasted for about five centuries and was destroyed by the Mongols in 1258. However, its demise was not abrupt; it began to weaken much earlier due to the resistance of marginalized groups, sectarian rebellions, and the emergence of local caliphates (especially in North Africa, Egypt, and Syria).

mihna: a harsh trial or Muslim inquisition

The Arabic term *mihna* refers to a troubling hardship, testing adversity, or challenging trial. It is pronounced "MEH-nuh" and refers to an important episode in Muslim history often described as the inquisition. In 833, the Muslim caliph Ma'mun was politically powerful, but his religious authority over Muslims was being challenged by the growing power of the religious scholars (**ulamaa'**), especially by the scholars of the **hadith**. They were known as the people of the hadith (ashab al-hadith), who cherished Muhammad's traditions. The people of the hadith (also known as traditionists) elevated the hadith reports as reliable and authentic accounts from Muhammad's time. They also produced abundant hadiths that made up the core of Islamic sources. Since their role was revered by

Muslims, these traditionists became significantly powerful. They were viewed as the religious arbiters of Muslims, which undermined the religious authority of the caliph. Consequently, Ma'mun sought to weaken their power. His plot was to force the people of the hadith to give up their ultimate source of authority: the hadith. He planned to have them declare their defeat as scholars by forcing them to accept the position of their intellectual opponents.

The opponents of the traditionists were a group of Muslim scholars known as the Mu'tazilites. They were committed Muslims who sought to make sense of matters related to Islam by relying on rationalism, philosophy, and plain reason. While the Mu'tazilites were devoted to the causes of Islam, they were openly willing to question the reliability and authenticity of traditions. Thus, they had many clashes with the people of the hadith, the lovers of traditions. One crucial disagreement between the two groups concerned the Quran's creation. The traditionists insisted that the Quran was uncreated, eternally existing with Allah. The Mu'tazilites argued that the Quran must have been created at some point in history because it does not make sense that two eternal beings coexisted. This was a considerable religious and intellectual dispute.

Caliph Ma'mun used this dispute for his own benefit, particularly to establish himself as the religious authority in the land. He launched a procedure of questioning, specifically targeting the traditionists. This religious test was known as the mihna. If a given traditionist continued to insist that the Quran was uncreated, he was sent to prison and harshly persecuted. If he forsook his position, which was basically an admittance of defeat and a declaration of the validity of the Mu'tazilites' position, he was spared and released. While Ma'mun was not necessarily fond of the Mu'tazilites and their arguments, he realized that the only way to undermine the powerful status of the people of the hadith was to force them to forsake their most important tool, the one that made them so powerful—the traditions.

Four months after he enforced the mihna, Ma'mun died. However, his two immediate successors continued to enforce the mihna, hoping to suppress the religious authority of the traditionists. After these two caliphs, a third, named Mutawakkil, came to power. He was not necessarily fond of the traditions or the traditionists, but he may have grown weary of conflicts. Mutawakkil abolished the mihna, thus essentially declaring the traditionists winners and making them the powerful arbiters of religious matters in Islam. They became the earliest manifestation of Sunnism as we know it today, while the Mu'tazilites and their arguments faded over time.

ISLAMIC FAITH
AND BELIEF

─────────

This section highlights terms related to Islamic beliefs and convictions. Many Muslims define Islam as a religion of two spheres: one of worship and another of practice—the first encompasses their relationship with the deity and the second their relationships with other people. This rather lengthy section focuses on worship, devotion, and their deity, scripture, and prophet. The entries also describe how Muslims view non-Muslims and their status under Islam and how Muslims are instructed to treat them. Finally, the terms explore matters of eschatology, especially the afterlife, with its punishments and rewards.

Allah: Islam's deity

Allah, pronounced "al-LUH," is the standard Arabic word for the deity. The noun *Allah* was known among the Arabs in pre-Islamic times. Today, as in pre-Islamic times, Arabic-speaking Jews and Christians use the term *Allah* to refer to the God of the Bible. While Arabic-speaking Jews, Christians, and Muslims may refer to the deity they worship using the same noun, they clearly understand his character and deeds in significantly different ways.

In Islam, **tawhid** (strict monotheism), or Allah's unicity, is the deity's most important distinction. It describes his singularity and oneness, denying any plurality in his character. This concept is in opposition to polytheism and the association of partners with the deity (shirk). However, according to Muslim traditions, before Muhammad, Allah was known among the Arabs, and according to their understanding, there were three female lesser deities, identified as his daughters: al-Lat, al-Uzza, and Manat. Among the idol worshipers of Arabia, Allah's daughters were known as influencing goddesses who were capable of interceding for humans by bringing their requests to Allah. These goddesses, moreover, were at the center of the infamous incident of the satanic verses, when Muhammad was reportedly deceived by Satan and affirmed that the pagan goddesses were valid intercessors. Nonetheless, with the formation and development of Islamic theology, Allah became distinctly singular—one and only one. This understanding became a pivotal and crucial part of Islamic identity.

In practice, most Muslims know Allah through his reported names. These names are his attributes—what he is and what he does. Muslims call them the most beautiful names (al-asmaa' al-husnaa). The Quran refers to Allah's beautiful names four times but never specifies them or indicates their number (Q 7:180; 17:110; 20:8; 59:24). Three centuries after Muhammad's death, a hadith emerged tracing back to Muhammad himself and indicating that Allah has ninety-nine marvelous names. The hadith even lists the names. Some of the names match the names and attributes of the God of the Bible, such as creator, forgiver, holy, merciful, almighty, kind, generous, judge, and so forth. However, the ninety-nine names include some attributes that are distinctively Islamic. Allah is the proud one (al-mutakabbir), the humiliator (al-mudhil), and the harmer (al-daar). Overall, Muslims cherish these names. Part of their worship and prayer involves reciting them repeatedly to gain Allah's favor and protection.

Among Muslim thinkers, some question the list and dispute many attributes included in it. They rightly observe that some attributes are not based on the Quran and that the Quran mentions some attributes that did not make the list. According to some traditions, the list was never fixed—scholars, in different generations, reportedly added to and removed from the list. Not surprisingly, Shiite Muslims are adamant regarding some of Allah's names that serve their sectarian goals. For Shiites, there is no question that Allah's names include the names of the infallible Shiite **imams**. In fact, for Shiites, Allah's names include the name Ali—the name of the first and major Shiite imam, who was the cousin of Muhammad. To support their claim that Ali is one of Allah's names, Shiites argue that the name Ali means "the highest one." Because many believers view the recitation of Allah's names as a crucial act of devotion and adoration, questioning the list raises doubts about an important element of Islamic worship.

tawhid: strict monotheism or Allah's absolute unicity

The term *tawhid* is the most distinguishing and foundational Islamic term. It denotes the divine unicity or strict monotheism. It is pronounced "taw-HEED" and is associated with an Arabic verb that means "to make one or unify." Technically, it is a reference to unitarianism, in contrast to polytheism or the belief in divine plurality, diversity, or multiplicity. Tawhid is thus the opposite of shirk—that is, polytheism or ascribing partners with Allah. For Muslims, Allah is one and only one.

Tawhid, as a doctrine, identifies Allah as unmatched—there is none like him. However, despite the importance of tawhid in Islam, the Quran does not mention the term. It never even mentions its verb, *to unify*. Still, the Quran does include verses that reflect the oneness of the deity, stating that there is no deity other than Allah (Q 2:163; 12:110; 21:8; 37:35; 41:6; 47:19). In fact, the shortest **sura** (chapter) in the Quran is known among Muslims as the tawhid chapter. It declares that Allah is one and only one, who has not begotten and has not been begotten (Q 112).

Because Shiites accept and seek the intercession of the **imams** (especially Ali), pious people, and prophets, Sunnis accuse Shiites of shirk. Shiites, on the other hand, insist that only intercession sought from idols should be rejected, and they refer to the Quranic affirmation that Allah accepts and permits the intercession of some (Q 20:109). While Muslims insist that Muhammad believed in Allah—in the one and only deity—even before he received the divine revelations, Muhammad's history reveals a different picture. It highlights the controversial incident known as the satanic verses, when Muhammad reportedly approved of and praised female pagan goddesses and told his companions that the intercession of these goddesses was acceptable.

Many medieval Christian thinkers questioned the doctrine of tawhid, particularly the Muslim insistence on strict monotheism in relation to Allah's attributes, especially before he created the world. If Allah has always been merciful, these Christian thinkers wondered, was he merciful even before creating the universe? The answer has to be affirmative, or there would be change in the deity—which is impossible and unacceptable. If Allah was merciful before the creation, then to whom was he merciful? Christian thinkers found in the doctrine of the Trinity an answer to this question, while Muslim theologians struggled to provide a solid argument. In the same vein, these Christians questioned the Muslim claim that the Quran is uncreated and existed eternally with Allah. If there are two eternal beings, Christians asked, is this shirk and in opposition to the claims of tawhid? If there is no plurality in Allah, various questions in Islam remain unanswered.

yawm al-qiyaama: the Day of Resurrection

The term *yawm al-qiyaama* refers to the Day of Resurrection, where *yawm* (pronounced "yowm") is "day" and *al-qiyaama* (pronounced "al-KEE-yah-muh") is "resurrection." In Islam, yawm al-qiyaama is when humans will be judged based on their works. Muslims refer to yawm al-qiyaama as the last day, the day of judgment, the day of punishment or reckoning, or simply the hour. The Quran contains a **sura** (chapter) titled "Qiyaama" (Q 75). It exhorts Muslims to be eager for the hereafter and discourages unbelief in the resurrection of the human body (vv. 3–4), which is evident in how people commit sins (vv. 5–19). It rebukes people who love the world and forget about life after al-qiyaama, and it reproaches those who do not believe in Allah's power to resurrect humans (vv. 20–40). The Quran exhorts believers to do good deeds to prepare for yawm al-qiyaama. The belief in yawm al-qiyaama is significantly important; it is one of the Six Articles of Faith, the basic beliefs of every Muslim.

According to most Muslim scholars, there are many signs for yawm al-qiyaama. The signs include the emergence of three major men: Mahdi, the antichrist, and Jesus. Mahdi is identified as one of Muhammad's family who will appear to establish justice on earth before yawm al-qiyaama. Shiite Muslims believe Mahdi will reappear, while Sunnis argue he will be a new man—from the descendants of Muhammad—who will emerge at the end of time. After Mahdi emerges, the antichrist will come. He is known in Muslim tradition as al-Dajjaal or al-Maseeh al-Dajjaal, where the word *al-Maseeh* means "Christ." Traditions claim that al-Dajjaal will be a horrifying man with one eye. He is the enemy of believers who will attempt to persuade them to kufr (unbelief or infidelity). After al-Dajjaal spreads injustice and corruption in the land, Allah will have Jesus (Isa) descend from heaven—since he never died and was taken up to heaven instead of being crucified—to fight al-Dajjaal. Jesus will judge people justly and will rebuke Christians who forsook the correct worship. Jesus will break the cross, kill the pig (prohibit the eating of pork), and call people to Islam. In addition to the coming of these men as a sign of yawm al-qiyaama, there will be cosmic signs. Before yawm al-qiyaama, a heavy smoke on earth will appear. The earth will also swallow up huge areas in their entirety—some in the East, others in the West, and a few in Arabia. The tradition reveals that the last day will not come until the sun rises from the west. Some traditions claim even more signs, including the disappearance of mountains, the bursting of oceans, earthquakes, darkened stars, and so forth.

The sequence of the events of yawm al-qiyaama is not clear, but Muslim scholars deduce some details from hints in the Quran and **hadith** traditions. Clearly, there are some similarities between Islam and the pre-Islamic faiths in their descriptions of the Day of Resurrection. After the signs, Muslims believe that a trumpet will sound and the dead will rise. Then all people will be pushed together in a narrow path during a unique event called al-hashr (the gathering or the pushing of people together). Then all people will be judged and sent to either paradise (**janna**) or hell (**jahannam**).

qadar: unquestioned divine fatalism, decree, and predestination

The term *qadar* refers to the predestination of Allah. It is pronounced "kahd-dar" and denotes divine control of everything, emphasizing Allah's complete and total foreordaining and decreeing of all that happens, both good and bad. It is often rendered as "unquestioned divine decree" or "total fatalism." Linguistically, the noun is based on another that refers to Allah's magnificent power and mightiness. The term is important, as it is the last of the Six Articles of Faith among most Muslims. These articles of faith are the basic beliefs every Muslim should embrace: the belief in Allah's oneness, his angels, his books, his prophets, his Day of Resurrection, and his qadar.

In practice, Muslims treat the term *qadar* as complete fatalism. For them, qadar means that Allah measured and estimated everything and then assigned the detailed specifics about life from eternity past. Qadar means that Allah, because of his divine knowledge, knew, wrote, willed, and decreed everything in advance. He dictated everything that takes place in life. What he decreed, Muslims believe, is all written in al-lawh al-mahfouz (the protected celestial tablet) (Q 22:70; 56:78; 85:22).

A controversial aspect of qadar is that evil human actions are prescribed. When Muslims do bad or evil deeds, they may refer to qadar as the reason for their actions, as if they had no control. This is a unique aspect of Islamic predestination and appears to contradict human free will. This aspect of qadar appears in the Quran when it refers to evil humans and **jinn** (genies)—who do wrong by deceiving one another—and indicates that if Allah had *not* willed and predestined, they would have never done the wrong deeds (Q 6:112). The verse continues by presumably instructing Muhammad to leave the wrongdoers alone without intervening. This aspect of qadar also appears in how the Quran speaks of the enemies of Muhammad, declaring that if Allah willed, he would have given the enemies power over his people (Q 4:90). The point is that nothing happens without Allah's ordinance and complete control. While this might indicate that humans have no free will, Muslim scholars still insist that the belief in qadar does not oppose human free will (Q 2:286; 78:39).

rasul: a divinely sent messenger or apostle

The term *rasul* refers to a messenger or apostle sent by Allah to humankind. It is pronounced "ra-SOOL," and its plural form is *rusul*. The term is based on a verb that means "to send or to designate as an envoy" and is related to a noun, *risaala*, which means "a message." Muslims believe that rasul is very close in meaning to **nabi** (prophet); however, a rasul is someone who is given a divine message or revelation that appeared in a heavenly scripture. Arguably, in Islam, every rasul is a nabi, but not every nabi is a rasul. Thus, Moses, David, Jesus, and Muhammad, according to Islam, are all messengers (rusul), since they all received divinely revealed scriptures—the Torah, the Psalms, the Gospel, and the Quran, respectively.

The term *rasul* appears in the Quran over two hundred times, and its plural form, *rusul*, appears over ninety times. Sometimes rasul refers to an angel sent by Allah to a human (Q 11:69). In many cases, the Quran does not seem to distinguish between rasul and nabi. Moreover, although there are many messengers, the divine message sent to all of them is the same—**tawhid**, strict monotheism. However, the Quran as Muhammad's message is unique. It not only matches and confirms previous revealed messages but also expounds on them and actually surpasses and controls them (Q 2:91; 3:3; 5:48; 6:114; 10:37). In one Islamic understanding, all divinely revealed messages reflect tawhid, even the Torah and the Gospel. Nevertheless, Muslims claim, Jews and Christians altered the message to align with their wicked desires.

Muslim traditions contain conflicting reports concerning the number of messengers sent by Allah. The general claim is that Allah sent thousands of prophets and hundreds of messengers. In one hadith attributed to Muhammad, he claims that 120,000 prophets—including 313 messengers—were sent by Allah. In another, the numbers are 114,000 and 315. In a different hadith, Muhammad insists that he was the final in a chain of one thousand prophets. The Quran explicitly mentions twenty-five people who could be identified as prophets and messengers, out of whom, some Muslims claim, there were thirteen messengers. Some of these are biblical figures, while others are not. According to Muslim traditions, Allah sent a messenger to every nation on the planet (Q 16:36; 35:24); however, Muhammad was uniquely sent as a messenger with a message suitable for all humankind (Q 34:28).

nabi: a prophet

Linguistically, the term *nabi*, pronounced "nab-BEE," refers to a proclaimer of a divine command. It can refer to a person foretelling the future or merely conveying a divine instruction to a specific people group at a point in time. In Islam, a nabi is sent to a particular group of people with a command from Allah—not a heavenly book—to help them improve their lives. These prophets, Muslims believe, are often given supernatural abilities from the deity to support their calling.

In Muslim traditions, a nabi is a man, not a woman. If a nabi received a divine book, then he was a **rasul** (messenger). The Quran identifies some heavenly revealed scriptures: the Torah, the Psalms, the Gospel, and the Quran. There are also two ambiguous references to scriptures (suhuf) of Abraham and Moses. The message of all these books is **tawhid**, the strict oneness of Allah.

Muslim traditions contain contradicting numbers for Allah's prophets, varying between 120,000, 124,000, 114,000, and even 1,000. All these prophets, we are told, were followers of Islam—that is, Muslims (Q 42:13). The term *Muslim* basically refers to submission to Allah. They were sent to call people to the worship of the one deity, but people rejected and persecuted these prophets; consequently, Allah had to send other prophets to proclaim the same message.

According to traditions, Adam was the first prophet and Muhammad the last. Some Muslim traditions claim that there were five arch-prophets: Noah, Abraham, Moses, Jesus, and Muhammad. While on the one hand Muslims claim that the messages sent by Allah were all the same, on the other hand, they still insist that Muhammad's message surpassed and eclipsed all previous messages. This is why the **Quran** identifies Muhammad as "the Seal of the Prophets" (Q 33:40). For Muslims, this title distinguishes their prophet as the proclaimer or conveyer of the last heavenly religion. The title also means that anyone claiming to bring a post-Muhammad prophecy is false—there can be no prophet after the final prophet.

'isma: inerrancy, infallibility, and immunity from error

The term *'isma* refers to immunity from error. It is pronounced "eye-smuh" and denotes infallibility and the inability to sin or make errors. The term is important in Islamic thought, as it shields prophets from error: they are given 'isma by **Allah** against fallibility and sin, and therefore they are immune from mistakes. There is disagreement among Muslims concerning the scope of this 'isma—whether it is complete in all matters or covers only the reception and delivery of revelations. In practice, some limit the 'isma to matters of divine proclamation—a prophet is protected by 'isma only when he is proclaiming scripture—but most Muslims believe that a prophet cannot err in any matter in life. In fact, Shiite Muslims add the twelve **imams** to the list of prophets and call them the infallible imams, all of whom are immune from any error whatsoever. This is why Muslims cannot fathom how a biblical prophet—think of David with Bathsheba—can be portrayed in the Bible as committing a sin, let alone that of adultery.

The Quran never mentions the 'isma of the prophets. This is a concept that was developed by later Muslim scholars. In fact, the notion of a complete and supreme 'isma is contradicted by some reports in Islam's traditions. In one case, Muhammad was reportedly deceived by Satan and uttered nondivine words that praised pagan goddesses. These words made their way into the Quran and were later erased by Allah and abrogated. While this tradition appears to depict Muhammad as fallible, it is not the only tradition that sheds doubt on the concept of 'isma in Islam. Other traditions portray Muhammad as being harmed by the evil magic of his enemies, to the extent that he began to hallucinate, imagining he did things he never did. In general, Shiite Muslims appear much more adamant and specific about the concept of 'isma. Some Shiite scholars claim that the doctrine of 'isma was advanced by the sixth imam, Ja'far al-Sadiq (702–765), who founded the well-known Shiite **madhhab** (school of thought).

wahy: a divine revelation

A wahy, pronounced "WAH-yuh," is a divine revelation. The term refers to a divine act of giving instructions to chosen people—prophets and messengers—whom Allah himself selects to make his will known to humans. The term *wahy* is technically defined by its source, channel, and target: Allah, the prophet, and humans, respectively. In this sense, Muslims understand the wahy as infallible. Allah revealed his will in different ways. Sometimes he used a mediator—an angel—and other times he spoke through a veil. Allah also spoke face-to-face with his chosen human. This occurred only once, according to Islamic traditions, when Allah allegedly met with Muhammad and gave him the ordinance of the ritual prayer (**salat**).

Muslims understand the term *wahy* in connection with another important term: *tanzeel*. Tanzeel literally means "the coming down" of the wahy. For Muslims, the wahy of the Quran was dictated to Muhammad through a process of tanzeel, in which the exact speech of Allah came down on Muhammad, who delivered it to his audience under the protection of the deity. This is why, Muslims argue, a wahy cannot involve any errors.

Another Islamic term is close in meaning to *wahy* but differs in important ways: *ilhaam*, which literally means "inspiration." Ilhaam is the divine whisper in the heart of humankind. It refers to valuable insights, stimulations, or instincts that come to the mind of a believer, mostly as a sign or result of a divine intervention. Ilhaam, unlike wahy, is not viewed as a divine dictation, nor is it infallible. For many Muslims, Allah sometimes sends ilhaam to a believer's heart and mind in the form of dreams. Through ilhaam, a Muslim may take action or choose between variable paths.

jinn: genies

The Arabic term *jinn*, pronounced "jihn," refers to nonhuman and nonangelic beings that can be good or evil. The term is based on a verb that means "to hide, cover, or make disappear." The term *jinn* is plural and is usually rendered as "genies" in English. Its Arabic singular form is the masculine *jinni* and the feminine *jinniyya*. Before the advent of Islam, the Arabs seem to have believed in the existence of jinn, as evidenced in Arabian folklore that depicts jinn as creatures from the unseen world who have access to and can influence the seen world. With the advent of Islam, the belief in the existence of jinn continued to flourish among Muslims, with some adjustments to the literary features describing them.

The Quran relates that jinn were created of smokeless fire, while humans were created of clay (Q 55:14–15). Allah created jinn, like humans, for no other purpose than to worship and serve him (Q 51:56). Satan comes from jinn (Q 18:50). Some jinn were servants of King Solomon, who powerfully trapped them in bondage (Q 34:14). Muhammad, says the Quran, was sent by Allah to preach to jinn and humans (Q 6:19). Due to the importance of this topic, the Quran contains an entire **sura** (chapter) with the title "jinn" (Q 72). In this sura, jinn speak words that permeate Islam's scripture. Some Muslim commentators claim that the sura was revealed as a response from jinn against humans who accused Muhammad of receiving his revelations from jinn instead of from Allah. In this sura, jinn report that they heard the astounding Quran recited and that they believed in its guidance and forsook polytheism. They also declare that among jinn are Muslim believers and infidels. In opposition to those who claim that Allah had a son, jinn declare that Allah never had a wife or a child. The sura also reveals that jinn have influence in the seen world, as they can support humans, but they affirm that they cannot evade or overcome Allah's will or flee his sovereignty. After all, Allah's judgment will come to unbelievers.

Muslim traditions created more stories that formed the Muslim mindset concerning jinn. Relying on traditions attributed to Muhammad, many Muslims believe that some jinn have wings to fly between places and can actually do this significantly fast. Some believe that jinn can possess dogs, dragons, and snakes and can appear on dark nights to harm humans. Some Shiite scholars believe that when a human is born, a thousand jinn are also born—in fact, for every human, they claim, there is a twin jinni or jinniyya. Overall, most Muslims are afraid of jinn. They believe it is always important to end the ritual prayer (salat) with supplications to cast away jinn. If jinn touch a man, Muslims believe, they can harm him, causing any sort of sickness, including epilepsy, mental hallucinations, and delusions. Some believe that if a woman is barren, this is likely an effect of harmful jinn. Some Muslims believe jinn are active on certain days or in specific places. Even though jinn are unseen, they control the lives of many who believe in their existence and influence. Although the Quran claims some of them are good while others are evil, in general, Muslims believe jinn are largely harmful.

iman: the faith and the act of believing

The term *iman*, which appears in many verses in the Quran, describes not only the entirety of the faith as a set of beliefs but also the act of believing in what is revealed. Muslims thus use the term *iman* to refer to the totality of Islam as a revealed faith from Allah and to their heartfelt, trusting response to Allah's commands. The word *iman* is pronounced "ih-MAN." The term *iman* is a noun based on a verb that means "to trust" and "to be secured."

While all Muslims may agree that iman is the genuine belief in one's heart regarding what Allah revealed through Muhammad, Sunnis and Shiites differ on two points. First, in Shiism, this belief extends beyond Allah and what he revealed through Muhammad to include the teachings and guidance of the twelve infallible **imams**, who were the descendants of Ali (Muhammad's cousin and the rightful successor of Muhammad, according to Shiism). For Shiites, the infallible imams are the true implementers of the faith. They are the spiritual and political leaders of Muslims. No true application of iman can be done without the imams and their teachings and life examples. Second, Sunnis largely believe that conversion to Islam makes one a believer in the faith. For them, every Muslim is a believer. Many Shiite scholars disagree and insist on distinguishing between converting to Islam—as a public declaration—and the act of iman (i.e., truly believing in one's heart). The logic is that people can simply convert to Islam—by stating the **Shahada**, which is a sentence declaring belief in Allah's oneness and Muhammad's prophethood—without a sincere iman (belief) in the heart. For these Shiites, every believer is a Muslim, but not every Muslim is a believer. To make their point, these Shiites refer to some reported examples from the history of Islam in which many people converted to Islam out of fear and under coercion without having true iman in their hearts. Thus, according to this logic, a Muslim is different from a true believer in the faith; one can become a Muslim but not a believer. Among many

Shiite scholars, iman (true genuine faith) cannot be imitated. A son of a believing father is not born a believer. Faith is a matter of deep and genuine conviction in the heart. For these Shiite scholars, the first three successors (caliphs) of Muhammad were converts to Islam (Muslims) but not genuine believers in their hearts. They harassed Muhammad's daughter and stole the succession from Ali, who was the rightful leader designated by Muhammad.

All Muslims believe there are Six Articles of Faith (iman), which highlight the six basic, essential, and primary beliefs adopted by any follower of Islam. These articles define what Muslims actually believe, in contrast to the Five Pillars of Islam, which identify what Muslims practice. For Sunnis, the Six Articles of Faith are belief in (1) Allah's oneness, (2) his angels, (3) his books, (4) his prophets, (5) his Day of Resurrection, and (6) his **qadar** (predestination). The books are the scriptures revealed by Allah, such as the Torah, the Psalms, the Gospel, and the Quran, while the prophets are biblical and nonbiblical prophets, who—as some Muslim traditions claim—may reach tens of thousands in number. The last item of the six beliefs is qadar, which is Allah's complete power of predestining everything, good or evil. The first five articles of faith are largely similar between Sunnis and Shiites. However, Shiites replace the belief in qadar with the belief in the unseen world. For that choice, Sunnis accuse Shiites of not believing in Allah's complete determination and predestination, although Shiites actually do believe in qadar—they merely understand it differently and adopt a different article of faith to conclude their list.

Islam: submission and converting to a religion

The Arabic term *islam*, pronounced "is-LAM," refers to submission. It comes from an Arabic verb that means "to surrender, give in, or yield to someone or something." While some—especially in Western circles—may argue that the term *islam* means "peace," this is untrue. There is no indication anywhere in early Islamic texts that the term was ever used to convey that notion. The Quran and Muhammad's traditions use the term *islam* to describe the act of submission to the one and only deity and his commands. The term became the name of the religion of Muhammad, who, according to Muslims, received a divine revelation from Allah called the Quran. The religion is firmly built on the concept of strict monotheism, unitarianism, or divine unicity, known as **tawhid**.

In Muslim traditions, the term *islam* is linked with the verb *aslam*, meaning "to convert to the religion of Muhammad, Islam." We read in these traditions that a man aslam—that is, adopted Islam (converted, entered into Islam). We also read that a pious man who followed Muhammad had a praiseworthy islam—that is to say, his devotion within the religion of Islam was commendable. When Muslim warriors invaded non-Muslim lands, they offered the conquered people three options: accept Islam, fight, or pay the jizya (tax). Many non-Muslims chose islam (submission). They embraced Islam to avoid murder or financial burden. In these cases, conversion was coercive and submission was to save lives.

In practice, many Shiites—and some Sunnis—distinguish islam from **iman**. For them, islam refers to converting to a religion by publicly declaring a statement—the **Shahada**. However, iman refers to truly believing in one's heart. This means that someone can convert to the religion without sincere belief in their heart. In this rationale, every believer is a Muslim, but not every Muslim is a believer. More specifically, among Sunnis, to be a Muslim, one needs to practice the mandatory duties of Islam, known as the Five Pillars of Islam: the Shahada (profession), the **salat** (ritual prayer), the **zakat** (almsgiving), the sawm (fasting), and the **hajj** (pilgrimage). Shiites have ten pillars, and practicing these duties makes a person Muslim. Theoretically, people can do these actions without genuine faith in their hearts—and they would still be considered true Muslims. This is why Shiites insist on the distinction between islam and iman. One reason for their insistence is that throughout Islamic history, Shiites have been the minority, and they often suffered persecution under ruthless leaders who, for the most part, claimed to be Muslims although they mistreated their fellow Muslims.

kafir: an unbeliever or infidel

The Quran identifies a person as either a believer or an unbeliever (Q 64:2). It uses the Arabic term *kafir*, pronounced "KAF-fur," for unbeliever or infidel. Linguistically, a kafir is a person who is practicing or following kufr (unbelief or infidelity). In Islam, the term *kufr* connotes ingratitude to Allah's favor and is the opposite of believing in absolute monotheism (**tawhid**), the deity of Allah, and Muhammad's prophethood. Kufr means covering or suppressing the truth. A kafir is thus a person who denies the two basic parts of Islam's profession of faith (the **Shahada**—confessing and believing in Allah's deity and Muhammad's prophethood), either partially or entirely. This is clear in the Quran, which states that anyone who denies belief in Allah and his Messenger is an infidel destined for hellfire (Q 48:13).

In practice, the term *kafir* is very negative and has a stigma attached to it. In Muslim circles, no one is pleased to be identified as a kafir. In a few verses, the Quran allows unbelievers to live as they please (Q 109), but in many other verses, it instructs believers to fight and slay unbelievers (Q 9:5). This may indeed send mixed messages, but the matter is clearer in Muhammad's statements and traditions, where most often unbelievers (kuffar or kafirun) are despised and identified as targets for violence and destruction. Similarly, Muslims believe that a Muslim cannot fight another Muslim, but fighting an unbelieving infidel is permissible and in some instances commanded. The Quran warns believing Muslims against unbelievers, identifying them as the manifest enemies of Muslims (Q 4:101) because they are the enemies of Allah, his angels, and his apostles (Q 2:98; 4:37). After all, Allah hates any kafir (Q 3:32), and Muslims are not to take a kafir as a friend (Q 3:28).

Some liberal and progressive Muslims have attempted to dilute the negative stigma attached to the term *kafir*. They argue that a kafir is simply a denier of truth: just as a Christian is a kafir of Islam, so a Muslim is a kafir of Christianity. For these progressives, a kafir is still a human who deserves to live in honor and dignity. Among literalist Muslims— who follow Islam's sources by the letter—the matter is different: a kafir is an unbeliever who should be executed so that the faith and its practice remain pure. Undoubtedly, many religions, including Judaism and Christianity, divide people into believers and unbelievers. However, the stigma of being a kafir in Islam is unmatched in comparison to other faiths.

mu'min: a believer

The term *mu'min* refers to a believer and is pronounced "mo-min." In Islam, the term can refer only to a Muslim who has embraced Islam and has faith in their heart. The term is masculine, and its feminine form is *mu'mina*. In practice, the term *mu'min* is the opposite of **kafir** (unbeliever or infidel) and is based on a verb that means "to believe" and "to have a heartfelt conviction." Some Muslims—especially among Shiites—distinguish a Muslim from a mu'min. They believe that every mu'min is indeed a Muslim, but since anyone can declare the **Shahada** (Islamic creed or profession of faith) and become a Muslim without sincere and genuine faith in their heart, not every Muslim is a believer.

In the Quran, a person is either a mu'min or a kafir (Q 64:2)—there is no third choice. The Quran uses the term *mu'min* in its singular form fifteen times and in its plural form ample times. In one of the occurrences, the Quran makes the case that good works are not sufficient for someone to enter paradise (janna) unless the person is indeed a mu'min (Q 4:124; also 17:19; 21:94; 40:40). This suggests that only a believer who does good works can be admitted into eternal bliss. The Quran also states that one of Allah's most beautiful names is *mu'min* (Q 59:23). Since it is not plausible to consider Allah a believer, Muslim scholars usually take this to mean that Allah is the keeper or guardian of faith or the granter of security.

A severe dispute exists between Sunnis and Shiites regarding the term *mu'min*. Each camp largely views itself as mu'min and the other as kafir. Sunnis believe that many Shiites worship the **imams** and view them as infallible and exaggerate their veneration of Ali and the household of Muhammad in general—these beliefs are clear signs of infidelity from a Sunni perspective. Thus, Sunnis believe that Shiites are kuffar (plural of kafir). Shiites believe that belief in the imamate (leadership) of the twelve infallible imams is an essential foundation of the true faith—and since Sunnis do not believe in it, they are unbelievers from a Shiite perspective.

In Islam, a Christian or Jew is not a mu'min (Q 2:105; 59:2; 98:1). A non-Muslim is an unbeliever of Islam and thus a kafir of Islam. While Islam is not alone in identifying a human as either a mu'min or an unbeliever, in the Quran and Muhammad's traditions, a person who is a kafir is open to harsh treatment at times. This makes the term *mu'min* significant. However, some progressive Muslims attempt to dilute the stigma of being a kafir by arguing that a kafir does not need to be viewed negatively, because every human is a mu'min of something and a kafir of something else.

mushrik: a polytheist or one who associates partners with Allah in worship

In Arabic, a mushrik, pronounced "moosh-rick," is a person who as-sociates others with Allah in worship. Particularly, the term identifies a polytheist or associator who does not practice the strict monotheism (**tawhid**) of Allah. The plural of mushrik is *mushrikun*—a term repeated often in the Quran. Technically, a mushrik is not a polytheist who be-lieves in many gods but rather a person who associates equal deities with Allah. However, many simply identify a mushrik as a polytheist. In Islam, a mushrik is also a **kafir** (infidel or unbeliever) whose sin is shirk (polytheism). The committing of shirk makes a person a mushrik. The sin of shirk is often rendered as "associationism" or "polytheism." It is among the greatest and most grievous sins. It is an unforgivable sin in Islam, defined as the opposite of the most important doctrine in Islam, which is monotheism. Muslims view themselves as the people of tawhid and are completely opposed to shirk.

The Quran despises the sin of shirk and those who commit it and commands believers to wage war on all the associators (Q 9:36) and to slay them wherever they are found (Q 9:5). The Quran appears to identify some Christians as mushrikun (associators) because they believe in Jesus and Mary as gods equal to Allah (Q 9:30–31). Thus, some Muslim jurists charge Christians with the sin of shirk. If they believe in the doctrines of the Trinity and the incarnation, the jurists claim, these Christians are mushrikun (Q 5:72–73; cf. Q 5:116–17). In the same passage, the Quran accuses the Jews, too, of acknowledging another deity (by saying Allah has a son named Uzair); thus, they are also mushrikun. The terms *mushrik* and *shirk* are directed against any who associate partners or equals with the deity. While progressive Muslims may hesitate to identify Christians and Jews as polytheists or associators, the literal reading of some verses in the Quran complicates the picture—and the consequences can be weighty.

murtad: an apostate

The Arabic term *murtad*, pronounced "moor-ted," refers to a person who has turned away from or abandoned a previously followed path or commitment. In Islam, this is an apostate who abandoned Islam after being a Muslim for a period of time, whether the abandonment was for a different religion or no religion or whether the person was born Muslim or accepted Islam and then left it. In practice, a murtad commits apostasy, which is known in Arabic as ridda or irtidaad. Both terms are viewed negatively in all Islamic texts.

The Quran threatens a murtad with eternal punishment under Allah's wrath (Q 16:106–9). However, there is no clear penalty in this life. In contrast, Muhammad's traditions are clear that whoever abandons Islam must be killed. This is one reason why all schools of Muslim jurisprudence agree that a murtad is to be punished by death. This is the case among Sunni and Shiite scholars, although they vary concerning their willingness to grant a chance for repentance.

In practice, ridda or irtidaad can occur by voicing a statement, by committing an act, or by adhering to any inner conviction against Islam. For instance, if a Muslim denies the doctrine of **tawhid** (strict monotheism) either by stating it openly or by believing it in their heart, this is considered outright apostasy. If a Muslim desecrates the name of Allah or Muhammad or defiles the text of the Quran, this act makes them a murtad; they thus deserve capital punishment. In some Muslim circles, mere doubt in any matter of faith is an act of apostasy.

The death sentence—as a punishment for apostasy—is supported not only by the command attributed to Muhammad but also by a historical incident known as the Apostasy Wars, or the Ridda Wars. After Muhammad's death, many Muslims abandoned Islam and neglected to pay the special tax (**zakat**) to the Muslim government under the first caliph, Abu Bakr, who succeeded Muhammad on the day of his death. In response to their abandonment of Islam, Abu Bakr launched brutal wars to bring them back to Islam or to execute them. According to Islamic histories, some of those killed were committed Muslims who merely rejected Abu Bakr's commands. But among Sunni Muslims, Abu Bakr is viewed as a hero who defended Islam against apostasy. His actions influence what many Muslims believe today about capital punishment for apostasy.

ahl al-kitab: the people of the book, Jews and Christians

The term *ahl al-kitab*, pronounced "ah-l al-kee-TAB," is mentioned in the Quran over fifty times in different forms. It means "the people of the book" or "scripture people," in which the Arabic word *ahl* means "people," and *al-kitab* means "book or scripture." While the Quran does not specify precisely who these people are, Muslims often understand the term as referring to Jews and Christians, who received divine scriptures before the advent of Muhammad. Still, Muslims claim that the term can also include believers in any heavenly inspired religion, including those who believed in the scriptures given by Allah to David and Moses, since they both were prophets of Allah who came with the same message of **tawhid** (strict monotheism). Among some scholars, ahl al-kitab also include Sabians (Mandaeans) and Zoroastrians (followers of Zarathustra, also known as Zoroaster, who founded this religion and was identified by his followers as a prophet and apostle; died ca. 550 BC). However, major Muslim jurists, past and present, believe the term *ahl al-kitab* primarily identifies Jews and Christians.

The term appears to honor believers of pre-Islamic heavenly revealed religions. The Quran states that some of ahl al-kitab are true believers (Q 3:110, 199; 5:59). But these true believers, says the Quran, do not associate partners with Allah (i.e., do not commit shirk), nor do they believe in the Trinity. Thus, Christians who believe in the Trinity are not considered true believers. In fact, true believers accept Muhammad and his message. After all, Muhammad was sent to all people with a message confirming and surpassing pre-Islamic heavenly revelations (Q 4:47; 5:15). Unbelievers among ahl al-kitab are portrayed negatively in the Quran. Muslims are warned against taking them as friends (Q 5:57). These unbelievers should be fought by Muslims until they accept Islam or pay the jizya (tax) while humiliated (Q 9:29). According to the majority of Muslim jurists, the Quran's opening chapter (**sura** 1) portrays Jews and Christians negatively. It refers to Muslims as followers of the rightful and straight path who received Allah's favor, distinguishing them from Jews, who received Allah's wrath, and Christians, who have gone astray. Indeed, while the Quran describes ahl al-kitab positively in some verses, in many others they are portrayed negatively since they rejected Muhammad's prophethood and did not accept the truth of the Quran (Q 2:105; 59:2; 98:1).

Muslim men are allowed to marry women from ahl al-kitab (Christian or Jew), whether the woman converts to Islam or not. Still, Muslim jurists discourage Muslim men from marrying a Christian or Jew unless the woman accepts Islam. As for Muslim women, they are allowed to marry only Muslims. As for any other religion, Muslims are not allowed to marry their followers unless the non-Muslim first converts to Islam by openly declaring the profession of faith (the **Shahada**).

dhimmi: a non-Muslim living under Islamic rule

After the Muslim armies conquered non-Muslim territories, the term *dhimmi*, pronounced "THIM-mee," was given to believers of different faiths to distinguish them from believing Muslims. A dhimmi was a non-Muslim who refused to convert to Islam but received a pact of protection (dhimma) by submitting to the rule of the Muslim conquerors. Linguistically, a dhimmi received the dhimma (protection) status—often rendered in English as "dhimmitude." Those dhimmis who received the dhimma status were often called ahl al-dhimma ("the protected people"). They included primarily Jews and Christians (also known as the people of the book) as well as followers of other religions such as Sabians and Zoroastrians. In return for protection, dhimmis, due to their continued adherence to their non-Muslim faith and their rejection of Islam, were obliged to pay a special tax (jizya). The Quran indicates that the jizya should be paid by non-Muslims—particularly Jews and Christians—while humiliated (Q 9:29). If they converted to Islam, they ceased to be dhimmis and received equal rights. While the terms of the dhimma pact are often explained as items of a protection agreement, they were arguably compulsory terms of surrender that the conqueror placed upon the conquered.

Muslim authorities did not apply the rules of the dhimma uniformly. The rules were enforced or ignored depending on the Muslim ruler of the time. Some Muslim rulers applied harsher treatment than others. The harsher treatment often traced back to an infamous Islamic document called The Pact of Umar, which was allegedly issued by Muhammad's second successor (caliph) and included humiliating protocols and restrictive instructions for non-Muslims living under Islamic rule. For example, Christian dhimmis were not allowed to preach Christianity to Muslims, nor were they permitted to repair their churches even if they were in ruins. They could not place a cross on top of their churches. They could not wear crosses or show sacred books of the Bible in the presence of a Muslim. Christians could not forbid any Muslim from entering their churches at any time. If a Muslim entered, Christians were to respect the Muslim and not recite liturgical services loudly. If Muslims were traveling, Christians needed to welcome them into their houses and host and feed them for up to three nights. To distinguish themselves from Muslims, Christian men were obliged to shave the front of their heads and maintain a distinctive style of clothing.

As Muslims continued to rule over a vast geographical region full of dhimmis, Muslim jurists sought to articulate, in more depth, the rules of the dhimmis. In the seventh and eighth centuries of Islam, the renowned Muslim scholar Ibn Qayyim al-Jawziyya (1292–1349) wrote an important work titled *Ahkaam ahl al-dhimma* (The Laws Regarding the Dhimmis). The book is sixteen hundred pages in Arabic and follows a pattern similar to that of The Pact of Umar. The Muslim jurist explains the relationship between Muslims and dhimmis and argues that Christians should not be given higher posts in the government and should be differentiated from Muslims by status, clothes, and even mode of transportation. Overall, the book still enjoys an authoritative prestige in many Muslim-majority lands. Some Islamic governments consider it influential, especially in legal matters concerning non-Muslims.

i'jaz: unequaled, unmatched, inimitable, in reference to the Quran

Muslims believe the Quran is unmatched in its revelation, content, and preservation. It is, for them, superior to any human speech. To describe the unique status of the Quran, Muslims use the term *i'jaz*, pronounced "ee-jazz." The Arabic noun *i'jaz* is based on a verb that denotes the impossible task of achieving or surpassing something. The rationale is this: due to the i'jaz of the Quran, one can never achieve anything like it. The term is often rendered in English as "inimitable," highlighting that the Quran cannot be imitated.

The term *i'jaz* is not mentioned explicitly in the Quran. However, several verses challenge the opponents of Muhammad to bring forth a verse, a **sura** (chapter), or a speech like that of the Quran (Q 2:23; 10:38; 11:13; 17:88; 52:34). Muslims call these verses the "challenge verses" and rely on them to argue for an inimitable Quran. Later generations of Muslims articulated the theological doctrine of the i'jaz of the Quran to present the Quran as the major miracle or sign of Islam. They claimed that the inimitable Quran was proof of Muhammad's prophethood and religious message.

To understand the need of Muslims to present the Quran as inimitable, one needs to consider the context of its reception. The text was proclaimed in a multireligious environment. In that setting, Christians and Jews provided lists of miracles performed by Jesus and Moses, respectively. Muslims, therefore, went in search of miracles associated with Muhammad, but the Quran insisted that he was not given any physical miracles—he was given only the Quran itself (Q 6:37; 11:12; 13:7; 29:50). If the only thing given to Muhammad was a text, then this text—the rationale goes—had to be inimitable. It had to be miraculous and unmatched.

The term *i'jaz* is related to another Arabic term, *balaagha*, which means "eloquence." Muslims view the Quran as beautifully constructed in an exceptional form of Arabic. Its balaagha and exceptional rhyming poetry, according to Muslims, caused the best nonbelieving Arab poets to fall silent. However, these claims are just that. No evidence for such assertions exists in any historical eyewitness accounts. The stories about the Arabs who were supposedly astonished by the Quran come from later Muslim sources. Some Muslim scholars—like Taha Husayn (1889–1973) and Ahmad Hasan al-Qubanji (1958–)—have even argued openly that the text of the Quran is less than perfect.

Suryaani: a dialect of Aramaic, a Semitic language

The term *Suryaani* refers to Syriac and is pronounced "soo-ree-YAN-nee." Suryaani is a dialect of Aramaic, which is often known as the language Jesus spoke. Suryaani is important in relation to the rise of Islam, because Middle Eastern Christians used Syriac in liturgy and writing in the seventh century. More importantly, scholarly research indicates a significant influence of Syriac on the Quran. While Muslims are adamant that the Quran as a text is in pure and clear Arabic, scholars disagree and demonstrate that the Quran contains many words with Syriac origins. Moreover, Muslim traditions include unique reports that may support these scholars' arguments. According to Sunni traditions, one of the most trusted scribes of Muhammad, Zayd ibn Thabit, wrote the revelations after Muhammad proclaimed them. Muhammad reportedly instructed Zayd to learn Syriac, and Zayd quickly learned it in seventeen days. He was also well-versed in Hebrew. Scholars rely on traditions of this sort to show the importance of examining foreign vocabulary in the Quran.

Scholars argue that the word *Quran* is not Arabic but rather comes from a Syriac term, *qeryana*, meaning "a liturgical text." Similarly, the word for a chapter in the Quran, **sura**, does not seem to be of Arabic origin. It is a Syriac word that means "writing," but it may also be of Hebrew origin. The importance of Syriac—as a language used by Christians during Muhammad's time—appears in a compelling argument advanced by some recent scholarship. For these scholars, the Quran was proclaimed in a context where Syriac was common, especially as a liturgical language used by Christians. If this was the case, these scholars argue, then the Quran was initially an oral discourse given in a mixture of Arabic and Syriac. When it was later documented, it was wrongly misunderstood as only Arabic. For these scholars, when some words in the Quran are difficult to understand as Arabic, we should try to understand them as Syriac. For these scholars, Syriac is a key language for unlocking many of the ambiguous words in the Quran.

sura: a chapter in the Quran

The term *sura* refers to a chapter in the Quran and is pronounced "SOO-ruh." The origin of the word is puzzling. For most Muslims, the Quran is a pure Arabic text, but this word appears to have a non-Arabic origin. Some scholars argue that *sura* is the Hebrew word for "a row in a list of segments." Others think *sura* is originally a Syriac term, simply referring to "a writing."

The Quran has 114 suras. They are arranged not in order of alleged revelation but by length—from longest to shortest—with some exceptions. For instance, sura 1 is not the longest, and sura 114 is not the shortest. Sura 2 is the longest, and sura 108 is the shortest. While most Muslims believe that Allah is the only one responsible for arranging the suras in their particular order, some claim it was Muhammad's decision and others claim that Muslim scholars in later generations chose the order. For conservatives adhering to traditions, the suras follow in precise order what is found in the original celestial tablet.

In the Arabic Quran, each sura has a title. Muslims, especially in the Arab world, cherish the use of these Arabic titles. Non-Arab Muslims attempt to refer to the Arabic title or simply use the number of the sura. Each Arabic title is derived from a major theme or figure found in each sura, although sometimes there is no clear connection between the title and the sura. There is general agreement that the titles were not present in the original text. Some of the titles—when translated into English—include "Table," "Cattle," "Women," "Spoils of War," "Mary," "Thunder," "Joseph," and "Catastrophe."

According to traditions, sura 1 is the greatest sura in the Quran. In practice, it is very important to Muslims, as it serves as the opening prologue to the entire Quran. It is titled "Al-Fatiha," meaning "the opening." Muslims must recite it in their daily prayer; otherwise, their prayer does not count. Ample traditions attributed to Muhammad claim significant reward for those who recite it. When cutting deals in the business world, some Muslims recite it to ensure the deal is blessed and confirmed by Allah, as a divine witness. While some Islamic traditions claim it has significant value, other traditions reveal that major companions of Muhammad insisted that sura 1 was not originally in the Quran. Moreover, Muslim scholars disagree on whether the sura was revealed to Muhammad in Mecca or in Medina. Some claim it was revealed very early in his prophetic career in Mecca, while others argue it came down from Allah after Muhammad emigrated from Mecca to Medina—over thirteen years after his prophetic career allegedly began. Some Muslims attempt to reconcile the discrepancy by claiming sura 1 was revealed twice—once in Mecca and again in Medina. Such contradictions are not unusual in Muslim traditions, resulting in ambiguity and uncertainty regarding the specifics of major Islamic topics.

aaya: a verse in the Quran or a miracle

The Arabic word *aaya* refers to a statement in a **sura** (chapter) in the **Quran**, although it can also refer to a supernatural miracle. In Islamic terms, the word refers to a verse in Islam's scripture. It is pronounced "'EYE-ya," and its plural form is *aayaat*. The Quran is divided into 30 parts, which include 114 chapters (suras), each of which is divided into aayaat. The verses vary in length. The longest verse is called the Debt

Verse because it explains matters related to loaning money to another person (Q 2:282). This verse occupies almost a complete page in the Arabic Quran and consists of 128 words. The shortest verse is less clear, as many verses consist of only two letters—like ta ha (Q 20:1) and ya' siin (Q 36:1)—and a few other verses are made up of only one or two words (e.g., Q 55:1; 55:64; 89:1; 103:1).

A **hadith** attributed to Muhammad identifies the greatest verse in the Quran as the Seat Verse, which magnifies Allah's seat, emphasizing that it encompasses the heavens and the earth (Q 2:255). Following in Muhammad's footsteps, Muslim scholars identified several unique verses in the Quran. Thus, we have the Light Verse, which indicates that Allah is the light of the heavens and the earth (Q 24:35), and the Sword Verse, which instructs Muslims to slay polytheists wherever they are found (Q 9:5). The Best of Creatures Verse identifies those who believed and did righteous works as the best of creatures (Q 98:7). The Jizya Verse instructs believers to fight unbelievers from the scripture people (often identified as Jews and Christians) until they pay the jizya (tax) while humiliated (Q 9:29). Muslims believe that the first aaya revealed to Muhammad was "Read in the name of your Lord who created" (Q 96:1). Some believe that the last verse revealed to Muhammad was the Perfection Verse, in which Muhammad declares to Muslims that on that day he perfected the religion (Q 5:3).

In the Arabic Quran, the number of an aaya follows it. An English translation of the Quran—which is considered by Muslims to be not a true Quran but a translation of its meanings—places the number of the verse before the aaya. The common way of citing the Quran uses the letter *Q* followed by two numbers separated by a colon. The first is the sura's number, while the second is that of the aaya.

mushaf: a set of pages containing Allah's revelations

The term *mushaf* is important in the study of the Quran. It is pronounced "moos-hahf" and refers to a set of pages in which Allah's revelations are written. Its plural form is *masaahif*. Most Muslims use the terms *mushaf* and *Quran* interchangeably; however, this is inaccurate, as there is a major difference. The word *Quran* refers to Allah's revelations to Muhammad. When these revelations are written down, the book that contains them is called a mushaf. Thus, technically, the Quran is not written. The Quran does not use the term *mushaf*. It uses a similar term close in meaning, *suhuf*, which refers to sheets, papers, or scriptures (Q 20:133; 53:36; 80:13; 81:10; 87:18–19).

Sunni scholars generally argue that Muhammad did not see a mushaf in his lifetime—he only proclaimed the Quran (revelations), and his companions wrote them on various materials, including stones, camel bones, and palm tree leaves. These materials were never compiled in one mushaf—Sunnis claim—during Muhammad's life. After his death, two collections of these materials were made: one by the first caliph, Abu Bakr, and another by the third caliph, Uthman. The result is a mushaf by Abu Bakr (compiled two years after Muhammad's death) and another by Uthman (compiled twenty years after Muhammad's death). The traditions about these collections are full of gaps and leave many questions unanswered, but Sunnis assume they were identical and that Uthman's mushaf is the final perfect text—that it is the exact copy of the Quran found in the celestial tablet and also the exact copy we have today. Undoubtedly, these claims are just that. They are not supported by evidence or by Muslim traditions themselves.

Shiite Muslims mock these Sunni claims concerning the two collections of the Quran. For Shiites, there were many masaahif (books claiming to include the Quran) during Muhammad's time and also after his death. There was also, Shiites argue, a mushaf of **Imam** Ali that was checked and endorsed by Muhammad to ensure it conveyed the divine revelations properly. For Shiites, Muhammad would never have entrusted the task of compiling the revelations to anyone except his cousin and reliable friend, Ali. Today's Shiites accept the copy we have, which is commonly—but not accurately—credited to Caliph Uthman, although they believe Sunnis manipulated the Quran to suppress praises of Muhammad's household, particularly Ali. Shiites commonly argue that the true mushaf included two **suras** (chapters)—not found in today's mushaf—in which Allah clearly endorsed Muhammad's designation of Imam Ali as his legitimate successor. Shiites insist in their important studies that the true mushaf of Ali will appear in the end.

Both Shiite and Sunni traditions reveal that the mushaf of Uthman was changed in later generations and that many masaahif appeared after the supposed completion of his mushaf. The Sunni traditions also highlight many missing verses, passages, and even entire suras in Uthman's mushaf as well as the existence of many competing **qira'at** (readings or variants). Thus, while today's Muslims claim that the Quran (mushaf) we have contains the totality of Allah's revelations, this claim is not supported by their own sources. Yet in practice, Muslims give oaths using the sacredness of the mushaf. When a Muslim wants to give the strongest oath, they say, "By the mushaf, I am telling the truth." The person uses the most honorable and trustworthy Islamic object to indicate their truthfulness.

qira'at: readings or variants of the Quran

The Arabic word *qira'at*, pronounced "kee-rah-AWT," is a plural noun that means "readings" or "variant readings." The term refers to different canonical, religiously acceptable variants of the text of the Quran and is important for Muslims in the way they understand, interpret, read, and recite the Quran. For Muslims, these variants are all standard, official, and recognized as valid and acceptable for Muslims to use when reciting the Quran.

Muslims insist that the Quran is a clear Arabic text that came down to Muhammad and has been perfectly preserved without error or corruption. The majority of Muslims—especially Sunnis—believe that Muhammad never held a Quran in his hands, nor did he compile the revelations in one text during his lifetime. For them, the third caliph, Uthman, supervised the canonization of the Quran into a standardized text that was then distributed among Muslims in the empire. This Uthmanic copy of the Quran—known among scholars as the Uthmanic recension—became the standard, official Quran, which is, in the eyes of Muslims, the exact copy of the celestial tablet found in heaven with the deity. Muslims believe that the Quran they possess today is the exact copy that was standardized in the seventh century by Uthman. They claim that the copy they have today came down to them through many generations, since the time of Uthman, without any hint of change or corruption. Nonetheless, if we follow reports in the Muslim traditions, these claims are unsupported. Many competing qira'at (variant readings) continued to circulate based on the Uthmanic text.

Qira'at as a concept is not explicitly mentioned in the Quran. The idea of qira'at emerged many generations after Muhammad, presumably to address problems with opposing readings in the so-called Uthman copy. In fact, in the first three centuries of Islam, there was no official account of the qira'at. This was the case until the renowned Muslim scholar Ibn Mujahid (d. 936) attempted to reconcile the differences in copies of the Quran based on Uthman's official version. Surprisingly, Ibn Mujahid claimed that seven different Arabic qira'at of Uthman's version were equally valid. After him, some scholars argued there were actually ten—not seven—canonical qira'at. This belief was eclipsed by other scholars who claimed the number of valid qira'at was fourteen, before others claimed it was twenty.

Today, Muslims still claim that the differences between these variant readings are minor and do not in any way affect the text or its meaning. They attempt to dilute the differences by claiming that all variants lead to the same text, which is the exact copy of the heavenly original. However, these claims are just that. Scholars argue that there were different and competing qira'at both before and after the standardization supervised and enforced by Caliph Uthman. A glance at various qira'at reveals obvious differences between them in nouns, verbs, verb tenses, pronouns, number of verses, and so forth. Today, many variants circulate among Muslims. In fact, researchers have identified thirty-six variant copies of the Arabic Quran that exist today—all claiming to trace back to the copy standardized by Uthman and presumably matching an original in a celestial tablet. Therefore, despite the Muslim claims of a perfectly preserved Arabic text without any variation throughout the centuries, the existence of different qira'at challenges these claims. Different qira'at were accepted by Muslims for centuries, and they still are today.

naskh: abrogation, particularly in the Quran

For Muslims, the term *naskh* is crucial in interpreting the Quran. While the Arabic word *naskh* has many meanings, in relation to the Quran and its text, it simply means "the erasing, annulling, or cancelation of a ruling, verse, or command." The term is pronounced "nas-kh" and is often rendered as "abrogation."

The term *naskh* explicitly appears in the Quran in various verses, where we read that Allah abrogates a verse or causes it to be forgotten. He also replaces verses with similar or better ones because he is powerful and can control everything (Q 2:106). For many Muslims, these verses establish a doctrine of naskh, which defines abrogating verses and abrogated verses. From the earliest commentaries on the Quran, Muslim scholars used the doctrine to resolve apparent problems when texts opposed or contradicted each other. While the Quran never indicates which verses abrogate or are abrogated, Muslim scholars from the earliest days of Islam claimed that later verses—those revealed in the later stage of Muhammad's life in Medina—abrogated earlier Meccan revelations.

The main problem with this understanding of naskh is that most tolerant verses in the Quran are understood to be Meccan, while the Medinan verses are more concerned with fighting and **jihad** against non-Muslim enemies. For example, many Muslims believe that **sura** 9 is the last sura revealed in Medina—it's the last sura chronologically of the 114 chapters. Most Muslim commentators of the Quran claim that this sura abrogates over three hundred Meccan verses that seem to promote tolerant and mutual coexistence. For these scholars, the later verses abrogate the earlier ones—basically canceling their rulings and commands.

With time, Muslim scholars developed more sophisticated aspects of the naskh doctrine. They claimed that some Quranic commands are abrogated, although they remain in the text unchanged and unremoved. This is the case, for instance, with verses advocating peace and tolerance. The commands are annulled, but the verses themselves are still in the text. Other cases of abrogation involve the removal of a text from the Quran, but the command and ruling remain valid. A case in point is the verse regarding stoning adulterers—the verse is not found in the Quran anymore, because it was erased and abrogated, but Muslim scholars believe the ruling still applies. Ultimately, the Quran does not specify any method of abrogation, but Muslim scholars—generations after Muhammad—created tools and methods to resolve difficulties in the Quran. For the vast majority of Muslims, naskh happens when competing verses exist, at which time the later verse abrogates the earlier. Nonetheless, some modernist and progressive Muslims advocate the opposite, as they rely on the fact that the Quran itself never established a method.

umm al-kitab: the mother of the book

The term *umm al-kitab*, pronounced "ohm al-kee-TAB," literally means "the mother of the book" or "the scripture's mother," denoting the book's source. The term is uniquely Islamic and appears three times in Islam's scripture (Q 3:7; 13:39; 43:4). While the Quran is ambiguous in these verses, the term is used to refer to a foundational kitab (book) in heaven, existing with Allah. The existence of umm al-kitab with Allah clearly shows that he can eliminate from the scripture, which is presumably the original, anything that he wills. Although the Quran does not provide details, Muslim scholars have attempted to assign meaning to the term. Many have argued that umm al-kitab is a celestial tablet that serves as a heavenly writing—a celestial source that includes not only the exact original Quran but also the predestined actions of all humans of all times, all written and totally prescribed. Muslims believe that nothing can affect umm al-kitab; it is divinely protected and eternally preserved. Some secular scholars draw similarities between umm al-kitab and the Christian book of life (Rev. 17:8).

In the Quran, the term *umm al-kitab* seems associated with another term, *al-lawh al-mahfouz* ("the preserved, protected, or guarded tablet") (Q 85:22; cf. 56:78). This tablet, Muslims believe, has the exact words found in the Quran today (cf. **mushaf**). Theoretically, this tablet also has the same words of the Torah and the **Injil** and all other pre-Islamic scriptures, since all of them, Muslims claim, contain the same message that Islam brought. Muslims believe that the Quran we possess today is found eternally in a heavenly text, umm al-kitab or al-lawh al-mahfouz. Thus, it cannot be corrupted. These claims are just that. Muslim historical accounts and **hadith** traditions state that, during and after Muhammad's time, many texts existed and all claimed to be the Quran—there were many competing versions and texts, all using the term *Quran*. Moreover, traditions reveal that certain verses, passages, and entire **suras** (chapters) were not found in the text of the Quran after its canonization by the third caliph. Furthermore, in scholarly arguments, many question the validity of the doctrine of **naskh** (abrogation) in relation to the claims about umm al-kitab being a fixed celestial text. If abrogation is a valid process in the Quran, the rationale goes, then do the abrogated verses still exist in the celestial tablet? Muslim traditions do not provide specific answers to that question.

janna: a garden or eternal paradise

The Arabic term *janna*, pronounced "JAN-nuh," means "garden." As an Islamic term, it refers to the home of everlasting bliss, the eternal paradise. It is the opposite of **jahannam**, the place of fire and eternal punishment (Q 52:21). Unlike in biblical tradition, the Islamic janna—as the eternal home of the righteous—does not appear to be a location in heaven. Rather, it is described as a blissful place on earth, much like the garden of Eden. In fact, the garden of Eden is known in Arabic literature as the janna.

The Quran speaks of the janna in more than a hundred verses. We are told that the people of the janna will dwell eternally in it, as a divine reward for their good works during their lives (Q 4:57; 40:40; 46:14). Only those who obey Allah and Muhammad will inhabit the janna, which is the abode of all the prophets, righteous people, and martyrs (Q 4:69). Those who fear Allah will be admitted to the janna—it will receive them with gates wide open (Q 39:73), and the angels will welcome them with peaceful chanting and greeting because they endured in life with patience (Q 13:24). In the janna, all desires will be met and fulfilled (Q 25:16). While wine is forbidden for Muslims in this life, believers in the afterlife will enjoy cups and pitchers of pure wine emerging from a flowing stream (Q 56:18). As for food, the dwellers of the janna will enjoy every kind of meat they desire as well as a continuous supply of fruit from amazing trees (Q 36:56–57; 52:22). Believers in the janna will also enjoy streams flowing underneath them and will be rewarded with bracelets of gold and compensated with green garments of silk (Q 18:31). Believing men will be served by boys made eternal for them (Q 56:17). These believers will also be tended by youth—as fair as stunning and spotless pearls—who will be dedicated to fulfilling their wishes, running to and fro to serve them (Q 52:24). Furthermore, these believing men will receive beautiful **hoor** (virgins) as a reward (Q 52:17–20; 55:56; 56:35–38). Their beauty is evidenced by their large, piercing black eyes (Q 37:48).

In addition to the Quran, later Muslim traditions provide specifics about and detailed portrayals of the janna. In what appears to contradict the Quran, a tradition indicates that good works will not guarantee admittance to the janna, unless Allah—as he wills—approves and has mercy on the person. The people of the janna will enjoy food and drinks in it, but, traditions reveal, they will not need to pass excrement, blow their noses, or urinate. They will also have abundant power for sexual intercourse, as every male believer will receive the power of a hundred men. We are told that the janna has white dust from which arises an amazing aroma. The sun rises and sets in the janna, and there is a tree under which a believer can enjoy the shade for a hundred years. The janna is called the house of peace, eternity, and refuge. It is also the garden of red gold. A report attributed to Muhammad states that most people who dwell in the janna are poor, and very few are women; women make up most of the dwellers in the hellfire.

jahannam: hell, hellfire, or eternal damnation

As an Islamic term, *jahannam*, pronounced "ja-HAHN-num," refers to the place of eternal punishment for the unrighteous after death. As a destiny, it is the opposite of **janna** (paradise) and is often rendered as "hell." Jahannam is repeatedly mentioned in the Quran and in Muhammad's traditions. Although Muslims tend to claim that the Quran is in perfect Arabic, the term *jahannam* appears to be of Hebrew or Persian origin.

Jahannam is prepared for unbelievers and infidels (Q 3:12, 162; 4:55, 115; 8:36; 9:49, 68). If a Muslim kills another Muslim purposefully, the killer will go to jahannam (Q 4:93). Jahannam is for anyone who disobeys Allah and Muhammad (Q 9:63)—it is also for hypocrites (Q 4:140). Wicked humans and evil **jinn** (genies) will be consigned to jahannam forever (Q 7:179). Unbelievers and idolaters are the fuel of jahannam (Q 21:98). In addition to the word *jahannam*, the Quran uses several other terms to identify eternal damnation in hell. One other common term is *jaheem*, which is often rendered as "hellfire." Linguistically, jahannam refers to a bottomless pit, while jaheem is a severe burning fire. In the Quran, jahannam appears seventy-seven times, while jaheem appears twenty-five times. The Quran describes the people of the jaheem in several places (Q 2:119; 5:10, 86; 9:113; 22:51; 57:19). In addition to jaheem, the Quran uses various Arabic forms of fire to refer to the burning of the wicked in eternal punishment (Q 22:19; 33:64–65).

In Muslim traditions, the punishment of the unrighteous in jahannam is portrayed in more detail. The depictions often describe eternal torture using graphic literary features. Muhammad reportedly warned his people about the torment of hellfire, which begins, he claimed, with the torture of the grave immediately after death. In descriptions of the torture of the grave, traditions highlight physical, mental, and spiritual agony. Some of the reports claim that the unrighteous will be struck by an iron hammer, which if used on a huge mountain would immediately turn it to dust. In other traditions, the heads of the wicked will be shattered by rocks, their bodies clothed with fire and swallowed by the core of the earth, or they will be forced to swim in a river of blood. These images create significant fear and horror among the masses, especially cultural Muslims or followers of folk Islam, as they often understand these images literally.

hoor: beautiful virgins given to male believers in paradise

The term *hoor* refers to beautiful virgins in the afterlife. It is pronounced "hoh-oor" and is sometimes presented as hoor al-'een, where al-'een describes their large and beautiful eyes. The term overall refers to beautiful white virgins with large eyes and piercing black pupils.

Undoubtedly, the term meant a great deal to the Arab Bedouins during Muhammad's time, since they reportedly marveled at white women in particular. White women were sold as slaves for a higher price than nonwhite women. The Quran mentions the hoor several times (Q 44:54; 52:20; 55:72; 56:22). Allah promises believing men that he himself will marry them to these beautiful women (Q 44:54). To incentivize men with the rewards of the afterlife, Allah promises to give them these beautiful hoor, whose likenesses are as well-protected as jewels and pearls (Q 56:22–23). Muhammad's traditions also establish this unique reward for believing men in many **hadiths**, describing the astounding beauty of these women. In one tradition, Muhammad reportedly says that if a man suppresses his rage, then on the Day of Resurrection, Allah will call him to the very front of the line, ahead of all the believers, to choose all the hoor he likes.

Many wonder why the afterlife promises appear to incentivize mainly men. Muslim scholars claim that there must be similar rewards for women, but the Quran and Muhammad's traditions avoid their mention in order to protect women's chastity and modesty. Muslim scholars indicate that women are too reluctant to speak openly about their sexual desires. These claims might satisfy religious enthusiasts, but non-Muslim scholars have different suggestions. They view the Muslim texts as the product of male-dominant contexts and believe that the primary goal of these texts was to exhort men to go to war and devote themselves to political expansion. Nothing incentivizes Arab warriors like promising them what they desire as nomads in the desert—women, wine, spoils, trees, and rivers. This is precisely the depiction of paradise given to the Arabs in seventh-century Arabia.

ISLAMIC PRACTICES AND RELIGIOUS DUTIES

This section moves from what Muslims believe in their hearts to what they practice and do. It highlights their most important duties, the divinely prescribed obligations required of every Muslim. It explains their importance for religious piety among Muslims and indicates the differences in practices between Sunnis and Shiites. This section also explores various Islamic phrases that are often used by Muslims in the daily practice of their religion. The terms here also highlight matters related to how Muslims live out their faith—matters of learning, marriage, adultery, divorce, rituals, feasting, and preaching, among others. While the previous section explored matters dear to the hearts of Muslims, this section examines works they cherish, rituals they follow, and patterns they apply. These are important, as they set Islam apart from most other religions—they present it as a works-based religion revolving around obligatory duties that are described as divinely prescribed rituals.

Shahada: the Islamic creed or profession of faith

The Arabic word *Shahada* means "declaration or testimony." It is pronounced "shah-HAHD-duh" and refers to what is arguably the most important Muslim statement: the Islamic creed. For both Sunnis and Shiites, the Shahada is "There is no god but Allah and Muhammad is Allah's messenger." Muslims call it the double Shahada, because it includes two parts—one for Allah and one for Muhammad. The statement is a declaration of belief in the strict oneness of Allah (**tawhid**) as well as an acknowledgment and acceptance of Muhammad as Allah's messenger. Shiites prefer to add a third part—"and Ali is Allah's vicegerent or friend"—calling it the third Shahada (testimony). This third part is exclusively Shiite and emphasizes their strong devotion to **Imam Ali**, Muhammad's cousin.

For Muslims, the Shahada is the first pillar of Islam. Muslims often repeat the Shahada many times each day. They simply state the Shahada before doing any task as a way of obtaining Allah's favor or declaring piety. Muslims seek to state it as their last sentence before they die, as it ensures they are followers of Islam, which for them is the correct path. The Shahada is repeated in the **adhan** (the call to ritual prayer), the **salat** (the ritual prayer), and many other situations. In practice, any non-Muslim who openly states the Shahada becomes a Muslim. Whether a person genuinely believes in the religion or not, the pronouncement suffices. This is why Shiites in particular distinguish between sincere faith and the declaration of the Shahada. For Shiites, believing (**iman**) refers to a genuine conviction, while outwardly joining Islam (sometimes called conversion) might simply be an act of submission out of fear or disingenuous belief.

The Quran does not include the double Shahada. It refers only to the first part (e.g., Q 3:18); the double Shahada appears only in later Muslim traditions. The absence of the double Shahada in Islam's scripture has caused critics of Islam to question the legitimacy of the second part, which essentially elevates Muhammad next to Allah. Some consider this idolatrous (compare with Q 2:165). Doubts about the second part of the Shahada are strengthened by recent research demonstrating that, in the first half century after Muhammad's death, inscriptions, coins, and papyri did not include the second part of the Shahada. This has led some scholars to speculate that later Muslims added it, thus forging the profession of faith as it is known today.

salat: the ritual prayer

The Arabic noun *salat* is based on the notion of connecting with someone or something. It refers to the act of connecting with the deity—prayer, but not any kind of prayer. Mere supplications or petitions are indeed forms of prayer, but these are not called salat in Islam. *Salat* refers only to the divinely prescribed daily ritual prayer. For Sunnis and Shiites, the salat is one of the Five Pillars of Islam. The term *salat* is singular and pronounced "sah-LAHT." Its plural form is *salawat*. Muslims often claim that the word *salat* is pure Arabic, but research shows that the word has a Syriac origin and was commonly known before Islam as a reference to prayer.

For Muslims, there are five daily prayers (thus, salawat). To perform the salat, Muslims must face the **qibla** (the direction of prayer), which is the **Ka'ba** in Mecca. According to Muslim traditions, Allah prescribed these as religious duties (fard). They were initially fifty in number, but after Muhammad negotiated the number with Allah—based on a suggestion from Moses—Allah decreased the number to five to ease the load on Muslims. While the Quran does not designate a number, Muslim traditions indicate it. Some traditions claim that Gabriel taught Muhammad the salat, while others indicate that Allah taught Muhammad in the most sacred place above the seventh heaven.

The Quran uses the term *salat* in over sixty verses. In each one, the Quran exhorts Muslims to perform the prayer and commends those who pray (Q 2:3; 4:103; 20:132; 29:45; 87:14–15). To elevate its importance, the Quran insists that some of the dwellers of hell are there because of their failure to perform the salat (Q 74:42). However, the Quran does not specify the details of the salat. All these details stem from later traditions, which describe standing, kneeling, and bowing while stating particular religious statements. Because of the competing traditions, there are differences between the Shiite and Sunni performances of the salat. In practice, there are two kinds of salat: individual and corporate. The Friday Prayer—which is very important for all Muslims—is performed only in a corporate or congregational fashion in a mosque (**masjid**). Muslims believe that the salat is the strongest foundation of the religion of Islam. They also believe that practicing the salat is required before any other religious duty will be accepted by Allah. According to traditions, a salat in a mosque receives a higher reward from Allah than one performed at home. Similarly, a salat performed in the mosque at Mecca or Medina equates to thousands performed at home.

zakat: almsgiving, obligatory charitable payment

Like the **salat** (the ritual prayer), the zakat is a mandatory act of worship in Islam and is one of its pillars. It refers to a religiously mandated (fard) giving of a portion of a Muslim's possessions to serve fellow Muslims in need. The term is pronounced "zah-CAT." Scholars believe it is derived from a Syriac or Hebrew word and is not originally Arabic. The zakat is mandated only for Muslims, unlike the jizya (tax), which is obligatory for non-Muslims—particularly Jews and Christians—who live under Islamic rule. In Arabic, the noun *zakat* is positive and means "purification, growth, multiplication, or to make something praiseworthy."

These positive elements appear in the way Muslims understand the zakat. When Muslims say they are giving the zakat on their wealth, they mean they are purifying and multiplying their wealth by performing a praiseworthy act of sharing with their fellow Muslims. In practice, the giving of the zakat is a way for Muslims to purify their money. It is an act of piety. It sanctifies one's soul and brings Allah's favor. In cultural Islam, the giving of the zakat is viewed as a protection of one's wealth, since it is believed to distract evil spirits from harming one's property. It is also perceived as a preventive act against diseases and misfortune. For instance, when a Muslim man's property is harmed in any way, his peers may ask him whether he paid his zakat as a purification of his possessions. While non-Muslims often think of the zakat as a form of taxation, Muslims do not prefer this description; they view the zakat as a charitable donation.

In Islamic history, the zakat became mandatory for Muslims at the inception of Islam. After Muhammad's death, some Muslims refused to pay the zakat; consequently, Abu Bakr, Muhammad's successor, fought them as apostates because they rejected the fulfillment of one of Islam's major obligatory duties.

The Quran mentions the zakat in over fifty verses (e.g., Q 2:43, 83; 4:162). In more than half of them, it is combined with the salat as mandatory acts of worship (e.g., Q 22:41; 24:37). For those who pay the zakat, the Quran promises that they will be with their Lord and will have no reason to be afraid concerning the afterlife (Q 2:277). As with other terms, the Quran is often general and vague about the zakat, not specifying how much a Muslim should give, but the traditions provide specifics. While Muslims largely disagree on the portion, according to common estimates, capable adult Muslims should give about 2.5 percent of their accumulated wealth—above a certain threshold—in any given lunar year.

The channels of paying the zakat vary greatly among Muslims in different areas. The involvement of governments in mandating and collecting the zakat from Muslims differs between countries. While many Muslim lands do not make it obligatory, some enforce the collection of the zakat on their Muslim citizens.

Ramadan: the holiest Muslim month

The noun *Ramadan*, pronounced "rah-mah-DON," is the most important month for Muslims. In the **hijri** calendar, Ramadan is the ninth month, preceded by Sha'baan and followed by Shawwal. Ramadan can be twenty-nine or thirty days, and like all months in the hijri calendar, it follows the moon's shapes and phases. The Arabic word *Ramadan* seems to refer to severe hot weather or to extremely hot rocks after they have been exposed to the heat of the day. Muslims believe the name reflects the toughness of the heat on anyone fasting in the summer—although Ramadan may occur in winter, depending on the year.

For Muslims, Ramadan is the month of fasting. They believe that Allah ordained a mandatory fast for every adult Muslim from sunrise to sunset throughout the month. This makes the month unique. Its high esteem arguably relies on an assertion in the Quran that it is the month in which the scripture came down to Muhammad (Q 2:185). It is the only month mentioned explicitly by name in the Quran. While Muslims commonly argue that Allah gave the Quran to Muhammad during Ramadan, they disagree on what the verse actually means, as we are told in other references that the Quran descended to Muhammad in pieces over a period of twenty-three years, thirteen in Mecca and ten in Medina. Some Muslims claim that the Quran—as the entire revelation—came down to the first heaven during Ramadan but was given to Muhammad through Gabriel piece by piece over the twenty-three years. The high esteem of Ramadan for Muslims also stems from the belief that it includes a unique night—**laylat al-qadr**, the night of power—which is the best night in any given year. On this night, the gates of heaven are open, and Allah answers prayers and supplications and absolves sins.

In Islam's history, Ramadan is linked with momentous events. Two major battles led by Muhammad himself occurred during Ramadan: the Battle of Badr, when Muslims won over the pagans of Mecca, and a few years later the conquest of Mecca, when Muhammad suppressed his enemies and became the sole leader of the Hijaz, West Arabia. The month has added significance for Shiites. They believe it is the month when their first **imam**, Ali, was martyred and the month in which their second imam, Hasan, was born. Many Shiite traditions elevate the uniqueness of the month. They believe that the hidden imam, Mahdi, will reappear during Ramadan. For them, Allah opens the gates of heaven and puts the devils in chains during Ramadan to bestow favor on humans. In some traditions, every good work receives double rewards during Ramadan.

In practice, Muslims eagerly welcome the month. To mark the beginning of the month, they often have moon sighting gatherings. Muslim countries organize huge events to celebrate the beginning of the month as a communal occasion. Muslims usually congratulate each other immediately before and during the month, saying, "Ramadan Mubarak"—meaning "blessed Ramadan." During Ramadan, committed and devoted Muslims fast. In many Muslim countries, out of respect, even Muslims who are not fasting tend to avoid eating and drinking in public. Many who fast also read the entire Quran during the month. The Quran has 114 **suras** (chapters) and is divided into 30 sections; Muslims tend to read one section each day to complete the reading within Ramadan. The time of breaking the fast, known as *iftaar*, is an important social gathering for Muslim families, who plan meals together. Since doing good deeds is recommended in Ramadan, some wealthy Muslims set up huge iftaar tents in which they offer free meals to poor and needy people. Conversely, Muslims believe that transgressions receive severer divine penalties if committed during Ramadan.

laylat al-qadr: the night of power, glory, or destiny

For Muslims, the Arabic term *laylat al-qadr* refers to the most important and esteemed night in any given year. *Al-qadr* is often translated as "power," although it can also be rendered as "high esteem," "utmost glory," "divine destiny," or "extreme measure." The noun *laylat* means "the night of" and is pronounced "lay-lat," while *al-qadr*, pronounced "al-kod-der," is a noun that may refer to one of Allah's names or may reflect esteem or destiny; however, its specific meaning is ambiguous.

Laylat al-qadr is one of the nights of the month of **Ramadan**. Muslims believe that during the night of al-qadr, Allah brought down the Quran to Muhammad, but a Muslim dispute exists: Did Allah reveal the Quran in one night or over a period of twenty-three years, as other traditions claim? This is uncertain among Muslims. Some attempt to reconcile the claims by arguing that the Quran came down to the first heaven or to the heart of Muhammad on laylat al-qadr but took twenty-three years to be revealed to Muhammad piece by piece.

One reason for the night's high esteem is that the Quran has an entire chapter titled "Al-Qadr" (Q 97). It is a short **sura** with only five verses, but it advances the great status of laylat al-qadr, indicating not only that the Quran was sent down during it (v. 1) but also that it is better than a thousand months (v. 3). The sura claims that on laylat al-qadr Allah decrees his angels and the spirit—which is an ambiguous reference that some see as the Holy Spirit—to descend (v. 4), presumably to give favors to humans and apply every matter Allah decreed. The night is entirely a night of peace until dawn breaks through (v. 5). This sura has propelled Muslims to believe that on this night Allah opens the gates of heaven to bless humans and grant fulfillment of their supplications. However, the Quran never specifies when the night of power really is, nor does it indicate that the night is actually a specific night during Ramadan. Muslims concluded that laylat al-qadr is during Ramadan based on two verses; one indicates that the revelation came down during Ramadan (Q 2:185), and the other states that it came down on laylat al-qadr (Q 97:1). Most of what Muslims believe about laylat al-qadr comes from tradition, not the Quran.

In Muslim traditions, Allah revealed to Muhammad the exact date of laylat al-qadr, but Muhammad forgot it when he saw two Muslims quarreling. Since Allah did not repeat the date to Muhammad, later traditions sought to advance various options for it. Some Sunni **hadiths** claim that the night is one of the last ten nights of Ramadan. Others claim that it actually occurs in the last seven nights, or the last three. Some traditions specify that it can occur only on one of the odd nights of the last ten days of Ramadan. Some traditions advance an even more specific date, placing the night precisely on the twenty-seventh night of Ramadan. Many Muslims speculate that since traditions state that the best day of the week is Friday and that Allah loves odd numbers, if there is a Friday night, odd in number, during the last week of Ramadan, then it must be laylat al-qadr. Shiite Muslims, on the other hand, advance their own claims and traditions about the night. They mostly specify the nineteenth or twenty-third night of Ramadan as its specific date.

All Muslims view laylat al-qadr as the best night of the best month in any given year, although they do not know its precise date. Their attempts to discern and watch for laylat al-qadr stem from the fact that traditions insist it is a night when Allah absolves all human sins and grants them what they want. No other night in any given year is assigned this status.

hajj: a pilgrimage or pilgrim

Linguistically, hajj, pronounced "hahj," is a pilgrimage to any sacred place, but Muslims often use the term in relation to the pilgrimage to the **Ka'ba** (black cubic shrine) in Mecca. A Muslim performing and fulfilling the pilgrimage receives an honorary title by his fellow Muslims: hajj (the feminine version is *hajja*). The title is cherished by Muslims, who believe it is a significant honor to perform a hajj to the place where Muhammad presumably lived. After all, this hajj is one of the five divinely prescribed religious duties for all Muslims—there is no disagreement here between Sunnis and Shiites.

These religious duties are known among Sunni Muslims as the Five Pillars of Islam—the hajj is the fifth among them. Shiites, however, add to these five pillars several other practices. For Shiites, other places are also considered holy and sacred, including the shrine of **Imam** Ali in Najaf and that of Imam Husayn in Karbala, both in Iraq. Shiites are encouraged to perform a pilgrimage to these exclusively Shiite sacred shrines. Still, Shiites, like all Muslims, highly respect the status of the hajj to Mecca. However, due to political conflicts and religious disagreements, Shiites often voice dissatisfaction concerning the politicization of the hajj to Mecca, as it is supervised and controlled by Sunnis.

When performing the hajj to Mecca, millions of Muslims gather to follow specific rituals in fulfillment of their religious duties. All the rituals must be done within a specific period of time in the twelfth month of the Islamic lunar calendar, known as the **hijri** calendar, as it uses the hijra (emigration) of Muhammad as its starting point. These hajj rituals require five to six days to complete. This is why this hajj is known among Muslims as the major pilgrimage, in contrast to a minor pilgrimage, called umra, which requires only a few hours to complete and can be done any time of the year.

While the rituals of the hajj are many, they are not mentioned explicitly in the Quran. Rather, they were specified by later Muslim scholars and detailed in Muslim traditions. Among the rituals, Muslims begin the hajj by walking or running in circles around the Ka'ba in the sacred mosque, starting at the black stone. Muslims need to touch or kiss the black stone as a part of their fulfillment of the hajj. They must move around the Ka'ba counterclockwise. The rituals also include walking or running between two hills, Safa and Marwa, as well as throwing stones against Satan in a valley called Mina, because of the belief that Abraham did the same centuries ago.

The rituals of the hajj are greatly cherished by Muslims, and they largely consider them exclusively Islamic in nature. For Muslims, kissing a stone, walking in circles around a shrine, running between hills, and throwing stones against Satan are not pagan or idolatrous actions. Pilgrims follow the rituals because they are, for them, prescribed duties in Islam's traditions. However, scholars have identified similar rituals in pre-Islamic pagan Arabia, where Arabs had many Ka'bas; these scholars conclude that the pre-Islamic pagan rituals basically permeated Islamic religious duties. It appears that Islam adopted ancient Arabian rituals, with minor adjustments.

du'aa': a prayer request, petition, or supplication

The noun *du'aa'* refers to a petition—prayer request—from a human to Allah. It is pronounced "doo-WAH" and is different from the **salat**, which is the ritual prayer. For a Muslim to voice a du'aa', there is no need for ritual ablution (**wudu'**) or facing the **qibla** (the direction of the ritual prayer), although some Muslims may do so. Non-Muslims may conflate a du'aa' and the salat, but Muslims view them differently. When Muslims ask someone to pray for them, they use the term *du'aa'*. The noun *du'aa'* is singular; its plural form is *ad'iya*.

In the Quran, Allah encourages believers to voice a du'aa' and promises to listen. He presumably tells Muhammad to inform believers that he is near and that he hears the du'aa' of any among them (Q 2:186). The Quran refers to a testimony of Zachariah, who made a du'aa' to have a son; Allah answered by granting him Yahya (Arabic name for John the Baptizer) (Q 3:38–39; 19:3–7; 21:89–90). The prophet Job, too, in his affliction, made a du'aa', which Allah answered (Q 21:83–84; 38:41–42). The same is true for Noah (Q 21:76). Allah exhorts believers to make a du'aa' with humility and in privacy and quietness, because Allah loves those qualities and hates transgressors (Q 7:55). He declares to believers that he responds to them and listens to their du'aa' (Q 40:60).

The same notions appear in many of Muhammad's traditions, where he affirms that a du'aa' is a form of devotion to and worship of Allah. Muhammad reveals that the best worship is a sincere du'aa'. He reports that any du'aa' offered by a human is precious in the sight of Allah. In fact, Muhammad tells believers that Allah loves those who keep asking repeatedly, and he warns Muslims that Allah gets angry if appeals are not made in a du'aa'. Various traditions indicate that the voicing of a du'aa' should be accompanied by prostration. Some traditions claim that a good time for voicing a du'aa' is immediately after a person hears the **adhan** (the call to ritual prayer).

When voicing a du'aa', most Muslims look up to heaven and raise both hands in supplication as they make their petition or request. However, this practice, though widespread, is discouraged by a hadith attributed to Muhammad. He reportedly said that Muslims should not raise their eyes toward heaven while making a du'aa' or they would lose their sight.

wudu': a ritual ablution, water purification

The Arabic term *wudu'* is derived from words for "purity and shining splendor." It refers to a ritual cleansing, using water, that purifies a Muslim and makes them able to fulfill religious deeds, such as prayer or Quran reading. Wudu' is pronounced "woo-DOO," and as a cleansing ritual before prayer, it is mentioned in the Quran: Allah instructs believers to wash their faces, hands, and arms up to the elbows and to wipe their heads, feet, and ankles (Q 5:6). While Sunnis and Shiites agree on the essential parts of the ritual ablution, they disagree on minor issues regarding the sequence and manner of washing the hands and wiping the head and feet.

In practice, the wudu' is required before the **salat** (the ritual prayer), touching or reciting the Quran, and performing the circumambulation around the **Ka'ba** during the **hajj** (pilgrimage). The wudu' must be preceded by a declaration of intention by Muslims, indicating they aim to follow the purification ritual precisely for the fulfillment of a religious duty (fard). The intention is part of the ritual ablution itself—without the intention, the ablution does not count. If any of the body parts mentioned in the Quranic verse are not cleansed properly, a Muslim must repeat the process. According to Muslim scholars, an ablution is invalidated or spoiled by flatulence, urination, bleeding, menstruation, or sexual activities. When an ablution is invalidated, it must be repeated before a Muslim can perform any further religious activity.

Because the wudu' is concerned with the cleansing of only a few body parts, it is known among Muslim scholars as the minor or partial ablution. In some cases, the whole body must be washed. This is called ghusl and is needed in specific cases, including when women complete their menstrual period or after men ejaculate. In contrast to the wudu', the ghusl is known among Muslims as the total or full ablution.

basmala: a repeated phrase in the Quran invoking Allah's name

The basmala is one of the most important phrases in Islam. It is arguably the most cherished and is repeated by Muslims daily. It is pronounced "bahs-meh-luh." The phrase reads, "In the name of Allah, Most Gracious, Most Merciful." It is also rendered, "By the name of Allah, the All-beneficent, the All-merciful." The importance of the basmala stems from the fact that it is an essential part of the Quran. It occurs at the beginning of each **sura** (chapter), with the exception of sura 9, and is found twice in sura 27—once at the beginning and again in verse 30.

The phrase is important in Muslims' daily practice of the faith. They repeat it in various situations because they believe it strengthens the believer by providing divine favor and protection through the invocation of Allah's name. Sometimes Muslims recite the phrase before entering a dark place or prior to beginning a new task. When they are about to have a meal, Muslims tend to say the phrase to give thanks. Most Muslims—even non-Arabic speakers—tend to recite the phrase in Arabic in recognition and appreciation of the language of the Quran. In Arabic, the phrase is "Bismillah ar-rahman ar-raheem," where the word *bismillah* means "in the name of Allah," *ar-rahman* means "Most Gracious," and *ar-raheem* means "Most Merciful." Since the initial word in Arabic is *bismillah* (essentially two words, *bism* and *Allah*), some Muslims summarize the entire basmala by its first word, *bismillah*. Thus, the phrase is known as the basmala, which begins with *bismillah*.

While Muslims treasure the basmala as purely Islamic, recent discoveries of inscriptions in the Arabian Peninsula suggest that the phrase was largely known to pre-Islamic Arabs for centuries before Islam. Some even speculate it was a Christian or Jewish liturgical phrase, often repeated by Arabic-speaking believers. This suggests that the phrase is not exclusively Islamic and that Islam may have borrowed the phrase or its variants from earlier faiths.

The absence of the basmala from the beginning of sura 9 has sparked debate and speculation among both Muslim and non-Muslim scholars. This debate is important because sura 9 appears to be one of the most intolerant toward non-Muslims in the entire Quran, and some Muslim scholars use it to cancel and annul many other tolerant suras in the

Quran. Some claim that one or two verses of sura 9 have actually abrogated hundreds of verses in the rest of Islam's scripture. Some say that sura 8 and sura 9 previously were one sura and that the basmala was not added at the time the verses were divided. However, this raises questions about the collection of the Quran and whether sentences were added or removed. Some even question sura 9 altogether and say it was not part of the Quran—it was a later addition designed to legitimize attacking and waging war on non-Muslims. In fact, some Muslims debate whether the basmala—as a phrase repeated at the beginning of each sura—is actually part of the revealed text of each sura or was added later to establish an opening phrase for each sura. While the debate continues, the basmala is very important to all Muslims in their daily practice of their faith.

tilaawa: recitation, particularly of the Quran

The term *tilaawa* refers to the act of careful reciting, particularly of the Quran. It is pronounced "tee-LAH-wuh." Muslims are encouraged to practice the tilaawa of the Quran because it entails attention to the text and meditation on it. Unlike the mere reading of scripture, tilaawa suggests deep reflection on the verses. Linguistically, tilaawa reflects the belief that the text drives the reader to follow its direction—the text is a forerunner, while the reader is a follower. This notion often appears in how reciters tend to repeat phrases or verses several times as an act of devotion and contemplation. This is evident in the only verse in the Quran where the term *tilaawa* occurs: Allah gives the scripture to people who recite it in the best way a recitation can be done (Q 2:121).

To advance the superior value of the tilaawa of the Quran, many traditions emphasize its great rewards. Muhammad reportedly said that anyone who recites one letter of Allah's scripture will receive a tenfold reward. In another **hadith**, Muhammad affirms that excellent reciters of the Quran will be with the angels, and those who find difficulty in reciting it will be given double reward if they persevere in the attempt. Therefore, the ritual recitation of the Quran is of significant importance to Muslims. For many Muslims, the tilaawa itself appears to possess a marvelous supernatural influence—a way to gain Allah's favor and receive his protection against the evil one.

Some Muslims adopt the tilaawa of the Quran as their profession. This is the case particularly with Muslims who have strong and beautiful voices, as the public tilaawa involves the vocal rendition of the text with artistic melodies. Such a reciter—always a male—is called a qaari' or a muqri'. Both terms simply refer to a professional reader of the Quran who is capable of reciting it following the proper rules of tilaawa.

asmaa' Allah: Allah's names or attributes

The Arabic noun *asmaa'* means "names" and is pronounced "as-MEH." In connection with Islam's deity, the term *asmaa' Allah* simply means "Allah's names." Muslims understand these names as the most glorious names and as descriptions of Allah's attributes. If Muslims want to know Allah, they should seek to comprehend his names. They should learn them and meditate on them in worship. In practice, these names are adjectives conveying his majesty and emphasizing his perfect character and unmatched deeds toward humankind. Some Muslims—especially during worship and fasting times—repeat Allah's names quietly, almost murmuring. They recite Allah's names, meditating on his attributes, because they believe this is an important act of devotion, worship, and piety.

Muslims use another term to describe these glorious names of Allah: *al-asmaa' al-husnaa*, which means "the most beautiful names." The term *al-asmaa' al-husnaa* is found four times in the Quran (Q 7:180; 17:110; 20:8; 59:24). The Quran emphasizes that Allah has al-asmaa' al-husnaa and that believers should call upon him using these names (Q 7:180). Since Allah's absolute oneness (**tawhid**) is central to Islam, the Quran states that no one is like Allah and that he possesses al-asmaa' al-husnaa (Q 20:8). However, the Quran does not list or detail these names. Later Muslim scholars had to solve the problem and form a list. Several centuries after Muhammad, **hadith** scholars attributed a tradition to him that states that Allah has ninety-nine names. The list of names given in the tradition includes divine attributes comparable to those used in other faiths: Allah is generous, king, creator, forgiver, almighty, holy, protector, and so forth. Some attributes, however, are unique to Allah: he is the proud one (al-mutakabbir), the humiliator (al-mudhil), and the harmer (al-daar).

A controversy regarding the ninety-nine names exists among Muslims for at least two reasons: some of the names are not found in the Quran, and some attributes in the Quran are not found in the list. Throughout Islamic history, many Muslim scholars added attributes to the list or removed attributes from it, which brought the list under suspicion. In fact, Shiites believe that the names of the **imams** are part of Allah's attributes—even the name Ali, they claim, is one of Allah's names. Even the hadith scholar who initially narrated the tradition of the ninety-nine names and attributed it to Muhammad added a caveat after his list. He wrote that this tradition is weak and strange.

alhamdulillah: thanks and praise to Allah

The term *alhamdulillah* means "thanks and praise to Allah." It is pronounced "al-HAM-doo-le-leh." The term can be divided into various parts, where the word *al-hamdu* means "thanks and praise," *li* is the preposition "to," and *llah* is a variation of Allah. The term is significantly important in the daily life of a Muslim. Whenever Muslims receive great news, they shout in joy, "Alhamdulillah!" When the news is sad, the term is voiced in a tone of sorrow but in clear surrender to Allah's will and in affirmation of the concept of **qadar** (Allah's decree, fatalism). In Arabic-speaking countries where Christians exist (e.g., Jordan, Syria, Lebanon, Egypt), Christians say the same term as a form of praise to God. It is similar in meaning to the biblical term *hallelujah*.

In Islamic theology, giving Allah praise (al-hamdu) means elevating him above any shortcoming, limitation, or deficiency. This is evident in many verses in the Quran where the term *alhamdulillah* is explicitly mentioned. In the first **sura** (chapter), the Quran reads, "Alhamdulillah who is the lord of the worlds" (Q 1:2)—this is the first verse in the sura immediately following the **basmala** (opening line). The Quran also refers to angels praising Allah by using this term (Q 39:75). It uses the term *alhamdulillah* in exalting Allah as the creator of heaven and earth (Q 6:1) and as the deity who gave Muhammad the scripture (Q 18:1), who created the universe (Q 35:1), and who possesses everything in it (Q 34:1). The Quran also exhorts believers to say alhamdulillah when praising Allah, who did not take a son (Q 17:111) and who will show his signs to his people (Q 27:93).

Many **hadiths** attributed to Muhammad exhort Muslims to praise Allah using *alhamdulillah*. In one hadith, Muhammad is reported to have said, "Alhamdulillah who gave us food, drink, home, and protection." Another hadith reports that Muhammad said that *alhamdulillah*, as a phrase, adds to the scale of the good deeds of a Muslim, allowing the erasure of bad deeds from the final count between good and bad actions. The traditions state that Allah is pleased and satisfied when a human says *alhamdulillah* after drinking or eating. Any deed that does not begin with *alhamdulillah* is considered bad or will produce unfortunate results. This is why, in practice, Muslims often repeat the term many times on any given day. The term is one of the most repeated among Muslims.

The term *alhamdulillah* is associated with another noun, *shukr*, which means "thanksgiving" or "thanking" in a more general sense. In relation to the deity, Muslims give shukr to Allah. Another form is shukran, which means "thanks or thank you." The term *shukran* is used by Arabic-speaking people to convey the state of giving thanks; it simply means "thank you."

mashallah: what Allah willed

The Arabic term *mashallah* literally means "what Allah willed" and connotes that what Allah predestined has occurred. It is pronounced "ma-sheh-al-LUH" and encompasses three parts: the word *ma* is a particle that means "that which," and *shallah* is the shortened form of the two words *shaa'* and *Allah*, which mean "Allah willed." The term basically conveys that Allah's will is being done in human life. The word appears once in the Quran, which states that what Allah predestined or willed will come to pass because there is no power greater than him (Q 18:39).

In practice, like **alhamdulillah**, mashallah is often repeated by Muslims on many occasions. When Muslims see beautiful scenery, objects, or people, they exclaim, "Mashallah!" This means that the beauty of these things or people comes only from Allah's predestined will. When a Muslim begins a new job, their friends will exclaim, "Mashallah!" in congratulations and praise to Allah, as he willed the provision of a new job. Sometimes the word is spoken as a protection against evil. For example, upon seeing a lovely child of a friend, Muslims would want to ensure that any praise of the child comes with a protection from Allah.

They would say mashallah to convey that the beauty of the child is great, yet at the same time their exclamation becomes a declaration of Allah's protection over the child. This is because Muslims believe that praising a child's lovability or attractiveness can reflect an evil eye (a superstitious belief that jealous glances can bring misfortune) and attract harmful **jinn** (genies) to attack the child.

Mashallah is associated with another term, *subhaan-Allah* (pronounced "soup-HAN-al-LUH"), which literally means "glory to Allah" or "exalted is Allah." The term is used whenever a marvelous or beautiful scene is found, as it is a glorifying exclamation of praise. When Muslims view a newborn baby, they may declare, "Mashallah subhaan-Allah." When viewing a stunning mountain, they may declare, "Subhaan-Allah," as praise for the great creation. For the most part, *subhaan-Allah* is used to declare that Allah is exalted and worthy of praise for his marvelous deeds.

inshallah: Allah willing or if Allah wills

The term *inshallah* means "Allah willing" or "if Allah wills" and is pronounced "in-shah-al-LUH." Muslims use it primarily in the context of speaking of future plans: if Allah wills and if things move to that end, their plans will happen. The term appears in the Quran in the story of Abraham attempting to place his son as a sacrifice on the altar: his son said in obedience that he was ready to fulfill what Allah demanded of Abraham, and inshallah (Allah willing), his endurance and steadfast patience would prove true (Q 37:102). The Quran uses the term also in reference to people seeking true divine guidance (Q 2:70)—if Allah wills, they will be guided to the correct path.

The term *inshallah*, as used in Islam, is similar to the notion found in the Bible in the book of James. The text explains that, when making plans, Christians should say, "If it is the Lord's will, we will live and do this or that" (James 4:15). Likewise, the Quran commands believers not to make definite statements about future plans without adding "if Allah wills"—one should remember Allah always (Q 18:23–24). Thus, the term *inshallah* acknowledges Allah's **qadar** (decree, fatalism) and that everything that happens is already determined by Allah and written in a celestial book in heaven.

The term *inshallah* is linked to another common term, *bi'dhnillah* (pronounced "bi-izni-al-LUH"), which has the same notion and means "if Allah permits." A person may indicate, "I will see you tomorrow, bi'dhnillah [if Allah permits]." The term appears in the Quran, where the text marvels, "Quite often a small group [of soldiers] overcame a large one bi'dhnillah [by Allah's permission]" (Q 2:249). In practice, Muslims sometimes use the terms *inshallah* and *bi'dhnillah* to answer questions without giving a definite answer. If a shop owner does not want to commit to a specific date about fixing a car, he might simply say he will inshallah fix it soon. This answer avoids specifics and relies on the common understanding that nothing will happen unless Allah wills it. Similarly, a manager might indicate she will inshallah join the important meeting, although she is not planning to actually do so. By stating inshallah, she is essentially declaring—at least in her mind—that unless Allah wills otherwise, she will not be joining the meeting.

as-salaamu 'alaykum: peace be upon you

As-salaamu 'alaykum is a distinct Muslim greeting that literally means "peace be upon you." It is pronounced "as-sa-LEH-muh ah-LAY-koom," where the word *as-salaamu* means "peace" and *'alaykum* means "upon you." The phrase serves as the official greeting in Muslim circles. When Muslims meet anyone, they use this phrase as a greeting. In this context, it serves as a hello. The phrase appears in the Quran with variations (Q 6:54; 7:46; 13:24; 16:32). This explains its importance in Muslim life; it is the Islamic greeting found in Islam's scripture. While the phrase is plural in its grammar and literal rendition, it can be said to one person. As a response to this greeting, Muslims say, "Wa-'alaykumu as-salaam," which means "and peace upon you too."

In practice, there is a lengthier form of this greeting, *as-salaamu 'alay-kum wa-rahmatu-Allahi wa-barakaatuhu*, which translates to "peace be upon you, as well as Allah's mercy and blessings." This lengthier form is often used as a warmer greeting, although the shorter one is usually sufficient. For Muslims, the greeting itself grants security and safety to the person who receives it, as it conveys peace that shields and honors their possessions and dignity. In some conservative Muslim circles, the phrase should be said only to Muslims. The rationale is that "the peace" is one of Allah's names and that true peace can be given and received only by Allah's believers—nonbelievers do not enjoy this blessing. In these cases, if a non-Muslim greets a Muslim with *as-salaamu 'alaykum*, the Muslim may respond by saying, "The peace is only upon believers."

salla allahu alayhi wa sallam: may Allah send prayers and peace upon him, a phrase honoring Muhammad

Salla allahu alayhi wa sallam means "may Allah send prayers and peace upon him." The phrase is greatly important to Muslims, and they always say it after Muhammad's name is mentioned. It is pronounced "sul-LUH al-LUH-hu al-lay-hee weh sal-LUM." In it, the word *salla* means "pray," *allahu* means "Allah," *alayhi* means "upon him," and *wa sallam* means "and grant peace." In English circles, the phrase is often rendered as "peace be upon him," but this is incorrect, as the Arabic phrase is more descriptive and detailed and conveys a lengthier statement of reverence and regard.

In practice, the phrase is a salutation to Muhammad that declares astounding honor. This is why Muslims who do not speak Arabic do not translate it in their conversations but often say it in Arabic in an attempt to declare devotion and reverence to the unique name. The repetition of the phrase can occur many times in one conversation, but Muslims do not view this as redundancy—it is necessary to repeat the phrase. Some Muslims use a variant of the phrase, *alayhi al-salaatu wa al-salaam*, which means "the prayer and peace are upon him."

The phrase relies on a verse in the Quran where the text conveys that Allah and his angels send their prayers on Muhammad and exhorts believers to do the same by offering prayer and peace upon him (Q 33:56). While the phrase is cherished and admired by Muslims, it can be confusing to non-Muslims, as it is unfathomable for the deity to pray over a human. If Allah prays, then who listens? However, Muslims argue that Allah's prayer in this context refers to him granting favor, mercy, and blessings over Muhammad.

This phrase is mainly used by Sunni Muslims. While Shiites use it as well, they add a piece to it that conveys reverence of and devotion to the household of Muhammad (ahl al-bayt), as the infallible imams from Muhammad's family are important spiritual and political guides among Shiites. After the mention of Muhammad's name, Shiites say, "Salla allahu alayhi wa aalihi wa sallam" ("Allah prayed and brought peace upon him and his household"). In this addition, the term *aalihi* means "his household."

Muslims use an honoring phrase—a shorter one—upon the mention of any other prophet recognized in Islam. For instance, after mentioning Moses or Jesus, Muslims usually say, "Alayhi as-salaam," which means "peace be upon him." They often reserve the use of the lengthier phrase for Muhammad alone.

Allahu Akbar: Allah is greater, a glorification formula

Allahu Akbar, pronounced "al-LUH-hu ukk-bar," is exclusively Islamic and conveys the utter belief in the greatness of Allah. Linguistically, the phrase means "Allah is greater," without indicating the object against whom the comparison is made. By indicating that Allah is greater than any other being or thing—he is above any comparison and beyond any expression of greatness—the phrase highlights that Allah is the greatest in the universe. In many respects, the phrase is the unique motto or slogan of Islam in the same way that "God is love" is a slogan of Christianity.

The phrase received its status and power from reports from Muhammad's traditions. In a night journey, Muhammad allegedly flew on a winged horse-like creature to the seventh heaven. He was then taken alone beyond the holy veil to the very place of Allah. Once he entered, Muhammad heard the declaration "Allahu Akbar." If the phrase is repeated in the holiest place, Muslims believe, then it must be of the highest esteem. Moreover, when Muhammad sought to invade the Jewish settlement of Khaybar, he marched with his warriors against the land, and just before entering it, he declared, "Allahu Akbar, Khaybar is destroyed." The cry *Allahu Akbar*, we are told, terrified the Jews, and the Muslims won. Here the phrase appears in the Muslim traditions as a declaration of victory over nonbelievers—an exclusively Islamic shout for Allah and in fulfillment of his purposes.

The phrase is also important in the Quran and is associated with another important Arabic term, *takbir* (pronounced "tuhk-BEER"). The term *takbir* refers to the act of glorifying Allah by declaring him greater than and above every other being or matter. The word *takbir* simply refers to the utterance of Allahu Akbar. The Quran calls Muslims to takbir (Q 74:3; 17:111). Sometimes Muslims call on each other, saying, "Takbir," by which they mean, "Let's all together shout Allahu Akbar." The response is always a loud shout in one accord, "Allahu Akbar!" This shout reflects unity, strength, and agreement.

For any Muslim believer, the most desired hope is to follow the Quran and to emulate Muhammad; therefore, in practice, Allahu Akbar is significantly important. It is arguably the most repeated Islamic phrase by any Muslim on any given day. It is their shortest expression of Allah's glory and superiority. They repeat the phrase on various occasions, whether in relation to worship or nonreligious activities. It is a venerating phrase that includes Allah in a Muslim's daily activities. In worship-related matters, Muslims declare Allahu Akbar in the call to ritual prayer (**adhan**). They also voice it many times during the ritual prayer (**salat**). It is also repeated frequently during the pilgrimage (**hajj**)—if a Muslim cannot touch or kiss the black stone, pointing to the stone while shouting Allahu Akbar will suffice to achieve the ritual. At work or in normal daily activities, a Muslim may shout it as a devotion statement or a declaration of faith. To gain strength or a blessing while doing a tough task, a Muslim may shout Allahu Akbar in an attempt to receive Allah's support. Even upon seeing beautiful scenery, a Muslim may shout Allahu Akbar as a declaration of astonishment and amazement. In sadness or at funerals, a Muslim may whisper Allahu Akbar as a sign of distress. Thus, this short phrase serves as an essential part of the life of every Muslim. While it simply means "Allah is greater," its application can vary depending on worship and practice.

ihsan: acting virtuously, righteously, and kindly

The term *ihsan* is one of the most beautiful words in Arabic. It denotes the exceptional disposition of doing virtuous, righteous, and kind deeds. It is pronounced "ih-sehn." The term is very difficult to define in one word, as it is complex in its range of meanings, although all are highly positive. It means acting in a beautiful, perfect, and excellent manner due to virtuous qualities of the heart. To explain, one may assert that the deity shows his ihsan (goodness, benevolence, generosity, and kindness) to humans in perfect and excellent ways, and they should act similarly toward one another.

The Quran mentions the term explicitly in five verses (Q 2:178, 229; 9:100; 16:90; 55:60), and all drive the notion of kindness, righteousness, and good deeds. In fact, we are told that Allah commands justice, ihsan (virtuous conduct), and giving to relatives, while forbidding immoral conduct and tyranny (Q 16:90). Allah also appears to promise that those who act with ihsan will be rewarded with divine ihsan, presumably high-lighting their admittance to paradise (Q 55:60). Some Muslim jurists explain ihsan as the outward description of one's inner devotion. In this sense, the heart is driven by devotion, and this appears in ihsan through conduct and manners.

The beautiful notion of ihsan is described in a **hadith** attributed to Muhammad in which he places ihsan as third in sequence after **iman** (the act of believing) and **islam** (submission and conversion by affirming strict monotheism and Muhammad's prophethood). In this hadith, Muham-mad defines *ihsan* as acting in a pious manner as a way of worshiping Allah—as if the believer is always seeing and acknowledging Allah in daily matters. Even if believers are unable to acknowledge Allah in daily life, says Muhammad, they must understand that Allah sees everything and everyone; accordingly, they must act with ihsan—that is, virtuously and compassionately. One of the most commendable aspects of conduct in Islam is ihsan, which is doing good works exceptionally well as an indicator of virtue and righteousness.

baraka: a divinely given blessing

In Arabic, a baraka is a blessing. For Muslims, it is the divine good-ness affirmed in one's life. It is pronounced "BAH-rah-kuh." Baraka is singular—its plural form is *barakaat*. The root of the Arabic word *baraka* comes from the word describing the abundance of nourishment found in the belly or chest of a camel; this reveals how highly animals were valued by nomadic Arabs. The baraka is what every human seeks in life, as it indicates satisfaction of a person's needs. For Muslims, the baraka is bestowed only by Allah, who grants it to whomever he desires. The act of seeking the baraka is called tabarruk. Tabarruk is a daily practice among Muslims, often following the ritual prayer (**salat**) or coming before one begins an important task or a new adventure. When Muslims perform the tabarruk, this simply means they are raising a supplication toward Allah, as they seek goodness, reward, happiness, and the like.

For many Muslims, objects possess a special baraka. Merely touching these objects, Muslims believe, transmits divine favor. The Quran is among these objects. Not only reading it but also touching it is considered a source of baraka. Muslims tend to wash their hands before touching it, as they revere it and believe it possesses a metaphysical power. Some even kiss the Quran or touch it to their foreheads several times as a way of receiving its presumed divine influence. The same is true for the black stone in the Muslim holy shrine, **Ka'ba**, in Mecca. Muslims seek to touch the stone, believing it possesses supernatural power and unmatched baraka. While most Muslims do not question the Quran and the black stone as sources of baraka, other objects are questionable to many Muslims. For example, some Muslims seek a baraka by visiting or touching the graves of dead Muslims who were considered pious. However, in mainstream Islam, these practices are considered wrong and actually heretical.

tawba: repentance

The noun *tawba* means "repentance." It is pronounced "taw-buh" and is related to a verb that means "to switch direction" or "to return." Thus, as an Islamic term, *tawba* refers to changing one's direction by returning to Allah. The Quran includes many verses about tawba, mostly commending those who practice it. We are told that Allah loves those who are continually voicing tawba (Q 2:222). He calls believers to tawba so that they can experience success in life (Q 24:31). In an exhortation, Allah seems to instruct his messenger to relay to humans who committed transgressions that they must not despair but must trust in Allah's mercy, as he forgives sins (Q 39:53). In a unique verse, the Quran states that Allah "repents over" Muhammad and believers (Q 9:117). Muslims interpret this to mean that Allah absolves the sins of humans or accepts their return to him; however, if the prophet in this verse is Muhammad, then the inevitable conclusion is that he needed forgiveness—which would violate the claim of his infallibility ('**isma**).

While the Quran does not specify how to repent, Muslim scholars affirm that tawba requires serious remorse and the total intention to abandon the sin or forsake the bad deed. Still, they disagree on whether tawba guarantees divine forgiveness and complete annulment or cancelation of eternal punishment. Some Muslim scholars insist that tawba does not guarantee eternal forgiveness and removal of punishment. This is a result of the ambiguity of some verses in the Quran. In describing the need for tawba, the Quran exhorts believers to return to Allah, but the verse gives no specific guarantee of forgiveness—the text indicates that Allah might expunge the evil deeds to admit them to paradise (Q 66:8). In practice, because some sins have divinely ordained punishments (**hudud**), a sinner must give an open tawba in order for the penalty to be discarded. This is important in cases of apostasy (ridda). If an apostate openly provides tawba and publicly returns to Islam, their tawba will be accepted by the ruler and the punishment (hadd) will not be performed.

tawakkul: reliance on Allah

The term *tawakkul* means "dependence and reliance on Allah." It reflects a complete surrender to Allah's **qadar** (predestination) and divine prescriptions and is pronounced "tah-wah-KOOL." The term is common in daily practice among Muslims, as they view Allah as intervening in every detail of their lives. When affliction or misery occurs, a Muslim often seeks to live in tawakkul, which reflects a deep surrender to Allah's will in allowing the bad things to happen. If hesitating between options, a Muslim might be advised to live in tawakkul and simply choose the option that appears better. The term here indicates trust in the unknown divine plan, which allows good and bad to happen. For Muslims, tawakkul means confidence in the divine ordinances and dependence on Allah's wisdom. In some cases, this notion of tawakkul can result in passiveness, because whatever a human does, Muslims believe, cannot guarantee an outcome. This is one reason why some, in referring to tawakkul, may ascribe bad outcomes to divine will rather than seeing them as consequences of human mistakes. But Muslim scholars insist that tawakkul does not mean Muslims should not show diligence in life and work hard.

The term *tawakkul* is found in many passages in the Quran—always portrayed positively. The Quran states that Allah loves believers who live in tawakkul (Q 3:159) and commands complete tawakkul as a sign of belief in Allah (Q 5:23). It exhorts believers to put all their trust (tawakkul) in Allah, who never dies (Q 25:58; also 14:12). If believers put their devotion and tawakkul in Allah, he will prove totally sufficient for them (Q 65:3; also 73:9). In daily practice, when facing an unfortunate result, Muslims often voice the ending of a specific verse in the Quran, which states that Allah alone is sufficient and that he is the most perfect wakeel (provider or protector) (Q 3:173). Here Allah is the one upon whom tawakkul is commanded and commended.

jihad: striving in Allah's path and for his cause

In Arabic, the word *jihad*, pronounced "jee-had," is a noun that refers to exerting effort. It is the striving to reach certain goals or the struggling to achieve certain purposes. The term appears ample times in the Quran and in Islamic original sources. It is linked particularly to striving for the sake of Allah to accomplish his purposes. As an Islamic concept, the term refers to any effort, action, or even speech intentionally done to spread Islam as Allah's supreme religion. In Muslim historical writings, the term is often used to refer to the military actions of Muslims against non-Muslims. Here jihad refers to fighting in Allah's path and struggling on battlefields with religious goals, including preaching Islam in non-Muslim lands to liberate unbelievers from the darkness of religious unbelief. Thus, many Muslims, past and present, tend to describe jihad as sacred fighting for Allah's cause. In fact, the Quran and many traditions attributed to Muhammad identify a Muslim fighter in battles as mujahid, which is a noun related to jihad that literally means "a striver fighter in jihad." In the Quran, the faithful mujahidun (plural of mujahid) are promised the great reward of paradise (**janna**). They are praised as better than those who sit at home instead of going to war (Q 4:95). Moreover, the Quran clearly associates jihad with giving oneself as a martyr in battle (Q 9:20, also 9:10–17).

With the rise of waves of mysticism in Islam, later generations of Muslims used the term *jihad* to denote struggling with oneself for self-piety or striving against Satan. In this sense, jihad is used to refer to self-control and striving against one's evil desires. This is why, about five centuries after Muhammad's death, a new **hadith** emerged and begin to circulate for the first time. It alleged that Muhammad reportedly described two kinds of jihad: a lesser jihad, which is fighting in battles for Allah's cause, and a greater jihad, which is fighting with oneself. At face value, this hadith seems to elevate jihad with oneself above jihad in battles. While this hadith never appeared in earlier centuries or in the so-called reliable hadith collections, it became famous—especially among pacifist Muslim mystics who wanted to discourage military actions. In recent years, as the public profile of Islam has grown rapidly, many progressives and modernists relied heavily on this hadith to present jihad as mainly an act of self-piety and self-control—the aim was to discourage any association between jihad and holy war. However, in the original Muslim sources, the term *jihad* was always associated with fighting enemies in battle for the sake of Allah.

In Sunnism and Shiism, jihad is a mandatory religious duty (fard) for all Muslims. It can generally be of two kinds: defensive or offensive. The former refers to jihad for the sake of defending Muslims, their lands, their religion, or their scripture against any assault or criticism. This is why some Muslims act vigorously and angrily when they know or sense that the Quran or Muhammad—as the most venerated elements of Islam—are attacked or insulted. For these Muslims, jihad against the attackers is the most compelling reaction. The latter refers to initiating actions and campaigns to spread Islam by making its laws prevalent everywhere. This is why many Muslims in the west view the building of mosques and organizing campaigns of **da'wa** (Islamic preaching) as a form of jihad. It is based on the belief that Islam is the best religion for humankind in all times and places. Still, in Shiism, jihad has a significant importance, as it is identified as one of the most important practices of faith for any devoted Shiite. Many Shiite primary sources discuss jihad in painstaking detail, explaining its obligation for every Muslim, its reward, and the consequences of abandoning it. In practical terms, Muslims understand jihad as an honorable religious duty that encompasses many actions, including preaching Islam to non-Muslims, applying Islam and following its commands against evil desires, defending Islam against any criticisms or attacks, spreading Islam in non-Muslim lands, and fighting unbelievers for Allah's sake.

eid: a feast or holiday

The noun *eid* means "feast or holiday" and reflects a festive celebration. It is pronounced "eyed." For Muslims, there are two major Muslim holidays: eid al-fitr and eid al-adhaa. Both of these feasts provide time for Muslim families and friends to gather in celebration with a distinct religious meaning. The Quran uses the term *eid* in one verse, stating that Allah sends down a table full of food from heaven for people to enjoy and have an eid (festive celebration) (Q 5:114).

The first Muslim feast, al-fitr, is known as the minor eid, as it is celebrated for only one day immediately following the fasting month of **Ramadan**. On that day, Muslims come together for an eid after a month of abstinence from food every day from sunrise to sunset. The word *al-fitr* means "the breaking of the fasting." A major feature of this eid is the congregational prayer in the early morning, when Muslims go out in the streets and courtyards of large mosques and gather in rows behind an **imam** to perform the ritual prayer (**salat**) of the eid. In eid al-fitr, Muslims tend to give their **zakat** (obligatory charitable payment) to support the poor among believers. They also organize big family gatherings with a variety of food.

The second eid is known as al-adhaa, which means "sacrifice or atoning." It is the major Muslim holiday and lasts for four days. This eid commemorates Abraham's sacrifice of his son (Q 37:100–112). While the Quran does not indicate the name of the son, Muslim traditions largely disagree with biblical statements and indicate that the son was Ishmael, not Isaac. Like in the biblical accounts, however, Abraham did not sacrifice his son after all. The Quran states that Allah redeemed Abraham's son through a great sacrifice (Q 37:107). This is why Muslims commemorate the occasion by ritually sacrificing animals—either a cow, lamb, or camel, depending on how wealthy the person is. In most Muslim-majority countries, these sacrifices are made outside in the streets. The blood often covers large public areas. Sometimes Muslims immerse their hands in the blood and use it to mark their new houses or new cars in order to protect them from the evil eye by redeeming them through this action. (The evil eye reflects a superstitious belief that someone can harm another by a mere glance due to jealousy.) The meat of the sacrifice is often shared by Muslims, with a portion given to the poor and needy. One important aspect of this eid is that it is the time when Muslims travel to Mecca to perform the **hajj** (pilgrimage). After they conclude the hajj rituals in Muhammad's birthland, they celebrate the eid together by sacrificing animals. At both of these feasts, when congratulating each other, Muslims say, "Eid mubaarak," meaning "a blessed eid to you."

Ashuraa': a unique Muslim commemoration day

The word *Ashuraa'* refers to an important day in Islam. Muslims call it Yawm Ashuraa', which means "the Day of Ashuraa'." It is pronounced "ah-SHOO-ruh," and the noun is based on the Arabic word for "ten"; it is celebrated on the tenth day of the Muslim month of Muharram. While all Muslims treat the day as a religious commemoration, Sunnis and Shiites disagree on the focus of and the reason for the commemoration. Overall, the day has a higher importance among Shiites.

Sunnis simply claim that the day commemorates Allah saving Moses and the sons of Israel from Pharaoh by splitting the Red Sea and rescuing them from danger. In this sense, Ashuraa' is an Islamic celebration of the Passover. While this Sunni tradition is common and widely circulated, even some Sunnis acknowledge that the Shiite version is more accurate and religiously appealing.

For Shiites, the day commemorates the martyrdom of the third Shiite **imam**, Husayn, at the hands of the anti-Shiite **Umayyads**. Husayn was the grandson of Muhammad and the son of Ali and Fatima (Muhammad's daughter). About fifty years after Muhammad's death, in 680, the **fitna** (civil war) was raging. In the city of Karbala, the fight against Husayn was severe, and he and many of his family were massacred. Shiite traditions detail specific points about his wounds, sufferings, and bravery, highlighting a heroic and messiah-like martyr. They also paint a picture of betrayal by insincere Muslims who hypocritically conspired to massacre him. Shiite traditions further establish detailed prophecies voiced by Muhammad decades earlier concerning the specific locations of the wounds in Husayn's body, claiming that Muhammad, before his death, kissed Husayn's body where the wounds would be. Historically, the death of Husayn was consequential and foundational for the strengthening of the rule of the Umayyad Dynasty and the beginning of systematic targeting of and persecution against the household of Muhammad, the descendants of Ali.

In practice, Sunni Muslims celebrate on the Day of Ashuraa', while Shiites mourn, although some Sunnis still commemorate the martyrdom of Husayn. Sunnis say that fasting is recommended on that day, while Shiites oppose fasting on it. To commemorate the death of Husayn, Shiites observe some rituals, including reading the text of Husayn's martyrdom and spending the whole night at his grave in mourning. Most notably, some Shiites practice wounding rituals. They use sharp swords to wound their own heads and backs, then run in rows down the streets, all in an attempt to experience what Husayn suffered.

imam: a leader, yet with a particular significance among Shiites

Linguistically, the word *imam*, pronounced "ih-mam," refers to a leader. As a noun, it is associated with a verb that means "to lead," "to become a forerunner," or "to be the chief in a group." Sunnis and Shiites treat the term very differently. For Sunnis, an imam is generally a leader of any sort, but the term particularly refers to a mosque's leader who is responsible for leading the local congregation in prayer and spiritual teaching. The mosque's imam is often an educated person with a religious degree of some sort, although sometimes it can simply be an esteemed person who is chosen by his peers. In this case, the imam is often a charismatic preacher or a respected older sheikh (elder) who is socially acknowledged by the people of the community.

Among Shiites, the term carries more significance and esteem. For the vast majority of Shiites, the term refers to twelve infallible imams in particular. They are viewed as the legitimate spiritual and political leaders of the Muslims. These imams are Ali ibn Abi Talib (Muhammad's cousin and son-in-law) and his sons and grandsons from his wife Fatima (Muhammad's daughter). For Shiites, Ali was the divinely designated imam to succeed Muhammad, but he was betrayed by evil Muslims who stole the succession and gave it to Abu Bakr. Muhammad and these twelve imams, in addition to Fatima, are the infallibles, according to Shiism.

For Shiites, the twelve imams are the only source of guidance and teaching in Islam and are identified as "the household of Muhammad" (ahl al-bayt). After Ali, his two sons became the second and third imams, followed by other imams until the twelfth, who is known as Imam Mahdi. Shiites believe that Mahdi did not die. In 940, he went into a state of hiding or disappearing and is believed to still be alive, hearing and watching all life affairs. He is waiting to reappear to establish order and enforce justice. For Shiites, Imam Mahdi is the eschatological savior and will remain the final imam. No true justice, Shiites argue, will be established on earth without Imam Mahdi, who will found Allah's rule on earth.

In addition to being inerrant and infallible, the imams share special similarities, according to **Shiism**. All twelve imams come from Muhammad's tribe, the **Quraysh**. All of them—except Imam Mahdi—were martyrs who are now alive with Allah. All of them received the designation of the imamate (leadership) by Allah, who alone can designate an imam. Just like Muhammad, all the imams have the ability to intercede for Muslims in front of Allah. Shiites believe that, with the exception of Muhammad, all twelve imams are preferred in rank over all previous prophets. This is one reason why the imams are considered the reference, authority, and guidance among Shiites. Obeying the imams and their traditions is obligatory in Shiism.

Shiites—to avoid confusion—are reluctant to use the term *imam* with any of their regular leaders; they prefer to use the term *hujja* (meaning "knowledgeable or esteemed") or *marji'* ("a guide or reference"). In practice, among most Muslims, the term *imam* refers to only a male leader; however, in recent years, particularly in Western countries, liberal and feminist Muslims have advocated for and accepted female imams.

nikaah: marriage, a marriage contract, or sexual intercourse

The term *nikaah* refers to marriage, a marriage contract, or sexual intercourse. It is pronounced "nee-kay-ah." Linguistically, *nikaah* denotes interacting and bringing together. Among pre-Islamic Arabs, it referred solely to the act of intercourse. Some argue that it initially meant a marriage contract and was later used as a synonym for sexual intercourse. In the Quran, the term *nikaah* or its verb, *yankah*, is used for both meanings.

In using nikaah as a reference for sexual intercourse, the Quran states that if a man divorces his wife three times, he cannot remarry her again until she has consummated marriage with another man, after which a divorce would permit her to remarry her former husband (Q 2:230; 33:49). In referring to nikaah as a marriage contract, the Quran gives men the freedom to marry women of their choice, two or three or four (Q 4:3). This is one reason why Muslim jurists do not allow men to marry more than four wives at a time; however, this does not include concubines—they are given to men without limit. The Quran states that men are allowed to have a nikaah with virtuous single women, whether they are free or slaves (Q 24:32). Muslim scholars believe that the reference to single women in this verse indicates that, unlike men, women cannot have multiple husbands. The marriage contract can be made only by a legal Muslim official and in the presence of at least two witnesses.

Nikaah in Islam can be between only a man and a woman. Homosexuality is forbidden and punishable by death. For a divorce to occur, the man is required to make a statement declaring he divorces his wife, without any required witnesses present. The right to initiate a divorce belongs solely to the man, although in rare cases women have this right if explicitly indicated in the marriage contract. According to Islamic law, a woman is not free to remarry after losing her husband—because of either death or divorce—for a period of time, specified as three menstrual cycles. This period is called 'idda (meaning "a period of preparation or abstinence"). According to Muslim scholars, this is to protect the sanctity of offspring and to avoid a mix in genealogies.

talaaq: divorce

Talaaq, pronounced "tah-lock," is divorce in Islam. It is the termination or annulment of the **nikaah** (marriage contract). While a marriage necessitates the agreement of a man and a woman and their signing of the nikaah documents in front of a legal Muslim official, talaaq requires only a statement: "Go, you are divorced." The man has the power in Islamic law to initiate talaaq, except in rare cases. In practice, there are two kinds of talaaq: reversible or returnable, and permanent or binding. In the former, a man can remarry a woman without reissuing a nikaah—that is, without documenting the marriage again—as long as the reversing of the divorce occurred within the so-called 'idda period (three menstrual cycles). In the latter, a man cannot have a woman back as his wife. According to Islamic law, a man who divorces his wife three times cannot remarry her unless she consummates a marriage with another man (Q 2:230).

Talaaq is a serious matter in Islam, as evidenced by the attention given to it in the Quran and the hadiths. In addition to various passages on talaaq in the Quran (e.g., Q 2; Q 33), an entire **sura** (chapter) titled "The Talaaq" (Q 65) describes the specifics of talaaq, including rulings and warnings. The traditions also provide specifics on talaaq. In one tradition, we read that talaaq is the most detested **halal** (legally allowed) action for Allah, implying that even though it is legal to divorce, it is not recommended.

mut'a: a temporary marriage for male sexual benefits

Linguistically, the term *mut'a*, pronounced "moot-ah," means "pleasure and enjoyment." In Islamic practice, a mut'a is a legally permissible temporary marriage that does not require witnesses to be considered legal. A mut'a begins with a contract between a man and a woman whom he desires for mut'a. They agree upon a period of time for the marriage and specific financial compensation for her. The mut'a marriage dissolves after the agreed-upon time period, and it does not require a declaration of divorce. In legal and practical terms, a mut'a is mainly a means for male pleasure. While some view it as enforcing the male-dominant structure found in Islamic texts and strengthened by Muslim jurists, the practice itself—according to Muslim traditions—is implied and endorsed in the Quran (Q 4:24). Therefore, for many Muslim jurists, there is scriptural support for the practice.

Muslim traditions also seem to support the practice, which was reportedly performed during Muhammad's time. It was actually flourishing in pre-Islamic times as one of the various forms of unions practiced in Arabian culture. Islam did not abolish the practice but instead adopted and continued it as a permissible Islamic practice. Still, Shiites and Sunnis disagree on whether Muhammad, later in his life, abolished it. According to Sunni traditions, while it was allowed and practiced during the rule of Muhammad's first caliph, the second caliph decided to abolish it. Shiite Muslims—who view the first and second caliphs as evil—insist that mut'a has been widely practiced and that Muhammad never forbade it. This is why Shiite Muslims insist that the practice is totally halal and should be allowed in Muslim lands. For Sunni Muslims, the authentic tradition concerning mut'a indicates that Muhammad indeed allowed and forbade it several times but eventually forbade it before he died. For some Sunni Muslims, Muhammad allowed it in his early prophetic years, but in the final two or three years of his life, he abrogated it. Shiites adamantly disagree with this Sunni claim.

This debate between Sunnis and Shiites continues today. In Iran, the Shiite governing authorities legalized mut'a in the constitution, and it is widely practiced. A Shiite woman can be married to only one man at a time. A Shiite man can marry as many women as he desires in mut'a marriage in addition to the four wives allowed by the Quran and Islamic law. While Sunni scholars oppose mut'a, it is still practiced in many Muslim-majority lands today. In fact, Sunni jurists—though they do not promote or favor mut'a—have a somewhat similar form of marriage, called *misyar*, which they allow. Misyar follows almost the same pattern and requirements as mut'a, with the exception that it requires witnesses for the legal establishment of the contract and the pronouncement of divorce when dissolving the marriage.

Without a doubt, some modern and progressive Muslims as well as feminist Muslims—particularly in the West—despise the practices of mut'a and misyar. They view temporary marriage as void of the true meaning of marriage—with its commitment and responsibilities—and see it as religiously sanctioned prostitution. Still, with support from the Quran and Muslim traditions, the practice is flourishing and does not seem to be losing favor.

zinaa: adultery

The noun *zinaa* means "adultery" and is pronounced "zee-nah." By definition, *zinaa* refers to extramarital sex. It is sexual intercourse that a married man or woman has with someone other than their spouse. This is different from fornication, which is committed by an unmarried person. An adulterer must be married to a permanent spouse who is able to consummate the marriage. The sin of zinaa is one of the kabaa'ir (greater sins) in Islamic thought. However, producing proof of zinaa is difficult in practice, as it necessitates either a confession by the adulterer or the testimony of four male adult witnesses who themselves saw the act of penetration. If a man cannot be present as a witness, then two women can replace one man.

The need for four witnesses to prove zinaa is based on a passage in the Quran concerning Muhammad's wife Aisha (Q 24:11–20). When many Muslims accused her of cheating on Muhammad—after she spent time alone on a journey with an unmarried man—and asked him to divorce her, Allah reportedly gave Muhammad a Quranic revelation, rebuked the accusers, and instructed that four witnesses are required to prove zinaa.

The punishment of an adulterer in Islam is called hadd (punishment, boundary; plural **hudud**). The specific punishment is confusing, as there is a contradiction between the Quran and the **hadiths**. The Quran states that the penalty for zinaa is one hundred lashes (Q 24:2). The hadith traditions indicate that the second caliph, Umar, insisted that Allah revealed a verse in the Quran commanding the stoning of a person who commits zinaa. Umar added that Muslims used to memorize and recite this verse and that Muhammad himself carried out the punishment of stoning and his companions followed course. This verse is missing from today's Quran, although traditions state that it was among the revealed verses. The verse was evidently with Aisha on paper, but upon Muhammad's death, the Muslims were all occupied, which allowed a sheep to sneak in and eat it. Thus, the verse is not found in the text, and the Quran and the hadiths contradict each other. Muslim scholars have attempted to reconcile the discrepancy by arguing that the punishment depends on the age of the adulterers—young adults who commit zinaa should be stoned, while older people should be punished by a hundred lashes and then by stoning.

taqiyya: concealment of truth for a purpose

The term *taqiyya* refers to hiding one's convictions out of fear. It is pronounced "tah-KAY-uh" and is often rendered as "concealment" or "dissimulation." The noun *taqiyya* is associated with a verb meaning "to guard oneself out of concern." Taqiyya is a doctrine and a practice. Taqiyya is used in times of fear and affliction to protect oneself and one's property. If Muslims face a threat or danger, the rationale goes, it is permissible and religiously commanded to conceal the truth about one's beliefs. This is an acceptable taqiyya. Taqiyya is allowed to be used with Muslims and non-Muslims. For example, in times of hostility against Muslims, they can hide their religion and are allowed to perform rituals they do not believe in to avoid harm.

The taqiyya practice is a strong conviction among Shiites, who have practiced it throughout their history, as they have been treated poorly under anti-Shiite rulers. Sunni Muslims, on the other hand, often despise the practice and refer to it as explicitly Shiite. Nonetheless, many medieval Sunni authorities adopted and allowed the taqiyya practice. Both Sunni traditions and Islam's scripture refer to it. The Quran uses the term *taqiyya* in a specific verse, which instructs believers to refrain from taking unbelievers as friends or allies, except in cases when one fears harm (Q 3:28). This verse is often used by Sunnis and Shiites to affirm and establish the practice, and it was later explained by many Muslim scholars who emphasized that it is religiously permissible for one to protect oneself from attackers or wrongdoers by concealing the truth. To support the practice, some Muslims refer to incidents in Muhammad's life when he approved and allowed the use of taqiyya. In Muhammad's **sira** (biography), after he emigrated from Mecca to Medina, some of his companions needed to return to Mecca to retrieve their possessions. They used taqiyya to protect themselves against the Meccan pagans, and Muhammad reportedly allowed them to lie about knowing him to protect their lives.

In modern times, some Muslims—especially modernists—began to reject the doctrine. They argue that taqiyya is a form of lying and that Islam does not permit it, as it suggests that Islam allows hypocrisy and deceit. This view is, in a sense, a reaction to severe criticisms of Islam. Still, many proponents of the practice dilute the meaning of taqiyya and argue that it is not a lie but simply a form of diplomacy.

khutba: a sermon, particularly in a mosque

Linguistically, the Arabic word *khutba* means "sermon or speech." It is pronounced "KHUT-buh." Among Muslims, a khutba is often the sermon given by a religious leader, especially the **imam** of a local mosque. Since for many Muslims Islam represents both a governing authority and a form of worship, a khutba often informs Muslims on matters of faith and religion but also extends to political and social matters. The person who delivers a khutba is known in Arabic as a khatib. Throughout the history of Islam, a khatib has always been a man. Only in recent years, and in a few very progressive mosques in the West, have some begun to advocate for female imams and preachers. This suggestion is unacceptable in mainstream Islam.

A khutba relies on the Quran and Muhammad's **hadiths** to exhort Muslims. The most important khutba for Muslims is the one delivered in the mosque during the Friday noon corporate ritual prayer (**salat**). For Muslims, Friday is the most blessed day in any given week, and traditions claim that praying with fellow Muslims in corporate prayer will bring more rewards from Allah. This is why the Friday prayer and sermon are highly regarded by Muslims. The tradition of the khutba in general—and of Friday prayer in the mosque in particular—traces back to the days of Muhammad in Medina. He reportedly used to gather his believing companions in the courtyard of his home to teach them Islam. In his sermons, he explained matters of worship, interpreted the Quran, and exhorted them to **jihad** (striving in Allah's path). Even today, Muslim preachers follow Muhammad's example as they deliver a khutba to their Muslim audiences.

Although Muslims venerate the tradition of Muhammad delivering sermons, the Quran does not refer to any of Muhammad's sermons. In fact, we do not have textual accounts of any khutba of Muhammad, except his alleged final one, which was documented centuries after his death. If Muhammad truly lived in Medina for over ten years, and if he delivered a khutba every Friday, he presumably preached over five hundred sermons. None of them are recorded. While we have access to thousands of traditions compiled centuries after his death, no eyewitness of Muhammad ever transcribed any of his sermons.

Still, the khutba tradition is cherished and followed by most Muslims today. In some Muslim-majority countries, Friday is the most important day. While not all Muslims take it as a day off, many close their businesses during the Friday noon prayer, walk to local mosques in groups, and sit in lines to listen to the Friday khutba. As they listen to the khutba, they not only learn about worship and faith but also are guided to adopt specific political views and adhere to particular social sympathies.

hijab: a head covering or veil for women

The Arabic word *hijab*, pronounced "hih-JAHB," refers to a curtain
or veil, specifically that which aims to hide or cover something. The
noun is based on a verb that means "to cover, separate, or protect." In
practice, the term *hijab* almost always refers to a piece of cloth wrapped
mainly around the head and neck of a woman. In pre-Islamic times,
various traditions mandated that women cover their heads. Muslims
today disagree as to whether a hijab is a religious obligation (fard) prescribed by Allah for all Muslim women. The Quran refers to the word
hijab—as a general reference to covering or hiding—in various verses
(Q 7:46; 17:45; 19:17; 38:32; 41:5; 42:51). None of these verses explicitly
refer to a woman covering her head. However, one verse, known among
Muslims as the Hijab Verse, refers to a hijab in connection to women
covering (Q 33:53). The verse addresses believers in their interactions
with Muhammad's wives. It mandates believers—if they need something
from one of Muhammad's wives—to offer their requests from behind
a veil. Muslims who support the wearing of a hijab as a mandatory
divine command understand this verse as a command for all women,
while objectors—who argue that a hijab is not mandatory—believe the
verse related only to the wives of Muhammad due to their roles among
believers. We should note that the verse does not explicitly mention
Muhammad but refers to the wives of the prophet; however, Muslims
believe the prophet in view is Muhammad.

While the Quran appears ambiguous regarding whether the wearing
of a hijab is a religious mandate for women, **hadith** narrations are more
direct and specific. In some hadiths, Muhammad appears to instruct his
wives to wear hijabs to cover themselves even when a blind man is present. Muslims understand this as a sign of modesty. In a tradition famous
among the supporters of the hijab, we are told that Muhammad's wives
used to go out together at night to relieve themselves. At that time, they
were not wearing hijabs. Some male companions of Muhammad were
furious, and they demanded that Muhammad ask his wives to cover
themselves. One of Muhammad's wives was a noticeably tall woman,
and men recognized her while she was relieving herself. This lack of
wearing a hijab continued, traditions claim, until Allah revealed the Hijab
Verse. Some traditions are more specific regarding what a veil should

cover, claiming that bodies, necks, and bosoms must be covered. Other traditions even include the mandatory covering of faces and hands with a form of a stricter hijab known as a niqab.

da'wa: calling people to Islam

The Arabic noun *da'wa* means "invitation." It is pronounced "DAH-uh-wah" and is related to a verb that means "to invite or to call someone into something." In Islamic practice, the term refers to the activity of inviting or calling non-Muslims to convert to Islam. It also reflects the act of Muslims correcting fellow Muslims or advising or inviting them to follow or adhere to proper Islam. The first meaning is the most common, reflecting the Muslim missionary duty to propagate, advance, and preach Islam. The Quran uses the noun *da'wa* in relation to Allah giving a da'wa for his people to leave their tombs on the last day (Q 30:25). It also uses the noun in reference to Allah affirming that he is near to his people and hears those who invoke a da'wa upon him (Q 2:186).

Muslims believe that Islamic da'wa is a religious responsibility for every capable Muslim. They believe that Muhammad was the best example of advancing the cause of Islam through his da'wa preaching. Many reports depict Muhammad sending da'wa letters or speaking with individuals, inviting people to embrace Islam. The reports about Muhammad's da'wa do not often include details of the statements he made, but they often involve him meeting with a person to call them to Islam or sending a convoy to invite a person to Islam. This pattern became a precedent for Muslims to follow.

According to Islamic traditions, in the earliest Muslim period, people accepted Islam after hearing the da'wa of Arab merchants who brought their trade to non-Muslim lands. In some instances, the da'wa was given following the military conquests led by Muslim armies. The conquered people, according to Muslim sources, were given one of three options: accept Islam, pay the jizya (tax), or endure fighting until the end. On these occasions, one cannot be certain of the content of the da'wa. The da'wa did not seem to involve the preaching of Islam's unique tenets or beliefs. Here coercive conversion linked to political surrender might have been the case. After the Muslim conquests, Muslims became the elite minority among the conquered population. Interactions between

Muslims and non-Muslims (e.g., Jews, Christians, and Zoroastrians) led to more da'wa preaching. It appears that many non-Muslims sought to join the elites, thus accepting their faith by converting to Islam.

jumu'a: Friday or assembling or congregating

The Arabic noun *jumu'a* means "gathering, assembling, or congregating." It is pronounced "joo-moo-AH" and is based on a verb that means "to gather, collect, or bring together." The noun *jumu'a* is the word for Friday in Arabic. Muslims consider Friday to be the most important day of the week, on which they gather in a mosque for communal ritual prayer (**salat**).

The Quran and Muslim traditions treat jumu'a in a special way. The Quran includes a **sura** (chapter) titled "The Jumu'a," in which Muslims are instructed, "O believers, when the call for prayer is made on the jumu'a (the Congregation Day), go forth to Allah's remembrance and leave the trading aside" (Q 62:9). This indicates not only the uniqueness of Friday but also the importance of the jumu'a corporate prayer. The jumu'a sermon (**khutba**) in a mosque (**masjid**) is by far the most important time for Islamic education among Muslims.

Many Muslim traditions convey the uniqueness and importance of Friday, seeing it as the most valuable day in any given week. Muhammad reportedly established the importance of Friday when he told his companions that Saturday was for the Jews and Sunday was for the Christians, but Allah guided the Muslims to Friday. Many traditions report that Friday is the most sacred day. Muhammad, Ali, and Fatima were each born on a Friday. Adam and Eve were created on a Friday. The Day of Resurrection will occur on a Friday. In fact, the traditions claim that Friday is Allah's day. Muhammad reportedly said that during a particular hour on Friday every human request of Allah is accepted. Many Muslim military victories occurred on Fridays. Many more exaggerated traditions add to the halo surrounding Friday. Allah doubles his favor and rewards for every good work accomplished on a Friday. Although Muslim traditions detail the horrors of the grave, a believer who dies on a Friday will not experience these terrors. Shiites believe that Ali married Fatima on a Friday—after all, it is the most glorious day. Muhammad designated Ali as his legitimate successor on a Friday. **Imam** Mahdi, who disappeared in 940, will reappear in the last days on a Friday. The infallible Shiite imams were martyred on a Friday due to its sacredness.

In practice, Friday is a formal Islamic holiday. However, in some Muslim-majority nations, Friday is not actually a day off. Still, Muslims cherish the day and its rituals and customs. Each Friday at noon, many Muslims walk together in groups to the local mosques to attend the main congregational prayer. Since mosques are sometimes incapable of receiving big crowds, they usually use the areas surrounding the mosques. They close the streets and place carpets on the asphalt to allow space for many Muslims to pray together and to listen to the important Friday sermon. It is likely that local non-Muslims find the closing of streets and the use of a mosque's loudspeakers for broadcasting the prayer and the khutba to be an inconvenience, but Muslims view it as both an essential religious duty and a theological statement of Islam's presence and priority in the land.

qibla: the direction of the ritual prayer

During the **salat** (the ritual prayer), Muslims face the qibla, the direction of prayer. The noun *qibla*, pronounced "kib-LEH," is based on the notion of facing a certain point or coinciding with it. Wherever Muslims go, they seek to determine the qibla if they want to perform their prayers properly. Not only the salat but also some other rituals necessitate facing the qibla. For instance, when slaughtering animals, the slaughterer must face the qibla for the meat to be **halal** (legally allowed). Muslims sometimes desire to bow or kneel as a sign of giving thanks to Allah for a particular matter. In these cases, it is recommended that they face the qibla. Some Muslim jurists suggest that one should also face the qibla when reciting the Quran or performing **wudu'** (ablution). The qibla is thus very important to Muslims for various ritual activities. However, the qibla changed at a certain point during the life of Muhammad.

During the first fourteen years after Muhammad allegedly received the divine revelations, the qibla was Jerusalem. This period included the entire Meccan career of Muhammad (thirteen years) in addition to one year in Medina after he and the Muslims emigrated. When Muslims interacted with the Jews residing in Medina, conflicts arose. Then, in 623, Allah reportedly revealed to Muhammad a Quranic instruction to change the qibla from Jerusalem to Mecca (Q 2:144). The specific point of the qibla in Mecca is the **Ka'ba**, the cubic shrine in the sacred mosque. Interestingly, this change of the qibla occurred toward the end of the second year after the Muslims resided in Medina, when there was still no sacred mosque and no monotheistic worship in Mecca. Some scholars question why Muslims would pray toward the place from which they were expelled. In addition, many Muslim traditions state that the Ka'ba was a place of pagan worship and idolatry at that time. It does not seem plausible, to these scholars, that Muslims were commanded to face a pagan place to pray. Some scholars suggest that, after the **hijra** (emigration) to Medina, it was inevitable for Muslims to break ties with the neighboring Jews—both faiths could not use the same point as their qibla. Thus, Muslims deviated from it. Still, this does not answer why and when the Ka'ba was chosen as the direction of prayer.

Today, there is a famous **masjid** (mosque) in Medina called the Two-Qiblas Mosque that contains two recessed spaces in the walls. One faces Jerusalem (northwest), and the other faces the Ka'ba (southeast). Muslims celebrate this mosque as a testimony to Allah's instruction to switch the qibla from Jerusalem to Mecca.

ibn: son; bint: daughter

The nouns *ibn*, pronounced "ibn," and *bint*, pronounced "bint," mean "son" and "daughter," respectively. The two nouns often appear in full Arabic names, as children are named in association with their parents—most often their fathers or clans. Still, some are identified in association with their mothers. If a person is named Ahmad ibn Hisham, this literally means that Ahmad is "the son of Hisham." In this case, Hisham can be the last name of the family or, in fewer cases, a reference to Ahmad's father. The same goes for the name Hind bint Hisham, which identifies Hind as "the daughter of Hisham." This form appears in the famous name of Muhammad's wife, Hafsa bint Umar. Her name associates her with her father, Umar. Sometimes the term *ibn* appears in a different Arabic form, bin (e.g., in the name of the Saudi crown prince Mohammed bin Salman).

The plural of ibn is *banu*, and the plural of bint is *banaat*. The plural forms often appear in constructs that mean "the sons of" or "the daughters of," although the male form is used more frequently. The name Banu Hashim refers to the people, descendants, or children of Hashim— "the sons of Hashim"—meaning the members of the tribe or clan of Hashim. In English, it can be rendered as "the house of Hashim" or "the Hashimites." Similarly, the name Banu Israel refers to the house of Israel, while the name Banu Abbas refers to members of the clan of Abbas—that is, the **Abbasids**. As for a feminine form, Banaat Moab refers to the female members of the Moab family or tribe.

abu: father; umm: mother

The nouns *abu*, pronounced "ah-boo," and *umm*, pronounced "ohm," mean "father" and "mother," respectively. Like **ibn** and **bint**, *abu* and *umm* often appear in names of Arabs, especially parents in association with their children. For instance, the first caliph in Islam was Abu Bakr. While his real name was Abdullah, after he had his son Bakr, he became identified in his circles as "the father of Bakr." This is quite common in Arab and Muslim circles, where the identification often refers to the firstborn. The name Umm Bakr means "the mother of Bakr"; this mother is named after her firstborn son, Bakr. In Arabic-speaking societies, it is common to identify a father (abu) or a mother (umm) by referring to their son, although referring to a daughter is not uncommon. For example, Umm Habiba ("the mother of Habiba") is identified in reference to her daughter Habiba. Abu Salmaa and Umm Salmaa are the parents of their daughter Salmaa.

Some names are more complex. For instance, Muhammad's wife was Aisha bint Abi Bakr. Her name was Aisha, and she was the daughter (bint) of Abdullah, who was identified in association with his son Bakr—that is, Abu Bakr. In her name, Abu is written as Abi due to an Arabic grammatical rule, although the meaning is the same.

abd: a male slave or servant

The Arabic noun *abd*, pronounced "abd," means "a male slave or servant." Its feminine form is *abda*, and its plural is *abeed*. The noun *abd* is associated with an Arabic verb meaning not only "to serve" but also "to adore or worship." Thus, the noun connotes subordination and service. The noun appears as a prefix in many Arabic names, especially in relation to Allah and his attributes. The name Abdullah is basically Abd-Allah, which means "the servant of Allah." The name Abd al-Rahim means "the slave of the merciful," where the word *Rahim* means "merciful," one of Allah's attributes, and *al* is the Arabic definite article. The name Abd Manaf—Muhammad's grandfather—means "the slave of Manaf." The name Abd al-Nabi means "the slave of the prophet," where *al-Nabi* means "the prophet." Similarly, Abd al-Rasul means "the servant of the apostle." Among Arabic-speaking Christians, a male can be named Abd al-Masih, which means "the slave of Christ," where *al-Masih* means "Christ" or, literally, "the Messiah." In Arab societies, until recently, owning slaves was a common practice supported by Islamic texts and precedents from Muhammad's **hadith** and **sira**. In most cases, the slave was named after his owner. Thus, Abd Hisham is "the slave of Hisham."

masjid: a mosque

The noun *masjid* means "mosque," which is the house of worship in Islam. It is pronounced "mass-jihd." The noun is based on a verb that means "to bow" or "to worship"; thus, masjid refers to the place where the act of bowing or worshiping occurs. In practice, Muslims can perform the ritual prayer (**salat**) anywhere. However, Muhammad reportedly encouraged Muslims to pray in a masjid more than in their homes, as a prayer in a masjid surpasses one performed at home, resulting in rewards twenty-five times greater. Each masjid has an architectural feature that indicates the **qibla** (the direction of prayer), usually a recessed space in the wall, which points worshipers toward the **Ka'ba** in Mecca.

The Quran uses the noun *masjid* over twenty-five times. One of the most important verses encourages Muslims to keep up and maintain Allah's mosques (Q 9:18). Many Muslims seek to build and maintain mosques in order to receive Allah's favor and rewards. In practice, Muslims respect mosques greatly and approach them as sacred places of Allah where worship is the only permitted act. Traditions drive such notions. We read that Muslims cannot enter a masjid with their shoes on but instead must go barefoot as a sign of respect. They are required to enter a masjid using the right foot, not the left, as it is believed that the right foot is holier. Menstruating women are not supposed to enter a masjid. A masjid cannot be sold to anyone, as it is believed to be owned by Allah (Q 18). Muhammad reportedly built the first masjid in Medina after the **hijra** (emigration); before that time he was persecuted by unbelievers and did not have the freedom to worship. Muslims also believe that he used the courtyard in his house as a gathering place for Muslims.

Among Muslims, a similar term is *jaami'*, which basically refers to a larger mosque. In a jaami', congregational prayers can be performed as well as the communal prayers of the major feasts of Islam. While a masjid is a place of worship in general where the five daily prayers can be performed, a jaami' is a mosque in which this is done in addition to community prayers.

For Muslims, the mere act of building a mosque, especially in non-Muslim lands, is a theological statement of Islam's superiority. The structure itself serves for these Muslims as a sign of Islam's hegemony, victory, and advance in the land. This is one reason why many Muslim groups in western countries seek not only to build new mosques—even in places where very few Muslims reside—but also to purchase church buildings and turn them into mosques and Islamic centers. When a mosque replaces a church, the Muslim logic goes, the message is clear: Islam surpasses the religion that was in place. The same logic accounts for why some Muslim-majority countries adamantly discourage the building of any non-Muslim houses of worship, for example, churches or synagogues. In countries like Morocco, Algeria, Libya, Egypt, and Saudi Arabia, among others, it is very difficult to obtain government permission to build a non-Muslim house of worship.

adhan: the call to ritual prayer

The word *adhan* means "declaration or announcement." It is pronounced "a-THAN" or "a-ZAN." Before the ritual prayer (**salat**), a Muslim—a man with a strong and loud voice—chants the adhan in a melodic manner. In Muslim countries, the adhan is usually broadcast through huge loudspeakers on high minarets, with the aim that all will hear it and join the ritual prayer. According to tradition, the adhan was first taught by

Muhammad one or two years after the **hijra** (emigration) to Medina. He instructed one of his companions, Bilal, to recite it loudly before the salat, calling believers to gather for prayer. Thus, the adhan is not a divinely revealed formula or text but instead a part of Muhammad's **sunna** (tradition). Still, Muslims believe that a form of the term *adhan* appears in the Quran, where it refers to an announcement from Allah and his apostle (Q 9:3).

The adhan includes fifteen short phrases: "**Allahu Akbar**" (repeated four times), "I testify there is no god but Allah" (twice), "I testify that Muhammad is the messenger of Allah" (twice), "Come [or hasten or hurry] to prayer" (twice), "Come to success" (twice), "Allahu Akbar" (twice), and "There is no god but Allah." This is the basic adhan; however, Shiite Muslims add two statements to it. They chant a sentence affirming Ali, "I testify that Ali is Allah's representative [or vice-regent]," two times following the statement declaring that Muhammad is Allah's messenger. This way the Shiite adhan includes a unique sentence affirming the Shiite belief in the imamate (leadership) of Ali. Moreover, they add another sentence that is not exclusively Shiite, "Come to [or hurry toward] the best of deeds," immediately before the final Allahu Akbar. For Shiites, this last sentence was approved by **Imam** Ali and demonstrates the diligence of the Shiites in doing good works.

Sunni Muslims believe these additions are **bid'a** (heresy) because the adhan as given by Muhammad includes only the fifteen initial sentences. Nonetheless, Sunnis add one sentence to the adhan before the dawn ritual prayer—"Prayer is better than sleeping"—which they repeat twice after saying "Come to success" twice. Shiites, unsurprisingly, consider this addition bid'a and do not accept or chant it.

madrasa: a school

The Arabic term *madrasa* refers to a school in general. In Islam, it is specifically an institution for teaching Islamic subjects, although some other topics may be discussed. The term is pronounced "MAHD-rah-suh," and its plural form is *madaaris* (compare with midrash in Hebrew), often rendered as "madrasas" in English. The noun *madrasa* is related to the Arabic verb *darasa*, which denotes studying and learning—and, in one of its forms, it means "to teach or to educate." This is important in regard to other Arabic terms related to the noun *madrasa*: a lesson is darsu, a student is daaris, and a teacher is mudarris.

In practice, a madrasa is often a section inside a local mosque where lessons are given to educate Muslims in matters of faith and practice. The teachers are often religiously educated and known as fuqaha'—they are experts in **fiqh** (comprehending Islamic law). Sometimes the children's madrasa is called a kuttaab; the term *kuttaab* is related to the Arabic verb that means "to teach someone basic writing." The term *madrasa* is also used for Muslim institutions of higher education where adults can study Islamic sciences and theology—in addition to other research fields—from an Islamic perspective. These institutions are sometimes located within a large local mosque but are often separate and operate as colleges or seminaries. They often include preliminary, intermediate, and advanced levels.

While Shiites may use the term *madrasa*, they prefer an exclusively Shiite alternative: *al-hawza al-ilmiyya*. The term *al-hawza* means "the container" or "the vessel," while *al-ilmiyya* refers to knowledge and science; therefore, the term refers to the place that contains and encompasses knowledge and information. For Shiite Muslims, al-hawza al-ilmiyya is a seminary or religious institution to advance **Shiism** and its doctrines and views. It usually includes several schools and covers various fields of knowledge, always with a sectarian convictional approach.

'awra: a body part to be covered, a private organ

The term *'awra* refers to a private part of a human. It is pronounced "our-uh." Linguistically, the word *'awra* refers to what shames someone or what one should hide due to incompleteness or undesirable vulnerability. In use, it simply describes the sexual parts of a human. The term is important in Islam because Islamic law has precise definitions concerning what *'awra* means for both men and women, and it must be totally covered.

The **sharia** (Islamic law) includes varying definitions of *'awra*, depending on scholars and their schools of thought. Sunnis generally believe that a man's 'awra extends from his knees up to his navel. Some scholars include the knees and the navel in the 'awra, while others

consider it only the area between them. If a Muslim man seeks to follow the prescriptions of the sharia, he must cover this area. Some Muslims argue that the knees should not be viewed as 'awra because in a
hadith, a pious companion described seeing the spectacular whiteness
of Muhammad's thigh. This indicates that Muhammad was not concerned about covering this body part above his knees. In this view, only
the private parts are 'awra. This discussion is important for religious
enthusiasts when making decisions about activities such as going to the
beach and playing soccer.

Islamic views concerning the 'awra of a woman are contradictory
and more complicated. What follows describes the most general claims.
In front of her husband, a woman has no 'awra at all, which means
there is no part that must be covered—she is even free to be unveiled. If
she is with other women, then her 'awra is the area between her knees
and her navel. Even if the woman is with her mother or sister, this
'awra must be covered if the woman wants to be within the boundaries of the sharia. In practice, this simply means that a woman is not
permitted to see the area between the navel and the knees of any other
woman. But when veiled women get together, they can unveil. Muslim
women remain fully dressed when they go to the beach because men
and women are present.

The 'awra of a woman relates to another important Islamic term:
mahram. The term *mahram* refers to a close male relative of a woman
whom she is not permitted to marry, according to the sharia. Mahram
is based on an Arabic noun that is close to the word *haram*, meaning
"forbidden." A mahram is a woman's father, brother, son, and nephew,
among others. According to the sharia, if a woman is with a mahram,
then her 'awra is her entire body with the exception of her face, neck,
and—some Muslims say—hair. If a woman meets any man who is not
a mahram, then her 'awra is her entire body without exception. This is
why conservative Muslim women are often fully covered by a niqaab, not
just a hijab (veil). In some ultraconservative Muslim circles, a woman's
voice is considered 'awra. This claim is based on traditions attributed
to Muhammad, and in practice it means that a woman's voice should
not be heard except by her husband. Many progressive and modernist
Muslims challenge the traditional Muslim views about 'awra, especially in relation to women. Some claim that a woman's 'awra is a valid

concept only when she is performing the salat (ritual prayer) or the hajj (pilgrimage), at which time she must cover; otherwise, regular clothes are sufficient. Some progressive Muslims even argue that a hijab is not mandatory for women in our day, as it was prescribed in the Quran only for Muhammad's wives due to their roles in his life and career.

ISLAMIC JURISPRUDENCE

⎯⎯⎯⎯⎯⎯⎯⎯⎯

This section is concerned with Islamic thought—particularly related to legal opinions and interpretations. It explains terms largely coined by Muslim clerics, scholars, and jurists in their attempts to explain and execute what they view as Allah's legal commands, commonly known as Islamic law or the sharia. Muslim thinkers—in responding to social, cultural, sectarian, and political questions—must derive answers from major Islamic texts. No answer emerges without sectarian or political bias, and no interpretation of religious texts exists apart from its context. Due to disagreements regarding presuppositions and views, Muslim interpretations clearly vary. Consequently, views and practices differ among Muslims.

This section explores terms that Muslim scholars and jurists use to define the two most important relationships in Islam: with the deity and with fellow humans. This section complements the discussions in the previous two sections—on faith and beliefs, and on practices and duties. This section tackles the various schools of Islamic law and how they address legal issues. It explains what is legally clean or permissible for Muslims and what is forbidden. It also explains the Muslim belief in divinely prescribed punishments for specific crimes, including apostasy, adultery, homosexuality, and consuming alcohol, among others. In discussing matters related to Islamic law and the interpretations pertaining to Muslims' relationships with others, this section defines concepts articulated by jurists—such as what a heresy is and what constitutes a Muslim land—and contrasts them with concepts in regions ruled by non-Muslims.

fiqh: comprehending Islamic sharia

In Arabic, the term *fiqh*, pronounced "fik-h," means "particular under-standing or thorough comprehension of a specific matter." As an Islamic term, *fiqh* refers to the religious process of learning, understanding, and identifying the rules of the **sharia** (Islamic law) as found in the Quran and Muhammad's **sunna** (tradition). In English, fiqh is understood as Islamic jurisprudence. As a legal process, fiqh aims to help Muslims comprehend the foundations of Allah's law (sharia) for the proper implementation of Islamic *worship* and *practice*.

A legal scholar who applies and teaches the rules of fiqh is called a faqih. A faqih should be—according to the vast majority of Muslims—a male. He is often rendered as a "jurist" in English, which is basically a scholar of Islamic law. The chief work of a faqih is to use the Quran and Muhammad's sunna to provide Muslims with the proper under-standing of Allah's precepts. Sometimes this understanding takes the form of a religious ruling (**fatwa**). A faqih who issues a fatwa is a mufti. In Sunni Islam, if a faqih does not find answers in these two major Islamic sources, then he should follow two more steps. First, he should examine previous religious rulings issued by generations of Muslim scholars to see if there has been a consensus (**ijmaa**) among them that could provide understanding to inform or solve the religious inquiry. If the ijmaa does not yield answers, then the faqih moves to applying a process of analogy (qiyaas) to reach a solution based on the rules of the sharia. For example, there is no ruling in Islamic texts about the use of heroin; however, there is an Islamic ruling forbidding the use of alcohol. Since alcohol and heroin both affect human reasoning, a faqih may conclude that the use of heroin is forbidden in Islam. While the Quran and Muhammad's sunna are the ultimate sources for the sharia and fiqh (understanding the sharia), the ijmaa and qiyaas—as two supplementary steps—are also of utmost importance to many Muslims, especially among the Sunnis.

For all Muslims, the Quran is inerrant and infallible. For most Muslims, Muhammad's sunna is also infallible because it is the speech of the infallible prophet; thus, they claim that it is a revelation (**wahy**) like the Quran. While the Quran and Muhammad's sunna are infallible for most Muslims, fiqh is considered fallible. It is a human process that relies heavily on interpretation and human reasoning. This process can err. Moreover, while Allah's law is unchanging, Muslims consider fiqh changeable based on the requirements of the time in order to serve the needs of Muslims. Still, Muslims largely respect works of fiqh produced by jurists from the medieval period. These works not only are authoritative for many Muslims regarding the process of fiqh but also dictate crucial decisions on belief and practice among Muslims even today.

madhhab: a school of thought

The Arabic word *madhhab* means "a path, route, way, method, or pattern of conduct." It is pronounced "MADH-heb," and its plural form is *madhahib*. In Islam, a madhhab is a method of interpretation one follows or a school of thought one adopts in order to understand the **sharia** (Islamic law). A madhhab is thus an acceptable and approved method of understanding Islam's principles. In practice, a major goal for any Muslim is to understand the prescriptions of the sharia. To achieve this goal, Muslims seek to follow a madhhab of the available and recognized madhahib within Islamic jurisprudence (**fiqh**).

There are many acceptable madhahib (schools of thought) in Islam, but Sunnis and Shiites do not follow the same ones. In Sunnism, there are four major madhahib. Each of them is considered orthodox and is named after its founder, who is often understood as an esteemed scholar who excelled in traditions and interpretation. The four founders of the Sunni madhahib are Abu Hanifa (699–767), who was born and lived mostly in Iraq; Malik ibn Anas (711–795), who was from Medina; Ibn Idris al-Shafi'i (767–820), who died in Egypt; and Ahmad ibn Hanbal (780–855), who lived and died in Iraq. The four schools of thought are therefore the Hanafiyya, Malikiyya, Shafi'iyya, and Hanbaliyya. Each of the founders is known among Muslims as an **imam** (leader), a term that reflects esteem and leadership. The general understanding among Muslims is that these founders largely relied on the Quran and the **hadith** traditions to make their religious decisions and interpretations.

For a Sunni Muslim, following any of these madhahib is acceptable as a way of understanding matters of worship and practice within the boundaries of the sharia. These four schools agree on most issues related to worship, but there are significant differences concerning practices, such as fulfilling the ritual prayer, allowing and forbidding the consumption of certain foods, and so forth. Regarding the influence of the four schools, the Hanafiyya madhhab flourishes roughly in Jordan, Palestine, and Egypt. The Malikiyya madhhab is common in Morocco, Egypt, and many other African countries. The Shafi'iyya madhhab is prevalent in Iraq, while the Hanbaliyya madhhab is common in Saudi Arabia as well as parts of Egypt and Syria. In general terms, the most lenient madhhab is the Hanafiyya, while the strictest is the Hanbaliyya.

In Shiism, there are various schools of thought, but the most important and famous traces its founding to Imam Ja'far al-Sadiq (702–765), who lived and died in Medina. His madhhab is called Ja'fariyya. He was the sixth infallible imam among Shiites—a decedent of Ali, Muhammad's cousin. His title, al-Sadiq, means "the truthful" and "the honest." Shiites highly esteem Imam Ja'far. Some even claim that he was a pioneer in believing and declaring that the earth is not flat but round. To demonstrate his esteem as a Shiite scholar, Shiites claim that the founders of the first two Sunni schools of thought—Abu Hanifa and Malik—both spoke highly of Imam Ja'far. They also claim that Malik spent many years learning from and being discipled under Imam Ja'far. Ja'far is credited with identifying and authorizing the reliable and sound hadith traditions among Shiites. He lived during both the **Umayyad** Caliphate and the early years of the **Abbasid** Caliphate. It is believed among Shiites that Imam Ja'far was poisoned by the second Abbasid caliph, Mansur.

ulamaa': scholars of Islam, the knowledgeable specialists

The Arabic term *ulamaa'* refers to scholars in any field of knowledge. It is pronounced "oh-leh-MEH." It is plural, and its singular form is *aalim*, which refers to a possessor of knowledge (ilm) who acquired it through a systematic study. As an Islamic term, it describes religious scholars in any Islamic discipline. They are also called "the people of knowledge" (ahl al-ilm). A scholar of the **hadith** tradition or a scholar of **fiqh** (comprehending Islamic **sharia**) is called an aalim. Commentators on the Quran are scholars of **tafsir** and thus also ulamaa'. The same goes for scholars of sharia who give **fatwas** (religious rulings)—they are ulamaa'. A mufti (one who issues a fatwa) is also an aalim. Simply, ulamaa' are scholars of Islamic knowledge who can define and teach Allah's laws based on evidence from the major sources of Islam: the Quran and Muhammad's **sunna** (tradition).

In practice, ulamaa' apply a legal process called ijtihad, which is a Muslim term meaning "to exert," to determine proper religious rulings for the benefit of Muslims. Within the major sects of Islam, the term *ulamaa'* is often preferred and used by Sunni Muslims. Shiite Muslims are usually reluctant to use the term, as they view ilm (knowledge) as ultimately given to and through the infallible **imams**. Shiites prefer a different term to refer to a scholar of the religion: *marji'*. The term literally means "a knowledgeable esteemed reference of Islam."

The majority of Muslims highly respect ulamaa' and often view them as protectors of the purity of belief and Islamic knowledge. This respect is amplified among Sunni Muslims, who cherish Muhammad's sunna. This high esteem has historical roots in the ninth century, when many of the Muslim ulamaa' opposed the powerful caliph who sought to control them by undermining their traditions. Ulamaa' endured many years of persecution from the caliphal power until they eventually won the dispute, although many gave their lives as martyrs. Ulamaa' who endured or survived the caliphal persecution became the earliest Sunnis, also known as "the people of the hadith." They ultimately became the arbiters of religious knowledge.

Most Muslims obey and respect ulamaa'. Their unique status is often based on a loose reading of a verse in the Quran. The verse instructs believers to obey Allah, the messenger, and those in authority among them (Q 4:59). Muslims commonly believe that ulamaa'—and, in a similar sense, government officials—are the people of authority among Muslims and should therefore be obeyed and respected. However, obedience to ulamaa' is not without limits. Muslims cannot obey ulamaa' in matters or decisions that contradict the Quran or Muhammad's statements. For many social, cultural, and political reasons, ulamaa' differ greatly in their decisions—although they all claim to rely on the same authoritative texts. In some Muslim countries today, ulamaa' are closely connected to the dominant political powers. They teach in government-sponsored universities and issue fatwas (religious rulings) that often match the opinions of their rulers.

hudud: boundaries or divinely prescribed punishments

The Arabic term *hudud* means "boundaries" and is pronounced "hoh-dood." Its singular form is *hadd*, which refers to a religious limit for Muslims—if crossed, it is punishable by Allah's decrees. Muslims often speak of the hudud of Allah when they refer to his prescribed limits or what he prohibited and designated as punishable offenses. The Quran uses the term *hudud* in association with rules—for example, between a husband and a wife—that should not be violated (Q 2:187). In practice, since hudud are boundaries set by Allah, the term itself became associated with punishments for offenses under Islam. Muslims use the term to refer to penalties for specific crimes under the **sharia** (Islamic law). The rationale is that divine punishments should be applied by Muslim rulers if the sharia is applied literally. Although the executer of these specific punishments is the Muslim ruler, the punishments are viewed as divine penalties.

Based on the Quran and the **sunna** (Muhammad's tradition), Muslim jurists identified several major crimes that deserve punishment under the sharia: murder, adultery, consuming alcohol, theft, robbery, and apostasy. Some jurists add false accusation and homosexuality to the list. For Muslims, these crimes threaten the political and social orders in Muslim society, and thus Allah's laws identify them as boundaries never to be crossed. Muslims claim that the application of divinely prescribed punishments for these offenses preserves life against murder, reason against drunkenness, faith against apostasy, lineage against adultery, and property against theft. The punishments are largely identified by statements in the Quran or the **hadith** tradition and can be applied only by the Muslim ruler or the Muslim judge in the land.

In applying Allah's hudud, there are some variations among Muslims—but they often follow similar patterns. For instance, adultery is to be punished by either flogging or stoning (both are prescribed in Islamic sources, with a clear contradiction between the Quran and the hadith). Consuming alcohol and false accusation are penalized by eighty lashes. A thief or highway robber receives the amputation of a hand or foot, or both on opposite sides (Q 5:33). Apostasy and homosexuality are punishable by death. These are some of the prescribed hudud in Islam. Not all Muslim-majority countries apply the hudud. Many adopt one form or another of Western systems of laws. Still, some Muslim countries—including Sudan, Iran, Saudi Arabia, and Afghanistan—adopt and apply the hudud in full or in part.

aqida: a conviction of doctrine or dogma

The term *aqida* refers to a strong belief in a particular matter. The term can be used in any field, but in Islam it is often used concerning the religious tenets and theological commitments of the faith. It is pronounced "ah-KEE-duh." It is singular, and its plural form is *aqaa'id*, which denotes a set of beliefs, doctrines, or religious creeds. In Arabic, the word *aqida* is derived from a noun meaning "a strong tie" or describing the action of firmly tying a rope around a stick. The word also denotes a contract. Therefore, aqida is viewed in Islam as tying a Muslim to the true path of faith.

In practice, aqida is what a Muslim believes. It is the set of beliefs taught and practiced in the life of a believer. Muslims cherish this word and use it often to describe the purity and superiority of Islam. Their Islamic aqida is the collective dogma and articles of faith to which they adhere. For example, Muslims believe that **tawhid** (the belief in one god, strict monotheism) is an important aqida. Trusting the **sunna** (tradition) of Muhammad as the best example to follow in life is also a crucial aqida. Belief in the afterlife and in the unseen world is also an important aqida in Islam.

Among Muslims, the term *aqida* is often linked to another, *din*, which means "religion" and is better understood here as "religious living." While the term *aqida* relates to a heartfelt belief and inner commitment or conviction, the term *din* refers to the outward application, the public

living and practice of aqida. The term *din* is often linked to the application of the **sharia** (Islamic law), both in worship and in relationships.
In many Islamic circles, the terms *aqida* and *din* are used repeatedly
and regularly.

umma: the unified Islamic community

The term *umma* means "community" and is pronounced "OHM-
mah." It is significantly important for Muslims, particularly for their
self-perception and their portrayal of themselves to non-Muslims. They
view themselves as one unified and united community, in contrast to
all unbelievers. In essence, the term is used to describe Muslims as one
community, unmatched in its beliefs and practices. Muslims present
themselves as the matchless umma of Muhammad, the umma of **tawhid**
(strict monotheism), the umma of believers, and the umma of al-islam
(the true submission to Allah). It is the most unique and unparalleled
community.

The term receives its significance from the Quran's designation of
Muhammad's followers as the best umma to ever exist or be raised in
humanity (Q 3:110). The verse makes the umma of believers supreme
among other people because they instruct the performing of good
works and prohibit wrongdoing. The same verse contrasts believers
with **ahl al-kitab** (the people of the book, presumably Jews and Christians) and asserts that the latter do not believe and the majority of
them are wicked. In another verse, Allah appears to talk to Muslims
about the unified umma. He reveals that this is your umma; it is one
umma and I am your Lord, so fear me (Q 23:52; also 21:92). Similarly,
Muhammad's traditions establish the concept of the one unified umma.
He reportedly stated that Muslims are all equal and their blood is
precious—they are one hand against all others. Believers should stick
together and care for each other because they resemble one human
body—if a member of the body is unwell, then the entire body is unwell. While this statement resembles biblical accounts (1 Cor. 12:26–
27), it establishes for Muslims a unique sense of unity that surpasses
religion to include social and cultural solidarity. Even the second caliph,
Umar, is reported to have said that the Arabs were the most humiliated
people group, but Allah raised them up and made them a superior

people through Islam. This reflects the Muslim understanding of the superiority of the umma of Islam when compared to other people groups or belief systems. While *umma* is a religious term, it definitely goes beyond spiritual beliefs to cover social and cultural spheres of life.

In practice, the term reflects Islamic nationalism. For Muslims, Islam—as a unifying belief system—replaces individualism and national identity. A Muslim in New York, Nigeria, or Thailand would proudly claim to be a member of Muhammad's umma. The concept is political in its essence. It creates a mindset whereby there is a unique bond between believers, despite their different languages, ethnicities, and cultures. While the theoretical understanding of the term *umma* may suggest that Muslims live in social and cultural equality among themselves, this is hardly the case in Islamic societies, where social classes and economic differences are a significant part of the daily lives of Muslims. Thus, within the one Muslim umma, despite idealistic religious claims, social boundaries and cultural particularities do influence behaviors and daily decisions.

qadi: a Muslim judge

The noun *qadi* means "Muslim judge" and is pronounced "kah-dee." It is based on a verb that means "to discern or to judge." Its plural form is *qudaah*. The most important job for a qadi is to make decisions in matters related to the **sharia** (Islamic law), often issuing **fatwas** (religious rulings) to answer questions relayed by Muslims. Major legal decisions cannot be made by regular Muslims but instead require an educated Muslim qadi. In Sunni Islam, a qadi relies on the Quran and the **sunna** (Muhammad's tradition) to make sharia rulings. If these two sources do not provide adequate information, the qadi often searches previous sharia rulings to determine whether there was an **ijmaa** (consensus) of the Muslim **ulamaa'** (scholars of Islam) at any point concerning the matter.

In Muslim tradition, a qadi must be a free (not slave) male, well versed and educated in the sharia. This matter has become controversial in recent years, as some in progressive circles have begun to call for female judges. Conservative and traditionist Muslims insist that the position of a qadi is only for men, especially because the Quran states that men are the maintainers and protectors of women and that Allah has made some excel over others (Q 4:34). This is understood to mean that men are in charge of women—which, according to traditional views, does not allow women to be judges. This is also established for conservatives by the divine statement that men possess a degree of advantage over women (Q 2:228), which, for them, reflects guardianship and responsibility. The same is enforced by **hadith** traditions attributed to Muhammad in which he states that no people will ever prosper if they appoint a woman to be in charge of their affairs. In practice, Muslim scholars insist that not only textual evidence but also the nature of women discourages their appointment as judges. They would have to work with men and in mixed settings, which would violate their privacy according to the sharia. In many Muslim-majority countries today, the government appoints qudaah in agreement with its political, sectarian, and social requirements.

ribaa: money interest, usury

The term *ribaa* refers to interest on money and is often rendered as "usury" in English. It is pronounced "re-bah." Linguistically, *ribaa* refers to an excessive increase in a particular matter. When people place their money in a bank and it receives interest, this is ribaa. In Islam, taking the ribaa is **haram** (forbidden). Muslims are encouraged to deal with Islamic **halal** (legally allowed) banks, not with banks that use the ribaa-based system.

Based on many verses in the Quran and numerous hadiths, Muslims believe that Allah prohibited ribaa. In the Quran, Allah warns believers that when they use ribaa to gain wealth, there will be no increase for it in Allah's sight (Q 30:39)—he will not bless it. Allah permits trading but explicitly forbids ribaa, and he equates those who deal in ribaa with those who will be ashamed on the judgment day as those deceived by Satan's touch (Q 2:275). For Muslims, this particular verse is an ultimatum against usury and loan interests, although other verses forbid ribaa as well (Q 2:278; 3:130; 4:161). In Muhammad's traditions, he reportedly cursed people who used ribaa and those who encouraged it. Based on the verses in the Quran and Muhammad's **sunna** (tradition), many Muslims consider ribaa one of the major transgressions and great sins. In practice, since ribaa is haram, many Muslims who want to follow Islam's rules refuse to invest in non-Islamic banks or stocks. In some conservative Muslim circles, a denier of the haram of ribaa can be labeled a **kafir** (infidel) or a **murtad** (apostate).

Of course, modern banking creates a challenge to Islamic laws in this regard. In response, modernist and progressive Muslims have attempted to establish fatwas (religious rulings) suitable for the day. In one argument, Muslims insist that ribaa was a practice used by pagan Arabs to steal from each other in the **jahiliyya** (pre-Islamic age of ignorance) and is not similar to modern banking. Still, in some Muslim-majority countries, banks that claim to operate under Islamic law do not practice ribaa. These banks declare that they follow only sharia-related methods of trading and profiting, although they still earn interest from currency exchange rates.

ijmaa: a consensus

The term *ijmaa* means "consensus," particularly in relation to medieval Muslim scholars and their views on particular religious matters. It is pronounced "ihj-mayah" and commands high respect among the vast majority of Muslims, particularly in **Sunnism**. It refers to the agreement of Muslims on a ruling or law of the **sharia** (Islamic law) if the Quran and the **sunna** (Muhammad's tradition) are unclear about it. It is a jurisprudence device for understanding the sharia, and it comes third—after the Quran and the sunna and before the concept of qiyaas (a process of analogy). If Muslims seek to establish a law, they first consult the Quran and the sunna. If the answer cannot be derived from these two sources, then they investigate whether scholars had an ijmaa on the matter at any point, especially in past generations.

Although an ijmaa carries less authority than the two ultimate sources of the sharia, it is of significant importance. Consider an important case related to the Quran. In early Islam, there were many companions of Muhammad, and each had a unique text of the Quran. These texts were not identical and contained variant readings. The caliph codified one copy, labeled it orthodox, and had every other copy burned. While the hadith tradition refers to parts and passages missing from this acceptable text of the Quran, an ijmaa made the text official and orthodox despite obvious omissions. This is how consequential ijmaa is. Moreover, even after Muslims adopted a consensus regarding this caliphal copy, a problem surfaced in later generations: variant readings of this accepted copy emerged. Muslim scholars agreed on seven, then ten, and finally fourteen acceptable variants while rejecting others. Their agreement—that is, their ijmaa—made a list of variant readings acceptable and orthodox while designating all others as unorthodox. This demonstrates the powerful tool of ijmaa, especially among Sunnis.

To support their insistence on ijmaa, Sunni Muslims argue that the Quran references the concept when it exhorts people to agree together about their decisions (Q 10:71; also 4:83) and when it refers to Joseph's brothers being in consensus (ijmaa) on one matter (Q 12:102). While many critics conclude that these verses do not explicitly establish ijmaa as a concept in determining sharia matters, Sunnis believe they do. They also refer to how the Quran calls believers to accomplish their life affairs by discussing, consulting, and agreeing together (Q 42:38; also 3:159). Although these verses simply refer to consultation, Sunnis insist that they legitimize ijmaa. In addition to sporadic hints in the Quran, Muslims rely heavily on one hadith attributed to Muhammad in which he declares his affirmation and trust in the consensus of his community. He conveys that Allah will always safeguard Muslims from any erroneous ijmaa.

In Sunni religious discussions, many may insist that a religious matter received the ijmaa of the **ulamaa'** (scholars of Islam), but in reality, this sort of ijmaa is elusive. Arguably, no religious matter—without a clear supportive text from the Quran and the sunna—can produce total agreement among Muslims. Still, the notion of ijmaa is widespread and powerful. It is not surprising that Muslims disagree on whose opinion matters in establishing an ijmaa.

In **Shiism**, the matter is different. While Shiites sometimes use the term *ijmaa*, it is not a source of their understanding of the sharia; it is used only in relation to the twelve infallible **imams**. If the imams—in their established traditions—agreed on a religious matter, then it received a legitimate ijmaa. For Shiites, there is no value or authority for any ijmaa outside the traditions and teachings of the imams.

fatwa: a religious ruling issued by a Muslim cleric

Whenever Muslims need religious advice in matters of belief, worship, or practice, they ask educated Muslim clerics (e.g., a mosque's **imam**). When a Muslim cleric hands down an Islamic legal opinion, this is called a fatwa, pronounced "FAT-wuh." The Muslim cleric who issues the fatwa is called a mufti. In mainstream Islam, a mufti is a man and cannot be a woman. Since Islamic texts are numerous, sophisticated, and mostly inaccessible to most Muslims, it is often difficult for the majority of Muslims to determine the proper Islamic direction in many life situations. This is why they need a fatwa. A Muslim man may ask for a fatwa as to whether it is permissible in Islam to work in the same shop with a Buddhist. Another may inquire if it is allowed in Islam to enter the house of a Jew and eat a meal together. A Muslim woman may seek a fatwa as to whether Islam permits her to remove her **hijab** (veil) at a party. A man may inquire whether burping during the ritual prayer will spoil the prayer and require him to repeat it. The questions presented by Muslims touch various spheres of life, including religion, politics, economics, and even social situations: May I vote for this candidate? Is it permissible to invest in stocks? May I marry a convert to Islam who still drinks alcohol and does not pray the five daily prayers? May I watch Hollywood TV shows?

A Muslim mufti often relies primarily on the Quran and Muhammad's tradition (**sunna**) to articulate a fatwa. After explaining to the questioner what Islamic texts state about the matter in question, the mufti often gives one of several answers to the question: **halal** (legally allowed), **haram** (forbidden), recommended, favored, disliked, or abominable. Not all fatwas are of the same authority. A fatwa issued by the imam of a local mosque is not equal in power to one issued by a professor of Islamic jurisprudence at a major Islamic university. Every fatwa receives its authority from the mufti issuing it. Today, Muslims can seek fatwas online, sometimes utilizing platforms such as YouTube. Due to the importance of fatwas to Muslims, some Muslim countries control the issuance of fatwas by founding an office that produces official fatwas. The office is usually called the House of Fatwa and is led by a mufti, called the grand mufti, hired by the government. This way the government ensures that major political and economic decisions in the country are controlled, especially because Muslims largely respect legal Islamic rulings. If a government wants to make something permissible, it might seek the issuance of a fatwa by the grand mufti to that effect.

Muftis sometimes issue a fatwa without any Muslim requesting a ruling. In this case, the fatwa serves as a public decision to guide the Muslim community. In 1988, after Salman Rushdie (1947–) published his novel *The Satanic Verses*, Muslim leaders were furious. The story had roots in Islamic texts and portrayed Muhammad in a negative way. Consequently, Iranian ayatollah Khomeini issued a fatwa accusing Rushdie of apostasy and blasphemy against Muhammad. Khomeini placed a bounty on Rushdie's head, basically permitting Muslims to kill him for the sake of Islam. Similarly, in 1998, Osama bin Laden reportedly issued a fatwa indicating it was permissible and actually desirable, based on Islamic legal texts, to target Americans, both civilian and military, and execute them.

halal: legally allowed; haram: forbidden

The terms *halal* and *haram* (pronounced "ha-laal" and "ha-rom") are important in Islamic legal theory. Linguistically, the word *halal* means "permissible or allowed," and it is related to a verb that means "to set loose" and "to permit." Under the **sharia** (Islamic law), halal is what Allah allowed and what a believer is permitted to use, do, and enjoy. Similarly, linguistically, the term *haram* is related to a verb that means "setting boundaries to cause something to be forbidden." If a food is haram, it is not permitted to be touched or consumed. However, the term *haram* has a deeper meaning that may appear contradictory due to its positive connotation. It indicates that something is untouchable or inaccessible due to greatness or majestic features. If a location is haram, it is not to be violated or harmed. This is why Muslims call the mosque in Mecca the haram mosque (al-masjid al-haram)—it is protected and sacred, and no offense or attack is permitted in it (Q 2:144, 198; 5:97). In the same vein, the Quran refers to some months in the year that are haram, which means they are protected and sacred—no one should violate their sanctity, and, in particular, fighting is not allowed during these months (Q 5:5).

In practice, halal refers to what is good and lawful that deserves Allah's rewards, while haram indicates what is forbidden, whose doer will be punished by Allah's wrath. For Muslims, the term *halal* is particularly important when preparing food, especially animal meat. A Muslim must perform a detailed ritual process to slaughter an animal according to the sharia. The slaughtering of the animal is called dhabh, and the slaughtered animal is called dhabiha. The halal slaughtering must begin with the pronouncement of Allah's name over the animal in fulfillment of a command in the Quran (Q 6:121). Some Muslim slaughterers declare the **basmala** ("In the name of Allah, Most Gracious, Most Merciful"). This is followed by the fast and complete severing of the animal's throat using a sharp knife, which ensures the cutting of the windpipe and jugular veins. Most importantly, because consuming blood is haram in Islam, after the slaughter, the animal must be hung upside down to ensure the complete pouring out of its blood. If the animal is not slaughtered according to these specific details, it is haram for Muslims to consume. This is why, in many Western countries, halal shops exist in places where Muslims predominantly live in order to provide them with meat that is slaughtered in accordance with the requirements of the sharia.

The Quran states that Allah has detailed for believers what he has declared haram (Q 6:119). While this suggests that the Quran is clear about what things and deeds are halal and haram, the matter is more complex than it appears. Muslim scholars often wrestle with decisions regarding what is halal and what is haram in the modern era. In their pursuit to issue religious rulings (**fatwas**), they established a complex system presenting a spectrum of choices that expand the main two options of halal and haram. If something is not explicitly haram but is to some extent questionable, they label it reprehensible or disliked. If a matter does not seem completely halal, yet there is no specific command about it in the Quran or Muhammad's **hadith** tradition, Muslim scholars may identify it as allowed with caution or cautiously recommended. Overall, the terms *halal* and *haram* are important among Muslims who seek to follow the precepts of the sharia. Some cultural Muslims find the details of halal and haram matters too complex to comprehend, let alone to follow.

bid'a: an innovation or invention in religion, heresy

For Muslims, the term *bid'a*, pronounced "bid-AH," refers to any invention in religion, whether by adding to or by removing from what has been received from Muhammad. If what Muhammad delivered to Muslims was basically the Quran and the **sunna** (his tradition), then the term *bid'a* covers anything outside these two spheres. A bid'a is thus any new—as opposed to traditional—view, teaching, or practice that emerges among Muslims. *Bid'a* is singular, and its plural form is *bida'*. When Muslims identify something as a *bid'a*, they mean that it is a novelty in Islam—a heresy that is not orthodox because it cannot be traced to Muhammad's deeds or teachings.

A bid'a is sometimes obvious, especially if a Muslim makes what is religiously considered **haram** (forbidden) to be **halal** (permissible), or vice versa. When one claims that Islam permits the consumption of alcohol, Muslims may outright describe the claim as a bid'a. However, in other instances, the term *bid'a* is used by Muslim scholars to dismiss a claim, teaching, or practice they disapprove of. They identify it as not a sunna, and thus it is a bid'a. Because Shiites rely on different traditions that they deem the sacred sunna—these contain not only Muhammad's teachings but also those of the infallible **imams**—Sunnis and Shiites differ on what is found in the sunna.

In practice, the negative connotation of *bid'a* in Islam stems from a hadith attributed to Muhammad. It emerged centuries after Muhammad's death and claimed that he once declared that every bid'a is misguidance and every misguidance will be in the hellfire. Therefore, Muslims are always concerned with any hint of bid'a in matters of worship or practice. This is one reason why Sunnis and Shiites often accuse each other of following a bid'a. For instance, Shiites observe some holidays to commemorate their infallible imams, and they permit visiting their graves. Shiites even offer sacrifices and vows directed to the infallible imams and practice intercession by calling on the imams to save them from affliction. For Sunnis, all these actions fall under the term *bid'a*, as they are not from the sunna. Similarly, Sunnis insist that during **Ramadan** and after the breaking of the fast, the corporate prayer in the mosque is a sunna and highly recommended for all Muslims. Shiites disagree and consider this a bid'a advanced by Umar, the second caliph, who did not follow Muhammad's conduct.

Sunnis sometimes distinguish between a mild bid'a and a severe one, depending on its influence and whether it is linked to worship or practice. However, there is no good bid'a—every bid'a is always haram (forbidden) and considered misguidance. For Sunnis, many non-Sunni forms of Islam—like **Mu'tazilism**, **Sufism**, and others—fall under the label of innovation in religion and thus are a bid'a.

maslaha: public benefit, utility, or welfare

The term *maslaha*, pronounced "moss-la-hah," means "benefit, utility, or welfare." It is related to an Arabic verb that means "to fix, repair, or improve." It is an important term in Islamic jurisprudence that is often used to help Muslims navigate their options. The maslaha is what achieves the greater benefit or well-being for Allah's people, Muslims.

For Muslims, an important goal of the application of the **sharia** (Islamic law) is to achieve maslaha—to repair and improve aspects of their lives. According to some Muslim jurists, maslaha is defined by the pursuit to protect Muslims' religion, souls, minds, children, and property. For instance, if a business seeks to open in a Muslim land that applies the sharia, Muslims will ask, Will this business protect Muslims' souls and children, or will it harm them in relation to the application of Islam? The answer would determine whether the Muslim land would allow the business to open.

The opposite of maslaha is mafsada, which simply means "damage, grievance, or injury." Maslaha and mafsada are very important for Muslim jurists, who serve Muslims by providing **fatwas** (religious rulings). In their pursuit to issue fatwas that align with the sharia, Muslim jurists seek to avoid any mafsada and to advance maslaha—that is, public interest and welfare for all Muslims. The fatwas of these jurists take into consideration the time and circumstances of their legal decisions. For example, some jurists may decide that, at this time, the declaration of **jihad** as fighting in Allah's path is maslaha for Muslims, while at other times they may affirm that it is a better maslaha to endure hardships and injustice until the right timing for jihad. In the same vein, at certain times some jurists may insist that it is maslaha to apply the hadd (punishment) of executing apostates in order to avoid any mafsada in the Muslim land; however, at other times the same jurists may find that the greater maslaha necessitates allowing apostates some time to change their minds. This is one reason why Muslim jurists speak of the canceled or abrogated maslaha, which was valid at some point but later annulled by legal decisions or divine revelations. One case in point is the Islamic perspective on consuming alcohol and gambling. At some point in Islam, the Quran declared that drinking wine and gambling provide some maslaha (benefit) for people (Q 2:219). However, on a different occasion, the same Quran insists that wine and gambling are evil, are of Satan's handiwork, and should be totally avoided (Q 5:90). Maslaha necessitated the change of the revelation and thus the religious ruling.

daar al-harb: the house of war; daar al-islaam: the house of Islam

The term *daar al-harb*, pronounced "DAR ul-HARB," literally means "the house of war." The term is the literal opposite of the term *daar al-islaam*, which simply means "the house of Islam" and is pronounced "DAR ul-ess-LAM." In Islamic **sharia** (Islamic law), the world is divided into two territories, the house of Islam and the house of harb (war). Some Muslims replace *daar al-harb* with *daar al-kufr*, which means "the house of infidelity" or "the house of unbelief."

In Islamic law, *daar al-islaam* refers to the territories where Muslims are ruling. Some Muslim scholars add a qualifier: daar al-islaam is the territories where the sharia is applied properly. This means that, for these scholars, a country ruled by Muslims that does not apply the complete sharia cannot be considered daar al-islam. In contrast, daar al-harb is any territory where non-Muslims rule and where the sharia is not applied. For Muslims, every place in the world is either the house of Islam or the house of war.

By defining territories as daar al-harb, Muslim jurists established the legal right to conquer these territories. While the Quran insists in some verses that war can be carried out only in self-defense (Q 2:190–91), medieval Muslims articulated the notion that Muslims can initiate war against daar al-harb. The rationale goes like this: If non-Muslims rule over lands adjacent to Muslim territories, then Muslim believers are in danger, as the enemy could attack at any time. Thus, attacking these non-Muslim territories is legally permissible and is considered a defensive and preventive war. The aim is for Muslims to be unbound by fear and able to worship freely in their land, which may involve demolishing the evil unbelief of non-Muslims.

In addition to these two abodes, Islam and war, some Muslim scholars added daar al-sulh. The term *sulh* means "pact or treaty." It is related to another term, *salaam*, which means "peace." *Daar al-sulh* refers to territories that arrange a deal with Muslims without converting to Islam. They are in a state of salaam with daar al-islaam. Whether there are two or three abodes is disputed among Muslims, especially because the Quran mentions no such divisions. Later Muslim scholars, in an attempt to encourage the conquest of non-Muslim lands to support caliphal desires for military expansion, created these terms. Modernist and progressive Muslims do not encourage these divisions and argue that the notion of daar al-harb has no bearing on our day. Still, some Muslims adhering to tradition believe that daar al-harb is a territory that should be attacked when Muslims are able and ready.

kalam: words, speech, or philosophical Islamic theology

The noun *kalam* refers primarily to speech and is pronounced "ka-LAM." The term is often used to refer to the Quran as kalam Allah—the word of Allah or his speech or utterance. While this is the basic meaning of the noun, later generations of Muslims used the term *kalam* to refer to theology in general. In this usage, Muslims see it as an Islamic science (ilm). An educated Muslim who practices kalam is known as a mutakallim. Its plural form is *mutakallimun*.

When Muslims refer to educational theology or apologetic rhetoric, they often use the term *kalam*. To them, it is the Islamic science of Allah and all that surrounds the divine. It involves advancing and defending the faith. Some of the earliest practitioners of kalam were theologians who attempted to defend Islam against charges by non-Muslims. Because kalam—in this sense—emphasizes rational argumentation, it is not surprising that, from the earliest generations of Muslims, kalam as science was associated with Mu'tazili scholars and the **Mu'tazilism** movement, which advanced rationalism and human reasoning over traditions. Arguably, kalam, as an Islamic science, is indebted in various ways to Greek philosophy. After all, Muslims lived and interacted with non-Muslims under the caliphate. Some of the caliphs supervised and organized disputation meetings between Muslims and non-Muslims in the caliphal court. An exchange of opinions and methods of theologizing was inevitable.

ISLAMIC MOVEMENTS

This final section focuses on sects and visions within Islam, highlighting the sectarian diversity within a significantly complex religion. The terms in this section are not related to how Muslims exist in different cultures or live as various ethnicities. Rather, they define theological divisions and divergent views within Islam as a religious system. The entries begin with the major Muslim sects, Sunnism and Shiism, explaining how they emerged in their historical settings and their differences regarding religious claims and interpretations. Most Westerners erroneously tend to think their disagreements are merely political. The section then tackles two famous Muslim visions, Salafism and Sufism—which sometimes clearly contradict each other. These are not sects per se but rather visions within the general body of Muslims. Next, the section highlights the modern movement of Wahhabism and explains it as an Islamic movement with religious and political roots. The next entries are Mu'tazilism and ahl al-Quran. The former is focused on rationalism, among other doctrinal beliefs, while the latter rejects reliance on traditions and embraces the Quran alone, thus operating as a sola scriptura movement in Islam. The section concludes with the Ahmadiyya, a recent Muslim sect. The entry highlights the group's uniqueness and how mainstream Islam views this sect. The discussions in this section demonstrate not only the existence of various visions and sects within Islam but also the severe contradictions among them. While Muslims tend to view themselves as one united body of harmonious believers, this is simply inaccurate.

Sunnism: the largest sect in Islam

Sunnism, pronounced "SOO-nee-ism," is the largest sect in Islam. A Sunni is a follower of that sect. The word *Sunni* literally means "an adherent of or devotee to Muhammad's **sunna**"—that is, his traditions and pattern of conduct. About 85 percent of Muslims worldwide claim to be adherents of Sunni Islam. In Sunnism, Muslims cherish Muhammad's traditions as the second authority after the Quran. These traditions, however, differ from those accepted by the other major Islamic sect, **Shiism**. Unlike Shiites, Sunnis revere some of the trusted traditions that come from narrators and compilers who were not necessarily friendly toward the household of Muhammad—particularly Ali and his descendants. Shiites accept only the traditions that support the household of Muhammad as the religious and political guides of the Muslims.

The importance of the sunna to Sunnism is unmatched, as Sunni beliefs and practices are largely built on the trusted ancient **hadith** traditions. Muslims look to the earliest generations for guidance, especially traditions attributed to Muhammad's companions (sahaaba). Most Sunnis believe that these forefathers (salaf) implemented Islam properly and that their traditions must be followed by those who seek to adhere to true Islam. Our knowledge of these forefathers—and what they did and said—is filtered through medieval Muslim scholars of the hadith. These scholars are known among Sunnis as ashab al-hadith, "the people of the hadith," and are often labeled as traditionists. They are the lovers and adherents of the hadith. They flourished in the ninth century and grew in power after developing numerous hadiths. They worked closely with the caliphal court and at its service. These traditionists became influential as arbiters of religious matters and were the earliest manifestation of Sunnis. Sunnis are followers of Muhammad's sunna, and what they follow or reject depends largely on the arguments of the Sunni traditionists and their opinions circulated through the generations. In Sunnism, the most trusted hadith collections are those by **Imam** Bukhari (810–870) and Imam Muslim (821–875). Although these two lived and wrote more than two centuries after Muhammad, Sunnis wholeheartedly accept their collections as reliable and trustworthy.

Politically, for most of Muslim history, Sunni Islam was in power— the rulers adhered to it and enforced it as the dominant belief of the empire. This created hostility toward non-Sunni Muslims, especially Shiites. Some mistakenly believe that the split between Sunnis and Shiites occurred immediately after Muhammad's death. However, according to Muslim traditions, it took at least a century for the Islamic sects to develop and begin articulating their views. After Muhammad's death, Muslims were either Shiite (supporters of Ali, in the political sense of the term) or anti-Shiite (mainly anti-Ali and his faction). During the first two caliphates, the **Rashidun** and **Umayyad**—until 749, almost a century after Muhammad—there were no Sunnis as we use the term now. Under the **Abbasids**, traditionists (lovers of the hadith) became powerful, especially after the failure of the **mihna** (inquisition). These traditionists became Sunnis and rapidly grew in power because of their cooperation with caliphal agendas. This is one reason why the Sunni version of Islam's history is more known, circulated, and dominant, even among most modern scholars of Islam. This version is simply that of the winner, the dominant group in power. The other version, that of the defeated and marginalized, often documented by Shiites, contains stark differences and competing features—historically and theologically—that shed light on the inner struggle between the two major sects of Islam.

Shiism: the second-largest sect in Islam

Shiism, pronounced "SHEE-ism," is the second-largest sect in Islam. It is largely the faction of supporters (shi'a) of **Imam** Ali, Muhammad's cousin and son-in-law. This faction believes that Ali and his eleven male descendants are the infallible imams who are the legitimate successors of Muhammad, politically and spiritually. A male follower is a shi'i, while shi'iyya is the feminine form. A mixed group of followers of the sect is simply rendered as "shi'a." The followers as a whole are Shiites.

While Sunnis account for about 85 percent of Muslims, Shiites make up about 13 percent. The other 2 percent comes from marginal factions or visions within Islam. Today, Shiism has various subgroups, including Twelvers, Ismailis, and Zaydis. The largest group is the Twelvers. They believe in the doctrine of imamate, which asserts that after Muhammad, authority among Muslims belonged to the twelve infallible imams, the descendants of Ali, who are called ahl al-bayt (the household of Muhammad). One difference between the Twelvers and the other two Shiite subgroups—the Ismailis and the Zaydis—is that they do not accept the same number of infallible imams; thus, the spiritual and political authority differs. Some believe in twelve, others in seven or five imams. Nonetheless, due to the large number of Twelver Shiites, it is common to refer to them as the shi'a in general. They are the vast majority in today's Iran.

Religiously, Shiites are skeptical of Sunni traditions and many of the Sunni theological claims. Shiites possess their own trusted collections of **hadith**, particularly four collections. These collections are attributed to both Muhammad and his household, specifically the twelve imams in addition to, for instance, Muhammad's daughter Fatima. The collections were compiled generations after Muhammad. To establish a halo over them, these collections were deemed sacred and authentic by various Shiite authorities, particularly during the time of the sixth imam, Ja'far al-Sadiq (702–765). The Shiite Ja'fari **madhhab** (school of thought) is credited to him. During the early period of Islam, roughly before Imam al-Sadiq, Shiism was not a rigidly formed theology—it is better viewed in that early period as the political zeal of the faction of Ali. Religious Shiism—devotion to and veneration of Ali and his descendants as religious and political imams—took generations to form as political zeal advanced religious contours and theological claims.

Politically, Shiites have been the minority for fourteen centuries. Under the Umayyads, Shiites were targeted and murdered—or at least treated poorly. Even though Shiites supported the Abbasid revolution against the Umayyads, they were soon marginalized and targeted by the Abbasid caliphs. Still, Shiites were able to seize power at certain times and in certain locations, such as the Fatimid Dynasty (909–1171) in North Africa and the Middle East, and the Safavid Dynasty (1501–1736) in Iran. Due to the minority status of Shiites for most of Islam's history, their voice does not permeate many of the available Muslim accounts. Their version of Islam is marginalized to a large extent and has been overshadowed by the Sunni version of Islam.

Sunni-Shiite relations are often less positive than some Muslims may claim. In Western countries, since both groups are minorities, there seems to be a relative harmony. In the Muslim world, the situation is different. Severe enmity and hostility often occur between the two sects. Each group views the other as untrue Muslims or heretics.

Salafism: a revivalist and reformist trend in Sunnism

Salafism, pronounced "SAH-la-fism," is a revivalist and reformist trend in **Sunnism** that emerged in the eighteenth century. The aim is to return to what was—in their view—the purest and earliest phase of Islam. The term *salafi* refers to a Muslim devoted to following and applying the teachings and traditions claimed about the salaf, the earliest generations of Muslims—the believers close in time to Muhammad who saw him and heard him teach. Thus, they are the best Muslims and should be imitated. But the term *salaf* is not limited to the eyewitnesses of Muhammad; it also includes roughly the three earliest generations of Islam. It includes the companions of Muhammad as well as those who learned from them after his death. Sometimes Sunnis identify the salaf as Muhammad's immediate companions, their followers, and the followers of their followers. For salafis, these earliest generations were ashab al-**hadith**, meaning "the people of the hadith" or "the lovers of prophetic traditions."

Salafis seek to adhere to the **sunna** (tradition) of Muhammad and his trusted followers, the salaf, often referring to them as al-salaf al-saalih, "the pious and faithful predecessors." Salafis believe that the salaf were the most pious Muslims, who applied Islam properly. Even though we read in the Muslim accounts that the earliest Muslims often fought and killed each other, sometimes over worldly matters, salafis view the salaf as unmatched. Any negative tradition about the salaf is tweaked or reinterpreted in order to present them as the best followers of Islam.

Among Muslims, the interpretations of salafis are known to be the strictest, harshest, and most rigid. Salafis closely adhere to the letter of Islam's sacred texts, particularly the Quran and Muhammad's sunna. They believe that al-naql (imitating the old tradition) should be elevated above al-aql (thinking, reasoning, or rationalism). For a salafi, reasoning and thinking can be accepted only when they agree with the traditions of the salaf. This is evident in how salafis vehemently reject any hint of bid'a (innovation) in the religion and strongly insist on following the Sunni hadiths and reported customs of the past. In their clothes and practices, they clearly rely on traditions that reflect the life and customs of seventh-century Arabia. This is exemplified in how a woman wears not a **hijab** (veil) but a niqaab (a complete cover). If a Muslim suggests even a minor deviation from the perceived tradition, salafis are often ready and willing to identify them as an infidel. For them, Shiites are unbelieving infidels whose eternal destiny is hellfire. Even some Sunni Muslims—who do not adhere to a literalist interpretation of the Quran and the sunna—are considered infidels by salafis, though arguably to a lesser degree. Of course, for salafis, any religion other than Islam is kufr (unbelief or infidelity). Most salafis follow the **madhhab** (school of thought) of Ibn Hanbal, known as the Hanbaliyya, which is the strictest among Sunnis. Salafis often condemn the other three Sunni schools of thought, viewing them as not solid enough. Not surprisingly, radical Islamic movements are most often a product or reflection of Salafism. Examples include **Wahhabism**, the Muslim Brotherhood, the Taliban, al-Qaeda, ISIS, Boko Haram, al-Shabaab, and others. They all emerged from a salafi interpretation of Islam and with an aim to revive the practices of the salaf in modern Islam.

Sufism: a mystical, ascetic vision in Islam

Sufism is frequently viewed as a sect in Islam, like **Sunnism** and **Shiism**, but this is an erroneous notion. Sufism, pronounced "SOOF-ism," is better understood as a vision in Islam. A Sufi is a Muslim who adheres to an ascetic vision in Islam called sufiyya or tasawwuf. This is basically Islamic mysticism or mystical Islam. A Sufi seeks to reach a closer experience with Allah through meditation and other practices and rites unique to Sufism. Some Muslims adopt mystical practices without calling themselves Sufis, while others identify as Sufis but practice the rituals of mainstream Islam without adhering to any significant mysticism. The noun *Sufi* is based on another Arabic noun, *soof*, which means "wool." Ascetics and mystics have been known to wear wool clothing, arguably to forsake the pleasures of the world and adopt tougher ways of living. The term *tasawwuf* is often understood to mean "dressing in wool." Sufis have largely been identified as the poor and forsaken.

Some argue that Sufism emerged as early as the first **fitna** (civil war), soon after 656, particularly during the reign of the **Umayyad** Caliphate, in response to the wicked practices of those who claimed to be Muslims yet sought power and worldly goods. Sufis, the rationale goes, rejected these Muslim practices and preferred to live as ascetics in pursuit of nearness to the divine. Some scholars argue that Christian monasticism influenced Islamic Sufism greatly. This might prove true based on the similarities between the two. Sufis cherish not only reciting the Quran but also—more importantly—meditating on it. They also observe a ritual called dhikr, in which they mention Allah and his attributes for a prolonged time in hopes of achieving a divine connection. Many Sufis follow rituals of bowing and kneeling for long periods, extending beyond the **salat** (ritual prayer). Sufis devote nights to praise and devotion, often weeping and lifting up constant supplications. Some Sufis seek closeness to Allah by practicing harsh fasting or severe hunger. Some observe long periods of silence and isolation. Unlike most mainstream Muslims, Sufis believe that the greatest **jihad** is not fighting or waging war but the jihad within oneself—the jihad of suppressing evil desires, practicing self-control, eliminating worldly yearnings, and coming near the divine.

A Sufi can be Sunni or Shiite. Sufis reject any attempt to call themselves a sect or even a **madhhab** (school of thought). They insist on identifying themselves as merely Muslim, and sometimes they add unique qualifiers, such as "the lovers of the divine," "the seekers of the true light," and so forth. Unlike mainstream Muslims, Sufis believe in the existence of special humans who have an unmatched connection with Allah. Sufis call a person of that stature a wali; its plural form is awliyaa'. In the Sufi understanding, a wali is a friend of Allah. A wali is not a god or a prophet but simply a human who achieved unique closeness to Allah and has developed several unique advantages. A wali can bestow favors on and grant blessings to fellow humans. A wali is not infallible but is similar to a saint. They can visit people in dreams or visions. Whether alive or dead, a wali possesses spiritual powers. This is why Muslims visit the graves of recognized awliyaa'.

Many methods of practice fall under the umbrella of Sufism. A method is called a tareeqa. Each tareeqa differs from the next based on the Sufi teacher who adopts it. Sufis refer to these different methods as mystical ways or Sufi orders. A Sufi order is a group of Sufis who gather together under the guidance of an esteemed sheikh (elder).

Sufis are despised, rejected, and loathed by mainstream Muslims, particularly by salafis and Wahhabis. Some medieval Muslim thinkers were unequivocally opposed to Sufism and identified it as a **bid'a** (an innovation, heresy). Many contemporary Shiites also oppose Sufism. Thus, Sufis are the ascetics, mystics, and pacifists among Muslims who are often loathed by those outside their Sufi orders.

Wahhabism: a movement in Sunnism that adheres to Abd al-Wahhab's interpretations of Islam

A Wahhabi is a Sunni Muslim who adheres to a particular theological interpretation called Wahhabiyya, often rendered as "Wahhabism." Wahhabism, pronounced "wah-HAHB-ism," traces its emergence and development back to revivalist and reformist Muhammad ibn Abd al-Wahhab (1703–92). He flourished in the Arabian Peninsula, particularly in the Najd region, and was a son and grandson of Muslim scholars who adopted a strict understanding of Islam, following the Hanbali **madhhab** (school of thought). Abd al-Wahhab was reportedly a devout follower of **Salafism**, seeking to imitate the earliest generations of Muslims. As a theologian, he stressed the preaching of **tawhid** (strict monotheism) and gathered many followers who initially called themselves muwah-hidun (confirmers of the unicity of Allah) but were later known by their opponents as Wahhabis. This is why adherents of this theological interpretation do not like to be called followers of Wahhabism.

The unity between political power and theological literalism occurred around 1745, when Abd al-Wahhab became a major theological guide and partner of Muhammad ibn Saud (1687–1765), one of the first found-ers of modern Saudi Arabia. This unity clearly conveyed the under-standing of Islam as both religion and political leadership. In this unity, Abd al-Wahhab was the religious **imam** (leader), while Ibn Saud was the political amir (commander). The politician was to shield and protect the theologian, while the theologian advanced the causes of the politi-cian and supported his rule through religious edicts. Abd al-Wahhab insisted on teaching tawhid as a distinct Islamic dogma. While teaching tawhid does not differ from any other Islamic strain of thought, Abd al-Wahhab and his followers emphasized tawhid as a theological sword and labeled any opponent a **mushrik** (polytheist). In dealing with his opponents, Abd al-Wahhab believed that his theological views were the orthodox path and that **jihad** must be waged against anyone who opposed his teaching. As a devoted salafi, Abd al-Wahhab believed that the first generations of Muslims interpreted and applied Islam properly, but those Muslims who came after them deviated from the straight path by adopting innovations and wrong practices. He insisted on following the **sunna** (tradition) of Muhammad as practiced by the salaf (pious forefathers) and their interpretations. In his preaching, he rejected various practices among Muslims of his day, such as partying, smoking, and playing music. He condemned painting and creating art, and he rejected designing statues of animals, humans, or angels. In some historical accounts, Abd al-Wahhab launched raids against fellow Arab Muslims and seized their possessions and lands after identifying them as polytheists and apostates.

For Wahhabis, Shiites have deviated from pure Islam and adopted kufr (unbelief or infidelity), particularly by allowing intercession through the imams and visiting their graves. Wahhabis insist on following the **sharia** (Islamic law) by applying the twofold practice of commanding right and forbidding wrong. They believe these are two divine commands, a general duty for all Muslims—not a select group of authorities—to maintain order in Islamic lands. Thus, Wahhabis often compel Muslims to strictly adhere to religious duties, such as performing the salat (the ritual prayer) in a masjid (mosque). In some cases, they execute wrongdoers publicly in clear application of the **hudud** (divine punishments). Critics view Wahhabis as rigid and radical extremists, while adherents of this theological interpretation view themselves as true Muslims and believers in tawhid.

Mu'tazilism: a rationalist movement in Islam

A Mu'tazili is a Muslim who seeks to make sense of theological arguments, primarily through intellectual reasoning. The term is often rendered as "Mu'tazilite" in English. A Mu'tazili is a part of the Mu'tazila movement in Islam, which is rendered as "Mu'tazilism" in English. It is pronounced "maw-teh-zeh-lism." The movement began as a political group and later developed and articulated its religious arguments. The political origins of the group explain its name. In the first **fitna** (civil war), during the fight between Caliph Ali's son, Hasan, and Syria's governor, Mu'awiya, many Muslims joined one of the two camps and declared the other unbelieving infidels. A group of Muslims, however, withdrew from the conflict. They refused to support either political party in the fight and were openly reluctant to identify any Muslim as an infidel. This third group became known as the Mu'tazila, which literally means "the withdrawers." This is the earliest manifestation of Mu'tazilism as a movement in Islam. Later, the group attempted to explain religious concepts through intellectual reasoning, especially under the major Mu'tazili thinker Wasil ibn Ata' (ca. 700–748). Many scholars argue that the Mu'tazila movement, in its insistence on rationalism, was clearly influenced by Greek philosophy.

A Mu'tazili is often willing to question the reliability and authenticity of Muslim claims, particularly circulated traditions. In Islam's history, Mu'tazilites often clashed with **hadith** scholars—known as traditionists or adherents of the hadiths—who elevated the authority of the hadith over human intellect. A major clash between the two Muslim groups concerns the eternal existence of the Quran. Traditionists insist that the Quran has eternally existed with Allah—it is uncreated. Mu'tazilites find this claim illogical, as there cannot be two eternal beings. They claim that the Quran is created. The clash was evident in the **mihna** (Muslim inquisition) of the 800s.

While Mu'tazilites historically elevated reasoning over mere acceptance of tradition, they were still committed Muslims and defended the causes of Islam. Some Mu'tazilites even wrote works against Christian doctrines that advanced distinctive Islamic claims. Mu'tazilites have three essential religious principles: **tawhid** (strict monotheism), 'adl (justice, in relation to Allah), and the concept of reward and punishment (or promise and threat) for human actions. While these three are considered foundational to Mu'tazilism, there are other important beliefs, including human free will, the createdness of the Quran, and the twofold concept of commanding right and forbidding wrong. Mu'tazilism also articulated a unique teaching regarding a Muslim who commits one of the greater sins (kabaa'ir), which include shirk (polytheism) and adultery. Mu'tazilites refuse to specify hellfire as a destiny for a Muslim who commits any of these greater sins. They argue that the destiny of such a sinner will actually be a position between paradise and hell.

In their earliest stages, Mu'tazilites were largely anti-**Umayyad** and supported the **Abbasids** in overthrowing them. However, for most of Islam's history, the Mu'tazila positions were marginal and mostly rejected in favor of traditionism. In modern Muslim discussions, the Mu'tazila positions stand in direct opposition to Sunnism, which elevates and cherishes the sunna (Muhammad's tradition). For many Muslims, a Mu'tazilite is considered a heretic (zindeeq).

ahl al-Quran: the people of the Quran

Ahl al-Quran, pronounced "ah-l al-kor-AHN," means "the people or adherents of the Quran," where the word *ahl* means "the people, advocates, or devotees." The term refers to a group of Muslims who take the Quran alone as their guide and authority and who reject the **hadith** traditions, either totally or partially. Members of this movement appear similar to advocates of sola scriptura in Christianity. In English, the group is often known as the Quranists. This is not a sect in Islam, like Sunnism and Shiism, but rather a vision or a trend that questions the reliability and authenticity of the hadith and insists on using the Quran alone in matters of religion. Ahl al-Quran are in stark opposition to ahl al-hadith, "the adherents of the hadith" or "the lovers of traditions." This may suggest that ahl al-Quran are, to some extent, similar to the Mu'tazilites, particularly in their evaluation of the hadith traditions; however, the rejection of the hadith among ahl al-Quran is more severe.

For ahl al-Quran, Allah's rules can be gleaned only from the Quran. It is totally reliable and complete, unlike invented hadith traditions, which were formed for political and sectarian reasons. For them, a Muslim cannot trust Muhammad's hadiths, because their narrators and compilers lived centuries after Muhammad and forged these traditions to meet caliphal needs. In their rejection, they argue that the hadiths insult Muhammad and Allah. For ahl al-Quran, the hadiths are responsible for all the manifestations of radical Islam in our day—manifestations that are far removed from the peaceful message of the Quran.

The ahl al-Quran movement is indebted to modern Muslim scholars who were able to swim against the current of Sunnism and the rigid commitment to tradition. One of the early influencers of ahl al-Quran was Ghulam Ahmad Parwez (1903–85), who was born in British India. He applied rationalism—thus, Mu'tazilite tendencies—in interpreting religious matters and challenged Sunnism and its traditions. Parwez rejected the so-called trusted hadith collections and questioned major Islamic beliefs, including the **salat** (the ritual prayer) and the **hajj** (pilgrimage). In his reliance on the Quran alone, he questioned major religious claims and practices advanced only through later traditions.

After Parwez, the ahl al-Quran movement is indebted to the work of Egyptian scholar Ahmed Sobhy Mansour (1949–). He completed his doctoral work at the prestigious Azhar University in Cairo and began teaching there, focusing on the Quran alone. He was challenged by Sunni religious scholars who marginalized him and accused him of heresy. This led to his imprisonment. After his release, he was forced into exile. He moved to the United States, where he began teaching his views to a small circle of followers.

Ahmadiyya: the community of Ghulam Ahmad, the youngest Islamic sect

The term *Ahmadiyya*, pronounced "ah-ma-DAY-uh," refers to the followers of the Ahmad path, which precisely refers to Mirza Ghulam Ahmad (1835–1908). It is the newest Islamic sect and was founded by Ghulam Ahmad in 1889. He is viewed by the members of the Ahmadiyya community as the awaited Mahdi and the true messiah, whose advent launched the truest manifestation of revival in Islam after generations of corruption and wickedness by those claiming to be followers of Islam. Ahmadiyya members openly seek to revive Islam. They view themselves as true Muslims but also as followers of both Muhammad and Ghulam Ahmad. In fact, some of them believe that Ghulam Ahmad is a reappearance of Muhammad. Most of the members believe that Ghulam Ahmad's son was his legitimate caliph (successor).

A follower of the Ahmadiyya sect is called an Ahmadi. As a group, they emphasize love and peace and discourage fighting and hostility. In contrast to growing religious radicalism, they advance mutual coexistence and respect. For Ahmadiyya, **jihad** cannot be achieved by fighting but only by peaceful striving for the good cause. Sunnis and Shiites largely consider them heretics and unbelievers. Many mainstream

Muslim scholars issue **fatwas** (religious rulings) against members of the Ahmadiyya community, refusing to permit marriages to any of their members, as they are considered unbelievers. For some mainstream Muslims, the Ahmadiyya movement began when British colonialists sought to divide Islam in the 1900s. They used Ghulam Ahmad—born in British India-Pakistan—and his teaching to dissuade true Muslims from the obligatory jihad against the British infidels. Due to their adoption of some mystical practices and peaceful approaches, many consider the Ahmadiyya sect a manifestation of **Sufism** or mystical Islam, only with an emphasis on the experiences and teachings of Ghulam Ahmad.

Sources Consulted

Islamic Texts

For studies on Islamic literature, see Fred McGraw Donner, *Narratives of Islamic Origins: The Beginnings of Islamic Historical Writing* (Princeton: Darwin Press, 1998), chap. 1; Chase F. Robinson, *Islamic Historiography* (Cambridge: Cambridge University Press, 2003), chaps. 1–2; Stephen Humphreys, *Islamic History: A Framework for Inquiry* (Princeton: Princeton University Press, 1991), chaps. 1–3; Ayman S. Ibrahim, *The Stated Motivations for the Early Islamic Expansion (622–641): A Critical Revision of Muslims' Traditional Portrayal of the Arab Raids and Conquests* (New York: Peter Lang, 2018), chaps. 1–2; Ayman S. Ibrahim, *A Concise Guide to the Quran* (Grand Rapids: Baker Academic, 2020), 8–10; Ayman S. Ibrahim, *A Concise Guide to the Life of Muhammad* (Grand Rapids: Baker Academic, 2022), 8–14; Michael Cook, *Muhammad* (Oxford: Oxford University Press, 1983), chap. 7; and Chase F. Robinson, *Empire and Elites after the Muslim Conquest: The Transformation of Northern Mesopotamia* (Cambridge: Cambridge University Press, 2000), chap. 1.

For important studies on the Quran, see Ayman S. Ibrahim, *The Stated Motivations for the Early Islamic Expansion (622–641): A Critical Revision of Muslims' Traditional Portrayal of the Arab Raids and Conquests* (New York: Peter Lang, 2018), chap. 5; Ayman S. Ibrahim, *A Concise Guide to the Quran* (Grand Rapids: Baker Academic, 2020), 1–60; Ayman S. Ibrahim, *A Concise Guide to the Life of Muhammad* (Grand Rapids: Baker Academic, 2022), 117–21; Jane Dammen McAuliffe, ed., *Cambridge Companion to the Qur'ān* (Cambridge: Cambridge University Press, 2006); Stephen J. Shoemaker, *Creating the Qur'an: A Historical-Critical Study* (Oakland: University of California Press, 2022), 1–69; Nicolai Sinai, *The Qur'an: A Historical-Critical Introduction* (Edinburgh: Edinburgh University Press, 2017); Gabriel Said Reynolds, *The Qur'an and the Bible: Text and Commentary* (New Haven and London: Yale University Press, 2018); Mondher Sfar, *In Search of the Original Koran: The True History of the Revealed Text* (Amherst, NY: Prometheus Books, 2008); and Oliver Leaman, ed., *The Qur'an: An Encyclopedia* (New York: Routledge, 2006). See also Ibn Warraq, ed., *What the Koran Really Says: Language, Text, and Commentary* (Amherst, NY: Prometheus Books, 2002); Ibn Warraq, ed., *The Origins of the Koran: Classic Essays on Islam's Holy Book* (Amherst, NY: Prometheus Books, 1998); and Michael Cook, *The Koran: A Very Short Introduction* (Oxford: Oxford University Press, 2000), chap. 1.

For a Muslim perspective on the Quranic text, see Muhammad Abdel Haleem, *The Qur'an: A New Translation* (Oxford: Oxford University Press, 2010).

For Shiite views on the Quran, see Meir M. Bar-Asher, "Shīʿism and the Qur'ān," in *Encyclopedia of the Qur'ān*, ed. Jane Dammen McAuliffe, 6 vols. (Leiden: Brill, 2001–6), 4:593–63 (hereafter *EQ*).

On hadith, sira, and traditions in general, see James Robson, "Ḥadīth," in *Encyclopaedia of Islam*, 2nd ed., ed. P. J. Bearman et al. (Leiden: Brill, 1960–present), 3:23ff. (hereafter *EI*); Alfred Guillaume, *The Traditions of Islam: An Introduction to the Study of the Hadith Literature* (Oxford: Clarendon, 1924); and John Burton, *An Introduction to the Hadīth* (Edinburgh: Edinburgh University Press, 1994).

On Shiite hadiths, see Jonathan Brown, *Ḥadīth: Muhammad's Legacy in the Medieval and Modern World* (Oxford: Oneworld, 2009), chap. 4; Etan Kohlberg, "Western Studies of Shi'a Islam," in *Shi'ism, Resistance, and Revolution*, ed. Martin Kramer (Boulder, CO: Westview, 1987), 31–44; Wim Raven, "Sīra," *EI*, 9:660–64; Wim Raven, "Sīra and the Qur'ān," *EQ*, 5:29–51; M. Hinds, "al-Maghāzī," *EI*, 5:1161–64; and F. C. De Blois et al., "Ta'rīkh," *EI*, 10:257ff. See also G. H. A. Juynboll, "Hadith and the Qur'ān," *EQ*, 2:376ff.; G. H. A. Juynboll, "Sunna," *EQ*, 5:163–66; F. Buhl, A. T. Welch, et al., "Muḥammad," *EI*, 7:360ff; J. M. B. Jones, "Ibn Isḥāk," *EI*, 3:810–11; and W. M. Watt, "Ibn Hishām," *EI*, 3:800.

On pre-Islamic scriptures according to Islamic views, see Ayman S. Ibrahim, *A Concise Guide to the Quran* (Grand Rapids: Baker Academic, 2020), 101–7.

On the sharia, see Wael B. Hallaq, *Sharī'a: Theory, Practice, Transformations* (Cambridge: Cambridge University Press, 2009), 1–354; and N. Calder and M. B. Hooker, "Sharīʿa," *EI*, 9:321–28.

Islamic History

On the historical episodes in this section, see Ayman S. Ibrahim, *A Concise Guide to the Life of Muhammad* (Grand Rapids: Baker Academic, 2022), 3–115; and Ayman S. Ibrahim, *A Concise Guide to the Quran* (Grand Rapids: Baker Academic, 2020), 21–23.

For a critical assessment of Muslim tradition and its reliability, see the valuable studies Patricia Crone, *Medieval Islamic Political Thought* (2004; repr., Edinburgh: Edinburgh University Press, 2014); Patricia Crone, *Slaves on Horses: The Evolution of the Islamic Polity* (Cambridge: Cambridge University Press, 1980); Patricia Crone, *Meccan Trade and the Rise of Islam* (Princeton: Princeton University Press, 1987); Chase F. Robinson, *Empire and Elites after the Muslim Conquest: The Transformation of Northern Mesopotamia* (Cambridge: Cambridge University Press, 2000); Chase F. Robinson, *Islamic Historiography* (Cambridge: Cambridge University Press, 2003); Erling Ladewig Petersen, *ʿAlī and Muʿāwiya in Early Arabic Tradition: Studies on the Genesis and Growth of Islamic Historical Writing until the End of the Ninth Century*, trans. P. Lampe Christensen (Copenhagen: Aarhuus Stiftsbogtrykkerie, 1964); and Herbert Berg, ed., *Method and Theory in the Study of Islamic Origins* (Leiden: Brill, 2003).

For scholarly studies on the Ka'ba and its history, see F. E. Peters, *The Muslim Pilgrimage to Mecca and the Holy Places* (Princeton: Princeton University Press, 1996), 3–41, especially p. 14 regarding the stone; G. R. Hawting, "The Origins of the Muslim Sanctuary at Mecca," in *Studies on the First Century of Islamic Society*, ed. G. H. A. Juynboll (Carbondale: Southern Illinois University Press, 1982), 23–48; J. Chabbi, "Mecca," *EQ*, 3:337–41; W. Montgomery Watt et al., "Makka," *EI*, 6:144–87; A. J. Wensinck and J. Jomier, "Ka'ba," *EI*, 4:317ff.; and G. R. Hawting, "Pilgrimage," *EQ*, 4:91–100. See also M. Gaudefroy-Demombynes, *Le pèlerinage à la Mekke: Étude d'histoire religieuse* (Paris: n.p., 1923); and Gerald Hawting, ed., *The Development of Islamic Ritual* (London: Routledge, 2017), especially C. Snouck Hurgronje, "The Meccan Feast," chap. 14, and Hava

Lazarus-Yafeh, "The Religious Dialectics of the Hadjdj," chap. 15; F. Buhl, "Ṭawāf," *EI*, 10:376; and W. M. Watt, "Kuraysh," *EI*, 5:434–35.

On the episode of the satanic verses in traditional sources, see *The History of al-Tabari*, vol. 6, *Muhammad at Mecca*, trans. W. Montgomery Watt and M. V. McDonald (Albany: State University of New York Press, 1988), 107ff.; and 'Abd al-Malik Ibn Hishām and Muḥammad Ibn Isḥaq, *The Life of Muhammad*, trans. Alfred Guillaume (1955; repr. Oxford: Oxford University Press, 1999), 165–67. For secondary studies on the satanic verses, see Ayman S. Ibrahim, *A Concise Guide to the Quran* (Grand Rapids: Baker Academic, 2020), chap. 19; Shahab Ahmed, *Before Orthodoxy: The Satanic Verses in Early Islam* (Cambridge, MA: Harvard University Press, 2017), chaps. 1–3; Shahab Ahmed, "Satanic Verses," *EQ*, 4:531ff.; William Montgomery Watt, *Muhammad at Mecca* (Oxford: Oxford University Press, 1953), 103; William Montgomery Watt, *Muhammad: Prophet and Statesman* (Oxford: Oxford University Press, 1961), 61; and Gabriel Said Reynolds, *The Emergence of Islam: Classical Traditions in Contemporary Perspective* (Minneapolis: Fortress, 2012), 24, 139–42.

On the episode of Muhammad's night journey, see the primary sources Ibn Hishām and Ibn Isḥaq, *Life of Muhammad*, 181ff.; Sahih al-Bukhari, 1.8.345; and Sahih Muslim, 1:313; and the studies Michael Sells, "Ascension," *EQ*, 1:176–81; N. J. Johnson, "Aqṣā Mosque," *EQ*, 1:125–27; B. Schrieke et al., "Miʿrādj," *EI*, 7:97–105; W. Montgomery Watt, "Ḥanīf," *EI*, 3:165–66; and Uri Rubin, "Ḥanīf," *EQ*, 2:402.

On the Islamic claims on the connection between Abraham's faith and Islam, see Francis E. Peters, *Muhammad and the Origins of Islam* (Albany: State University of New York Press, 1994), 120–25.

On the history of the early caliphate, see Tayeb El-Hibri, *Parable and Politics in Early Islamic History* (New York: Columbia University Press, 2010), chaps. 1–5; G. R. Hawting, "Umayyads," *EI*, 10:840ff.; and B. Lewis, "'Abbāsids," *EI*, 1:15–23.

On the events of Muhammad's raids in Arabia, see Ayman S. Ibrahim, *The Stated Motivations for the Early Islamic Expansion (622–641): A Critical Revision of Muslims' Traditional Portrayal of the Arab Raids and Conquests* (New York: Peter Lang, 2018), 66–119; Richard A. Gabriel, *Muhammad: Islam's First Great General* (Norman: University of Oklahoma Press, 2014), 86ff.; Francis E. Peters, *Muhammad and the Origins of Islam* (Albany: State University of New York Press, 1994), 211ff.; and Francis E. Peters, *Islam: A Guide for Jews and Christians* (Princeton: Princeton University Press, 2009), 68ff.

On the mihna, see Ayman S. Ibrahim, *Conversion to Islam: Competing Themes in Early Islamic Historiography* (New York: Oxford University Press, 2021), chaps. 2–4.

Islamic Faith and Belief

For a Muslim view of Allah in the Quran, see Fazlur Rahman, *Major Themes of the Qur'ān*, 2nd ed. (Chicago: University of Chicago Press, 2009), chap. 1; Gabriel Said Reynolds, *Allah: God in the Qur'ān* (New Haven: Yale University Press, 2020), 11, 46–49, 94–95, 105, 131–32, 177; and Shems Friedlander, Muzaffer Ozak, and Hamid Amidi, *Ninety-Nine Names of Allah: The Beautiful Names* (Grand Rapids: HarperCollins, 1993).

On terms and studies related to the text of the Quran (e.g., aaya, sura, mushrik, nabi, rasul, and i'jaz), see Ayman S. Ibrahim, *A Concise Guide to the Quran* (Grand Rapids: Baker Academic, 2020), 147–64 (terms) and 165–74 (resources); and John Renard, *Islamic Theological Themes: A Primary Source Reader* (Berkeley: University of California Press, 2014).

On the variant readings of the Quran, see Ayman S. Ibrahim, *A Concise Guide to the Quran* (Grand Rapids: Baker Academic, 2020), 55–60; Gabriel Said Reynolds, *The Qur'ān and Its Biblical Subtext* (New York: Routledge, 2010), 204ff.; Gabriel Said Reynolds, "'Uthmān," *EQ*, 5:408ff.; Frederik Leemhuis, "Codices of the Quran," *EQ*, 1:347–51;

James Bellamy, "Textual Criticism of the Qur'ān," *EQ*, 5:237–52; and Frederik Leemhuis, "Readings of the Qur'ān," *EQ*, 4:353ff.

On the history of the Quran, see Shady Nasser, *The Transmission of the Variant Readings of the Qur'ān* (Leiden: Brill, 2012); Andrew Rippin, *Approaches to the History of the Interpretation of the Qur'ān* (Oxford: Clarendon, 1988), 139–57; Andrew Rippin, "The Qur'ān as Literature: Perils, Pitfalls and Prospects," *British Society for Middle Eastern Studies Bulletin* 10, no. 1 (1983): 38–47; Harald Motzki, "Alternative Accounts of the Qur'ān's Formation," in *Cambridge Companion to the Qur'ān*, ed. Jane Dammen McAuliffe (Cambridge: Cambridge University Press, 2006), 61ff.; and Theodor Nöldeke et al., *The History of the Qur'ān*, ed. and trans. Wolfgang H. Behn (Leiden: Brill, 2013). For a Shiite perspective, see Mohammad Ali Amir-Moezzi, *The Silent Qur'an and the Speaking Qur'an: Scriptural Sources of Islam between History and Fervor*, trans. Eric Ormsby (New York: Columbia University Press, 2016), 1–73; and al-Sayyid al-Khu'i, *Prolegomena to the Qur'an*, trans. Abdulaziz Sachedina (Oxford: Oxford University Press, 1998), 23–80.

On tawhid, see D. Gimaret, "Tawḥīd," *EI*, 10:389ff.; D. Gimaret, "Shirk," *EI*, 9:485ff.; Ayman S. Ibrahim, *A Concise Guide to the Life of Muhammad* (Grand Rapids: Baker Academic, 2022), 117–21; and Ayman S. Ibrahim, *A Concise Guide to the Quran* (Grand Rapids: Baker Academic, 2020), 89–93.

On 'isma, see Ayman S. Ibrahim, *A Concise Guide to the Life of Muhammad* (Grand Rapids: Baker Academic, 2022), 61–64; W. Madelung and E. Tyan, "'Iṣma," *EI*, 4:182–84; and Paul E. Walker, "Impeccability," *EQ*, 2:505–7.

On jinn in the Quran and Islam, see Jacqueline Chabbi, "Jinn," *EQ*, 3:43–50; and D. B. MacDonald et al., "Djinn," *EI*, 2:546ff.

On dhimmi, see C. Cahen, "Dhimma," *EI*, 2:227–31; C. Cahen et al, "Djizya," *EI*, 2:559ff.; M. Long, "Jizya," in Gerhard Bowering et al., eds. *The Princeton Encyclopedia of Islamic Political Thought*. (Princeton, NJ: Princeton University Press, 2013), 283–84; Bat Ye'or, *Islam and Dhimmitude: Where Civilizations Collide* (Madison, NJ: Fairleigh Dickinson University Press, 2002), 33–80; and Bat Ye'or, *The Decline of Eastern Christianity under Islam: From Jihad to Dhimmitude* (Madison, NJ: Fairleigh Dickinson University Press, 1996), 69–99.

On terms related to paradise, heaven, and hell in Islam, see Christian Lange, *Paradise and Hell in Islamic Traditions* (Cambridge: Cambridge University Press, 2016), 1–164; Christian Lange, ed., *Locating Hell in Islamic Traditions* (Leiden: Brill, 2015); and Rosalind W. Gwynne, "Hell and Hellfire," *EQ*, 2:414–20.

Islamic Practices and Religious Duties

On practices and beliefs among Muslims, see Andrew Rippin, *Muslims: Their Religious Beliefs and Practices* (London: Routledge, 1993), chaps. 1–7; and Fazlur Rahman, *Islam* (Chicago: University of Chicago Press, 1966), 1–116.

On terms of practice, see E. Chaumont, "Wuḍū'," *EI*, 11:218–19; and L. Gardet, "Du'ā'," *EI*, 2:617–18.

On the Five Pillars of Islam, see Ayman S. Ibrahim, *A Concise Guide to the Quran* (Grand Rapids: Baker Academic, 2020), 158; Ayman S. Ibrahim, *A Concise Guide to the Life of Muhammad* (Grand Rapids: Baker Academic, 2022), 191; M. Plessner, "Ramaḍān," *EI*, 8:417ff.; G. Monnot, "Ṣalāt," *EI*, 8:925ff.; and Roxanne D. Marcotte, "Night of Power," *EQ*, 3:537–39.

On the hajj, see Ayman S. Ibrahim, *A Concise Guide to the Life of Muhammad* (Grand Rapids: Baker Academic, 2022), 42–47; F. E. Peters, *The Muslim Pilgrimage to Mecca and the Holy Places* (Princeton: Princeton University Press, 1996), 3–41; and G. R. Hawting,

"The Origins of the Muslim Sanctuary at Mecca," in *Studies on the First Century of Islamic Society*, ed. G. H. A. Juynboll (Carbondale: Southern Illinois University Press, 1982), 23–48.

On the basmala and Asmaa' Allah, see Ayman S. Ibrahim, *A Concise Guide to the Quran* (Grand Rapids: Baker Academic, 2020), 73–74; Ayman S. Ibrahim, *A Concise Guide to the Life of Muhammad* (Grand Rapids: Baker Academic, 2022), 122–27; William A. Graham, "Basmala," *EQ*, 1:207–11; and L. Gardet, "al-Asmā' al-Ḥusnā," *EI*, 1:714.

On tawba, see F. M. Denny, "Tawba," *EI*, 10:385.

On tawakkul, see Fazlur Rahman, *Islam* (Chicago: University of Chicago Press, 1966), 130; and L. Lewisohn, "Tawakkul," *EI*, 10:376–78.

On jihad in the Quran and tradition, see Ayman S. Ibrahim, *The Stated Motivations for the Early Islamic Expansion (622–641): A Critical Revision of Muslims' Traditional Portrayal of the Arab Raids and Conquests* (New York: Peter Lang, 2018), 199–204; Ayman S. Ibrahim, *A Concise Guide to the Life of Muhammad* (Grand Rapids: Baker Academic, 2022), 152–55; and Ayman S. Ibrahim, *A Concise Guide to the Quran* (Grand Rapids: Baker Academic, 2020), 123–26.

On eid, see E. Mittwoch, "'Īd al-Aḍḥā," *EI*, 3:1007–8; and E. Mittwoch, "'Īd al-Fiṭr," *EI*, 3:1008.

On Ashuraa', see A. J. Wensinck et al., "'Āshūrā'," *EI*, 1:705ff.

On imam, see Ayman S. Ibrahim, *A Concise Guide to the Quran* (Grand Rapids: Baker Academic, 2020), 153; and Ayman S. Ibrahim, *A Concise Guide to the Life of Muhammad* (Grand Rapids: Baker Academic, 2022), 186.

On women and the various kinds of marriage in Islam, see Leila Ahmed, *Women and Gender in Islam: Historical Roots of a Modern Debate* (New Haven: Yale University Press, 1992), chaps. 3–6; J. Schacht et al., "Nikāḥ," *EI*, 8:26ff.; Shahla Haeri, "Temporary Marriage," *EQ*, 5:232–34; W. Heffening, "Mutʻa," *EI*, 7:757–59; Shahla Haeri, *Law of Desire: Temporary Marriage in Shi'i Iran* (Syracuse, NY: Syracuse University Press, 1993), 1–73; and Sachiko Murata, *Temporary Marriage (*Mut'a*) in Islamic Law* (London: Muhammad Trust, 1987).

For a secondary study on the role of taqiyya in Shiism, see Etan Kohlberg, "Some Imami- Shi'i Views on Taqiyya," *Journal of the American Oriental Society* 95 (1975): 395–402.

On khutba and jumu'a, see Ayman S. Ibrahim, *A Concise Guide to the Life of Muhammad* (Grand Rapids: Baker Academic, 2022), 137–40.

On da'wa, see Ayman S. Ibrahim, *A Concise Guide to the Quran* (Grand Rapids: Baker Academic, 2020), 150; and Matthew J. Kuiper, *Da'wa: A Global History of Islamic Missionary Thought and Practice* (Edinburgh: Edinburgh University Press, 2021), 1–132.

On the qibla and Mecca, see J. Chabbi, "Mecca," *EQ*, 3:337–41; W. Montgomery Watt et al., "Makka," *EI*, 6:144–87; Ayman S. Ibrahim, *A Concise Guide to the Quran* (Grand Rapids: Baker Academic, 2020), 157; and Ayman S. Ibrahim, *A Concise Guide to the Life of Muhammad* (Grand Rapids: Baker Academic, 2022), 190; see also A. J. Wensinck and C. Schoy, "Kibla," *EI*, 5:82ff.; G. Fehérvári, "Miḥrāb," *EI*, 7:7ff.

On the adhan, see Ayman S. Ibrahim, *A Concise Guide to the Quran* (Grand Rapids: Baker Academic, 2020), 148; and Ayman S. Ibrahim, *A Concise Guide to the Life of Muhammad* (Grand Rapids: Baker Academic, 2022), 180.

On 'awra, see Khaled Abou El Fadl, *Conference of the Books: The Search for Beauty in Islam* (Ann Arbor: University of Michigan Press, 2001), 50, 293–97; and Irma Riyani, *Islam, Women's Sexuality and Patriarchy in Indonesia* (London: Taylor & Francis, 2020), chaps. 1–2.

Islamic Jurisprudence

For Muslim perspectives on jurisprudence, see Mohammad Hashim Kamali, *Principles of Islamic Jurisprudence* (Cambridge: Islamic Texts Society, 1989); and Khaled Abou El Fadl, *Speaking in God's Name: Islamic Law, Authority and Women* (Oxford: Oneworld, 2001), chaps. 1–5.

For a scholarly perspective on the disagreement between Shiism and Sunnism in matters of Islamic law, see Devin J. Stewart, *Islamic Legal Orthodoxy: Twelver Shiite Responses to the Sunni Legal System* (Salt Lake City: University of Utah Press, 1998).

On the formation of Sunni schools of law, see Wael B. Hallaq, ed., *The Formation of Islamic Law* (London: Routledge, 2004); Christopher Melchert, *The Formation of the Sunnī Schools of Law*, Studies in Islamic Law and Society 4 (Leiden: Brill, 1997), xiii–30; and Nimrod Hurvitz, *The Formation of Ḥanbalism Culture and Civilisation in the Middle East* (London: Routledge Curzon, 2002).

On the development of Islamic thought in general, see A. J. Wensinck, *The Muslim Creed: Its Genesis and Historical Development* (London: Frank Cass, 1965); William Montgomery Watt, *The Formative Period of Islamic Thought* (Oxford: Oneworld, 1998); and William Montgomery Watt, *Islamic Philosophy and Theology* (Edinburgh: Edinburgh University Press, 1962). For a Shiite perspective, see Liyakat Takim, *Shi'ism Revisited: Ijtihad and Reformation in Contemporary Times* (Oxford: Oxford University Press, 2021), 57–107; and Najam Haider, *Shī'ī Islam: An Introduction* (Cambridge: Cambridge University Press, 2014), 1–99.

On fiqh and the sharia, see Joseph Schacht, "Fiḳh," *EI*, 2:886–91; Joseph Schacht, *An Introduction to Islamic Law* (Oxford: Oxford University Press, 1982); N. J. Coulson, *A History of Islamic Law* (Edinburgh: Edinburgh University Press, 1999); and Wael B. Hallaq, *Sharī'a: Theory, Practice, Transformations* (Cambridge: Cambridge University Press, 2009).

On the sharia, see Abbas Amanat and Frank Griffel, eds., *Sharī'a: Islamic Law in the Contemporary Context* (Stanford, CA: Stanford University Press, 2007). For current trends and modern Muslim approaches to sharia, see Khaled Abou El Fadl, *Reasoning with God: Reclaiming Sharī'ah in the Modern Age* (London and New York: Rowman & Littlefield, 2014).

On ulamaa' and their important role in medieval Islam, see Ayman S. Ibrahim, *Conversion to Islam: Competing Themes in Early Islamic Historiography* (New York: Oxford University Press, 2021), chaps. 3–4; Muhammad Qasim Zaman, *Religion and Politics under the Early 'Abbāsids: The Emergence of the Proto-Sunnī Elite* (Leiden: Brill, 1997), chaps. 1–2; H. Laoust, "Aḥmad b. Ḥanbal," *EI*, 1:272–77; H. Laoust, "Ḥanābila," *EI*, 3:158–62; and C. Gilliot et al., "'Ulamā'," *EI*, 10:801ff. For the rise and function of the ulamaa', see Aaron W. Hughes, *Muslim Identities: An Introduction to Islam* (New York: Columbia University Press, 2013), 141ff.

For a modern Muslim perspective on Allah's hudud, see Mohammad Hashim Kamali, *Crime and Punishment in Islamic Law: A Fresh Interpretation* (Oxford: Oxford University Press, 2019), 21–62.

On aqida, see W. Montgomery Watt, "'Aḳīda," *EI*, 1:332–34; and Klaus Ferdinand, *Islam: State and Society* (London: Routledge, 1988), 62–63.

On the umma and qadi, see E. Tyan and Gy. Káldy-Nagy, "Ḳāḍī," *EI*, 4:373–75; F. M. Denny, "Umma," *EI*, 10:859–63; and George C. Decasa, *The Qur'anic Concept of Umma and Its Function in Philippine Muslim Society* (Rome: Pontificia Università Gregoriana, 1999), 9–135.

On fatwa, see E. Tyan and J. R. Walsh, "Fatwā," *EI*, 2:866–67; Ayman S. Ibrahim, *A Concise Guide to the Quran* (Grand Rapids: Baker Academic, 2020), 151; Ayman S. Ibrahim, *A Concise Guide to the Life of Muhammad* (Grand Rapids: Baker Academic,

2022), 149, 183–84; and Alan Verskin, *Oppressed in the Land? Fatwās on Muslims Living under Non-Muslim Rule from the Middle Ages to the Present* (Princeton: Markus Wiener, 2013).

On halal and haram in connection to the sharia, see the Muslim perspective in Mohammad Hashim Kamali, *Shariah and the Halal Industry* (Oxford: Oxford University Press, 2021), 17–48.

On bid'a, see J. Robson, "Bid'a," *EI*, 1:1199; Michael A. Cook, *Commanding Right and Forbidding Wrong in Islamic Thought* (Cambridge: Cambridge University Press, 2001), 320n93, 330, 354n118, 383, 498, 517, 555ff.; and Mehran Kamrava, ed., *Innovation in Islam: Traditions and Contributions* (Berkeley and Los Angeles: University of California Press, 2011).

On daar al-islam and daar al-harb, see A. Abel, "Dār al-Ḥarb," *EI*, 2:126; and Giovanna Calasso and Giuliano Lancioni, eds., *Dār Al-islām / Dār Al-ḥarb: Territories, People, Identities* (Leiden: Brill, 2017).

On maslaha, see M. Khadduri, "Maṣlaḥa," *EI*, 6:738–39; Abdul Aziz bin Sattam, *Sharia and the Concept of Benefit: The Use and Function of Maslaha in Islamic Jurisprudence* (London: Bloomsbury, 2015), 1–101; and Felicitas Opwis, *Maṣlaḥa and the Purpose of the Law: Islamic Discourse on Legal Change from the 4th/10th to 8th/14th Century* (Leiden: Brill, 2010), 1–26.

On kalam as an Islamic science, see L. Gardet, "Kalām," *EI*, 4:468; L. Gardet, "'Ilm al-Kalām," *EI*, 3:1141–50; and Richard M. Frank, *Texts and Studies on the Development and History of Kalām*, vol. 3 (London: Routledge, 2009). On Islamic philosophy from the ninth to the twentieth century, see Khaled El-Rouayheb and Sabine Schmidtke, eds., *The Oxford Handbook of Islamic Philosophy* (Oxford: Oxford University Press, 2017).

Islamic Movements

On Muslim sects, see P. Shinar and W. Ende, "Salafiyya," *EI*, 8:900ff.; A. Merad et al., "Iṣlāḥ," *EI*, 4:141–142; Yohanan Friedmann, "Aḥmadiyya," *EQ*, 1:50–51; and M. Sharon, "People of the House," *EQ*, 4:48–53.

On Sunnism and Shiism, see the important recent study Toby Matthiesen, *The Caliph and the Imam: The Making of Sunnism and Shiism* (Oxford: Oxford University Press, 2023).

On early Sunni thought, see Wilferd Madelung, "Early Sunni Doctrine Concerning Faith as Reflected in the *Kitāb al-Īmān* of Abū 'Ubayd al-Qāsim b. Sallām (d. 224/839)," *Studia Islamica* 32 (1970): 233–54.

On Shiism, see Heinz Halm, *An Introduction to Shi'ism*, 2nd ed. (New York: Columbia University Press, 2004), 1–153; and Moojan Momen, *An Introduction to Shi'i Islam: The History and Doctrines of Twelver Shi'ism* (New Haven: Yale University Press, 1985).

On Salafism, see Henri Lauzière, *The Making of Salafism: Islamic Reform in the Twentieth Century* (New York: Columbia University Press, 2016), chaps. 1–3; Henri Lauzière, "The Construction of Salafiyya: Reconsidering Salafism from the Perspective of Conceptual History," *International Journal of Middle East Studies* 42, no. 3 (2010): 369–89; and Quintan Wiktorowicz, "Anatomy of the Salafi Movement," *Studies in Conflict & Terrorism* 29, no. 3 (2006): 207–39.

On Sufism, see Annemarie Schimmel, *Mystical Dimensions of Islam* (Chapel Hill: University of North Carolina Press, 1975), 3–97; Seyyed Hossein Nasr, *The Garden of Truth: The Vision and Promise of Sufism, Islam's Mystical Tradition* (New York: HarperOne, 2007), 3–57; Seyyed Hossein Nasr, *Sufi Essays*, 3rd ed. (Chicago: Kazi Publications, 1999), 25ff.; A. J. Arberry, *Introduction to the History of Sufism* (London: Longmans, Green, 1943); Julian Baldick, *Mystical Islam: An Introduction to Sufism*, 2nd rev. ed. (London: I. B. Tauris,

2000), 1–84; and Carl W. Ernst, *The Shambhala Guide to Sufism* (Boston: Shambhala, 1997), chaps. 1–2 (definitions and sources of Sufism).

On the historical development of Wahhabism, see George S. Rentz, *The Birth of the Islamic Reform Movement in Saudi Arabia: Muḥammad b. ʿAbd al-Wahhāb (1703/4–1792) and the Beginnings of Unitarian Empire in Arabia* (London: Arabian Publishing, 2004), 23ff.; David Commins, *The Wahhabi Mission and Saudi Arabia* (London: I. B. Tauris, 2006), 1–103; Hala Fattah, "'Wahhabi' Influences, Salafi Responses: Shaikh Mahmud Shukri and the Iraqi Salafi Movement, 1745–1930," *Journal of Islamic Studies* 14, no. 2 (2003): 127–48; Joas Wagemakers, "The Enduring Legacy of the Second Saudi State: Quietist and Radical Wahhabi Contestations of *al-Walāʾ wa-l-Barāʾ*," *International Journal of Middle East Studies* 44, no. 1 (2012): 93–110; and Daniel Lav, *Radical Islam and the Revival of Medieval Theology* (Cambridge: Cambridge University Press, 2012). See also the modern perspectives on radicalism and jihad in Fawaz A. Gerges, *The Far Enemy: Why Jihad Went Global* (Cambridge: Cambridge University Press, 2005), 1–79, 151–249; and Jeevan Deol and Zaheer Kazmi, eds., *Contextualising Jihadi Thought* (London: Hurst, 2012).

On Muʿtazilism, see Ayman S. Ibrahim, *Conversion to Islam: Competing Themes in Early Islamic Historiography* (New York: Oxford University Press, 2021), chaps. 2–4. For the theological arguments of Muʿtazilism, see Josef van Ess, *Theology and Society in the Second and Third Centuries of the Hijra: A History of Religious Thought in Early Islam*, 5 vols., trans. John O'Kane (Leiden: Brill, 2017), 2:286ff., 3:483ff.; and Josef van Ess, *The Flowering of Muslim Theology*, trans. Jane Marie Todd (Cambridge, MA: Harvard University Press, 2006), 9ff., 79ff. On the emergence and development of Muʿtazilism, see Racha el-Omari, "The Muʿtazilite Movement (I): The Origins of the Muʿtazila," in *The Oxford Handbook of Islamic Theology*, ed. Sabine Schmidtke (Oxford: Oxford University Press, 2016) 130–41; and David Bennett, "The Muʿtazilite Movement (II): The Early Muʿtazilites," in *The Oxford Handbook of Islamic Theology*, ed. Sabine Schmidtke (Oxford: Oxford University Press, 2016), 142–58.

On ahl al-Quran, see Ayman S. Ibrahim, *A Concise Guide to the Quran* (Grand Rapids: Baker Academic, 2020), 134–37; Ayman S. Ibrahim, *A Concise Guide to the Life of Muhammad* (Grand Rapids: Baker Academic, 2022), 159–60; Gabriel Said Reynolds, *The Emergence of Islam: Classical Traditions in Contemporary Perspective* (Minneapolis: Fortress, 2012), 43, 91–92, 207–8; and Ali Usman Qasmi, *Questioning the Authority of the Past: The Ahl al-Qurʾan Movements in the Punjab* (Karachi, Pakistan: Oxford University Press, 2011).

On Ahmadiyya, see H. A. Walter, *The Ahmadīya Movement* (New York: Oxford University Press, 1918), 13–99; Spencer Lavan, *The Ahmadiyah Movement: A History and Perspective* (Delhi: Manohar, 1974), chap. 1; Simon Ross Valentine, *Islam and the Ahmadiyya Jama'at: History, Belief, Practice* (London: Hurst, 2008), chaps. 1–2; Yohanan Friedmann, *Prophecy Continuous: Aspects of Aḥmadī Religious Thought and Its Medieval Background*, Comparative Studies on Muslim Societies 3 (Berkeley: University of California Press, 1989); and Ayman S. Ibrahim, *A Concise Guide to the Quran* (Grand Rapids: Baker Academic, 2020), 149.

Resources on Islam

Muslim Primary Sources Available Online

www.sahih-bukhari.com
  An English translation of the most reliable traditions that are highly respected in Sunni Islam.
sunnah.com
  Offers fifteen trusted Sunni collections of Muhammad's sunna.
www.al-islam.org and www.shiasource.com
  Advance Shiite perspectives on Islamic history, theology, and practice. They include articles and digitalized books.
islamqa.info/en/
  An important Sunni website that answers jurisprudence questions from a conservative salafi perspective. It contains numerous religious opinions (fatwas).
www.altafsir.com
  Offers seven Quran commentaries in English.
www.searchtruth.com
  Offers a modern conservative commentary on the Quran by Islamist Abu al-A'la al-Mawdudi (1903–79), among other features.
corpus.quran.com
  In addition to a word search, offers many English Quran translations and provides tools on syntax and morphology for each word in Islam's scripture.

Muslim Primary Sources Translated into English

Balādhurī, Aḥmad ibn Yaḥyā al-. *The Origins of the Islamic State*. Translated by Francis Murgotten and Philip Khuri Hitti. New York: AMS Press, 1968.

Ibn Hishām, ʿAbd al-Malik, and Muḥammad Ibn Isḥaq. *The Life of Muhammad*. Translated by Alfred Guillaume. Oxford: Oxford University Press, 1999. First published 1955.

Ibn Qutayba al-Dīnawarī. *Faḍl al-ʿarab wa-l-tanbīh ʿalā ʿulūmihā*. Edited by James Montgomery and Peter Webb. Translated by Sarah Savant and Peter Webb. New York: New York University Press, 2017.

Ibn Rāshid, Maʿmar, and ʿAbd al-Razzāq al-Ṣanʿānī. *The Expeditions: An Early Biography of Muhammad*. Edited and translated by Sean W. Anthony. New York: New York University Press, 2014.

Suyuti, Jalal al-Din al-. *Medicine of the Prophet*. Edited by Ahmad Thomson. Rev. ed. London: Ta-Ha, 2015.

Ṭabarī, Abū Jaʿfar Muḥammad ibn Jarīr al-. *The History of al-Ṭabarī*. 40 vols. Edited by C. E. Bosworth et al. New York: SUNY Press, 1985–99.

Muslim Primary Sources in Arabic

The first date given in Arabic references is the year of publication according to Islamic Hijri calendar. The date that follows is the equivalent year according to the Gregorian calendar, which is more familiar to English readers.

Dhahabī, Shams al- Dīn al-. *Taʾrīkh al-Islām*. 52 vols. Edited by ʿUmar ʿAbd al-Salām Tadmurī. Beirut: Dār al-kitāb al-ʿarabī, 1413/1993.

Ibn Ḥanbal, Aḥmad. *Musnad*. 45 vols. Edited by Shuʿayb al-Arnāʾūṭ et al. Beirut: Muʾassasat al-risāla, 1421/2001.

Ibn Saʿd, Muḥammad. *Kitāb al-ṭabaqāt al-kabīr*. 8 vols. Edited by Muḥammad ʿAbd al-Qādir ʿAṭā. Beirut: Dār al-kutub al-ʿilmiyya, 1410/1990.

Ibn Taymiyya, Taqī al-Dīn. *Minhāj al-sunna al-nabawiyya*. 9 vols. Edited by Muḥammad Rashād Sālim. Riyadh, Saudi Arabia: Jāmiʿat al-imām Muḥammad ibn Saʿūd, 1406/1986.

———. *Muqaddima fī uṣūl al-tafsīr*. Edited by Muḥammad Shiḥāta. Cairo: Dār maktabat al-ḥayāt, 1490/1980.

Majlisī, Muḥammad Bāqir al-. *Biḥār al-anwār*. 110 vols. Edited by ʿAbd al-Raḥīm al-Shīrāzī et al. Beirut: Dār iḥiyāʾ al-turāth, 1983.

Muqātil ibn Sulaymān. *Tafsīr Muqātil*. 5 vols. Edited by ʿAbdullāh Maḥmūd Shiḥāta. Beirut: Dār iḥiyāʾ al-turāth, 1423/2002.

Qummī, ʿAlī ibn Ibrāhīm al-. *Tafsīr al-Qummī*. 2 vols. Edited by al-Sayyid al-Mūsawī al-Jazāʾirī. Qum, Iran: Muʾassasat dār al-kitāb, 1967.

Shāfiʿī, ibn Idrīs al-. *al-Umm*. 8 vols. Beirut: Dār al-maʿrifa, 1410/1990.

————. *Musnad*. 4 vols. Edited by Māhir al- Faḥl. Kewiut: Ghrās li-l-nashr, 1425/2004.

————. *Tafsīr*. 3 vols. Edited by Aḥmad al-Farrān. Saudi Arabia: Dār al-tadmuriyya, 1427/2006.

Suyūṭī, Jalāl al-Dīn al-. *al-Itqān fī 'ulūm al-Qur'ān*. 2 vols. Edited by Sa'īd al-Mandūb. Beirut: Dār al-fikr, 1416/1996.

Non-Muslim Sources

Hoyland, Robert G. *Seeing Islam as Others Saw It: A Survey and Evaluation of Christian, Jewish, and Zoroastrian Writings on Early Islam*. Studies in Late Antiquity and Early Islam 13. Princeton: Darwin Press, 1997.

Ibrahim, Ayman S., and Clint Hackenburg. *In Search of the True Religion: Monk Jurjī and Muslim Jurists Debating Faith and Practice*. Arabic critical edition and English translation. Piscataway, NJ: Gorgias Press, 2022.

Theophanes. *The Chronicle of Theophanes: Anni Mundi 6095–6305 (A.D. 602–813)*. Edited and translated by Harry Turtledove. Philadelphia: University of Pennsylvania Press, 1982.

Timothy's Apology for Christianity. Woodbrooke Studies: Christian Documents in Syriac, Arabic and Garshūni. Vol. 2, *Timothy's Apology for Christianity; The Lament of the Virgin; The Martyrdom of Pilate*. Translated by Alphonse Mingana. Cambridge: W. Heffer and Sons, 1928.

Encyclopedias

Atiya, Aziz S., ed. *The Coptic Encyclopedia*. 8 vols. New York: Macmillan, 1991.

Fleet, Kate, Gudrun Krämer, Denis Matringe, John Nawas, and Everett Rowson, eds. *Encyclodepia of Islam*. 3rd ed. Leiden: Brill, 2007–.

Gibb, H. A. R., et al., eds. *The Encyclopaedia of Islam*. 13 vols. 2nd ed. Leiden: Brill, 1954–2008.

Houtsma, M. Th., et al., eds. *Encyclopaedia of Islam: A Dictionary of the Geography, Ethnography and Biography of the Muhammadan Peoples*. 9 vols. Leiden: Brill, 1908–36.

McAuliffe, Jane Dammen, ed. *Encyclopedia of the Qur'ān*. 6 vols. Leiden: Brill, 2001–6.

Thomas, David, et al., eds. *Christian-Muslim Relations: A Bibliographic History*. 18 vols. Leiden: Brill, 2009–21.

Alphabetical List of Entries